Jesus

My Autobiography

Other Books by
Tina Louise Spalding

Great Minds Speak to You

Making Love to God

Jesus

My Autobiography

Jesus and Ananda through
Tina Louise Spalding

LIGHT Technology PUBLISHING

ISBN: 978-1-62233-030-0

PO Box 3540
Flagstaff, AZ 86003
1-800-450-0985
1-928-526-1345
www.lighttechnology.com

This book is dedicated to everyone who has known that there was more to Jesus's story, and especially to those who have suffered unnecessarily in his name. I offer this book to you in hopes that it will help heal any hurts you may have suffered and lead you into a more joyful and creative life.

Contents

Preface

TWO YEARS AGO ALMOST TO THE DAY, ANANDA, MY GUIDES AND NONPHYSICAL teachers, made themselves known to me in a month-long journey through extreme energy events, ecstatic tidal waves of experience, and profound personal realizations. This spiritual event is called a kundalini awakening, and it often heralds the beginning of new psychic and creative abilities. The name Ananda means bliss, and that is certainly what I felt during that introduction to channeling and the communication of messages from nonphysical consciousness that would eventually become my life's work.

During that blissful summer, I came to know Ananda as a consciousness, as friends, and as teachers. They continue to lead me along an unusual path of communications from the nonphysical realms in which they reside as a collective group consciousness. I am able to connect with them at any time and ask any question about my personal life, world events, and of course, burning spiritual concerns. They also have spiritual assignments for me that can be very challenging. This book is one of those assignments.

When I channel Ananda, I relax, take a deep breath, and surrender my conscious mind, allowing them to speak through me and use my voice, my body, and my energy to convey the messages they want us to hear. After transmitting two books and hundreds of hours of channeling sessions, I've learned that their teachings are impeccable and their ability to communicate for extended periods and to expound on many subjects with ease, intelligence, and humor is always astounding.

During the summer of 2013, Ananda helped me channel and give birth to *Great Minds Speak to You*, a collection of essays and recordings from twenty deceased, iconic personalities from the past few generations — names we've loved, hated, pitied, and envied. Their messages tell us about life, death, and the afterlife, encouraging us to open and grow and explaining to us how we limit ourselves and how our misunderstandings and incorrect beliefs slow our consciousness evolution and cause us prolonged and unnecessary suffering.

As a channel, I found this surrender to so many different energies to be a challenge and at times a bit unnerving; after all, every morning for a month, I spoke for a deceased being who had a message for the world, a message he or she wanted us to hear. But Ananda was always there, holding my hand, encouraging me, and introducing each and every one of those amazing beings. In that eclectic and unusual group of communications, one in particular stood out, so I'd like to write here a little bit about that unfolding relationship as a prelude to his story.

By the time I had channeled fifteen or so of those celebrity stories, I began to get a little worried about whom the twentieth person might be. I had an uneasy feeling. I knew it would be someone significant; it had to be. After all, when you've channeled Marilyn Monroe, John F. Kennedy, Michael Jackson, and many other famous and infamous beings, surely the finale had to be a grand showstopper! All I knew was that I didn't want it to be Jesus, but I had a feeling it would be.

On the day I channeled the final chapter, Ananda — as gentle, logical, and kind as usual — introduced the last participant. Sure enough, it was Jesus. They assured me that this was necessary, and they told me that this final essay was the real reason for the book — to let us know that death, as we see it, is the grandest illusion of all and that Jesus's original message, delivered to us so many centuries ago, is still the same. Everlasting life is available to us all. That final chapter was added to the book, and I sent it off to the publisher. However, that wasn't the end of the story — not by a long shot!

I realized then that I had already been a student of Jesus's teachings for a long time, and the understanding dawned on my still slightly resistant mind that I had been preparing for this assignment for the past decade. You see, I have been a long-time student of *A Course in Miracles*, an amazing spiritual document channeled in the 1970s that offers in great detail Jesus's true teachings without the distortions of ego, Church, or human limitation. For ten years, I had been a dedicated *Course* student and practitioner, but only as

I began to channel more information from that great mind was I able to see how I had been gently led down this pathway to channeling and eventually to speaking Jesus's own story.

So many fears surfaced from deep within my mind as I began to think about the implications of this material I was transmitting. I knew that I was heading into treacherous waters. After all, this was the kind of behavior for which people had been burned, judged as insane, or martyred — none of which sounded like much fun to me! How was I going to navigate these waters alone?

Just a week or two after the last chapter had been dictated, my two sons, Alex and Kieran, as well as my daughter-in-law Laura Jean, came to stay with me for two weeks — and a new teaching began. Each night for ten days or so, I channeled both Ananda and Jesus for these open-minded and adventurous young adults. It heralded the beginning of their personal spiritual educations. Following that intense excursion into spirit guided by Ananda and Jesus, they decided to move to my little island and begin their spiritual odysseys into the nondualistic teachings that were being transmitted through my voice and body but certainly were not from my consciousness. They too are now studying *A Course in Miracles* and are being readied for their unique spiritual journeys, guided and helped by great minds indeed.

I began channeling the text for this project in August of 2013. Daily, I would go into the peaceful state that allows channeling to take place, and Ananda would introduce JC (the affectionate term we use to refer to Jesus) and once again, encourage, soothe, or cajole me into the task at hand. It took almost another year for me to complete this most unusual story. I had to take breaks and put it aside when the idea of it overwhelmed me, but I kept coming back to the project, knowing that I am only the messenger — nothing more. Ananda told me that it would be a year in the making, and at the time I could not see why, but now I do. There is a certain process that the mind must go through when facing such huge shifts in consciousness, crossing forbidden boundaries, and actually integrating all this information; it simply takes time.

So I offer up this book to you with honesty and without an ounce of deception. I cannot verify the source. I cannot prove that this is true. All I know is that the story is not mine; it comes from a consciousness other than my own. Any changes have been extremely minor.

I ask you to come to this story free of judgment and open to hearing something new, something fresh. I have been transformed by these teachings that continue to flow, and my young, brave, and spiritual children have become enthusiastic and diligent students walking the path to peace with me, Ananda, and JC.

Christ consciousness is accessible and available to all of us. Jesus was gifted with access to it and attempted to teach the means to its attainment. Apparently his teaching ministry is not yet complete: He has more to tell us.

— Tina Louise Spalding, June 20, 2014

Introduction

I AM RETURNED TO CONNECT WITH THE WORLD. I HAVE COME TO SPEAK to you as a group, as a species, as a group consciousness that exists on this plane at this time. The stories in this book are not for recreation; they are to clarify and to heal the split, distorted perceptions that many of you are walking around with.

My name is Jesus. This is a very exciting opportunity for me as this being that you know as Jesus. I am at work in many places, many times, and many dimensions. This is not the only place that I am exerting my personality, as you call it, this focal point that you may converse with. I use my mental and spiritual connections all the time all over the world, for there are many beings who call my name. There are many beings who misunderstand what it is I stood for and what I represent, and this is why this book is being written: to clarify the message and to educate these beings. This was not my name in my lifetime, but I will use this word, as it triggers great joy and fear and causes great confusion and anger in its spoken form.

There is no reason for a word or a name to elicit such fear and joy, hatred and judgment. This gives you an idea that the name has been misused, for if a name is in alignment with love, with peace, and with joy, it only brings these feelings to the surface. My name has been contaminated and used to commit crimes. It has been used to subjugate people, to spread lies, and to deceive millions of people out of their true heritage, which is a divine, creative, and joyful existence.

Now, this seems a heavy and hard subject to talk about, but it is very important that the truth of my existence becomes known, for there are many, I am sorry to say, who labor under misconceptions and falsities of what I was, what my life meant, and what happened on that journey. There have been fabrications, there have been distortions, and there have been out-and-out lies.

There are, of course, some truths sprinkled in there, and so I am here to channel through this one we call Tina, this one we call the dear one. She is a vessel who offers up her physicality to transmit information that is of great import to your spiritual, mental, emotional, and physical health. She offers her body as a microphone, as a magnifier, as a megaphone, and as a producer of this material out of the goodness of her heart and out of the arrangements that she has made with all of us here to do this work and to spread the words of the nonphysical through her voice into the world so that you may hear them.

We are here to give you relief from your misperceptions. We are here to align you with truth so you might not suffer anymore. These histories, these stories, and these lies and fabrications distort your ability to connect with divine information. They distort your ability to relate to other human beings in a kind, compassionate, and egalitarian way. As long as these lies stand without contradiction and as long as they stand without a voice speaking up to tell the true story, then these lies and misperceptions, these untruths, will continue to distort the lives of honest, kind, and caring people who think they are doing the right thing because they are reading the "Word of God." This is not the truth.

The Bible is not the word of God, for there is much death; there is much killing; and there is much judgment, narrow-mindedness, and cultural distortions in that book that do not apply in God's world. They do not apply in the world of the Divine, the higher realms of light and love and joy and creativity. These are human stories that have passed through the lenses of many men and, unfortunately, few women. This text, these stories that you call the Bible, is distorted by cultural prejudices and power structures you are now oblivious of.

So I have come at this time, in this place, and through this being to speak *my* truth, to speak the story of my life — the *true* story of my life. Now, there are those in traditional religious circles who will say that this woman speaks blasphemy and that she is possessed by the devil, but this is not the case. This being is of a high vibration after much prayer and considered meditation and spiritual work — more than many of you who stand in judgment of her. She has practiced the art of forgiveness, the art of creativity, and the art of honesty and self-expression to a high degree and has, through this practice, cleared the way for these communications. So do not point a finger at her and attack her in any way, for she is clearer than those who attack her.

Those who attack her, even in thought, show a lack of clarity and a lack of understanding of my teachings. If you stand in judgment of this being, you are closed-minded; you are not practicing the principles that I taught when I was transformed on this physical plane many, many years ago. You are practicing the energy of the ego and the material world, and your self-righteousness is evidence of your lack of awareness, your lack of elevation in the vibrational sense. So if you come to this book with an air of judgment, superiority, or dismissal, know that these are reflections on you rather than on us and the dear channel who took down this information.

This is the truth: Judgment is the biggest crime that can be committed against yourself and against others. Whatever the judgment, you are judging against yourself in the sense that you disconnect from spiritual communication. You disconnect from the flow of abundance and love — that which you call God, the benevolent force that guides this universe and that guides the teachings and the processes that illuminate, help, and assist beings on their way to the higher realms.

The reason I am here is to take advantage of the clarity of this channel, of the liberalism that now pervades your culture, and of the technical developments that allow this information to be disseminated to millions of beings around the planet. Now is the time to step up and learn the true teachings of this one you call Jesus, this one you call the Christ, and to truly understand what my life meant, what I was here to accomplish, and why I lived the life I did.

I talk about the truth of my birth and the truth of my life. I cover some stories that are recounted in the Bible and tell you the true story of those events. I describe some of my personal traits, my human traits, and I define what I am, who I am, and why these things happened. You will be able to understand the truth, and you will begin this reconditioning, this retooling of your mind — of your thoughts and beliefs — on this subject of my life, my meaning, and my purpose, for it is a long process.

This story will begin the change. It will not *make* the change. It will facilitate turning the key in the lock, but you must open the door and walk through it into a new realm that is opened by this information. That is your responsibility. We can only bring you the message, this channel and I. We can only work together to transmit the information, but it is through your actions and your transformation that you will see a change in your world, a change in the subjective world that is manufactured from your beliefs, your thoughts, and your feelings.

This book will free you from the limitations of your conditioned mind, for there are many stories and tales about me that are not true. Many punishments have been devised to discipline those who do not follow rules attributed to me but that I never set. Many laws have been created that are not in alignment with what I taught. There are many institutions that you believe are good but were created to lessen your spirit and, in fact, were created to diminish your creative abilities. Many of these decisions were based on erroneous information about me and what my life meant and what its purpose was.

So the purpose of this book is to clarify, to tell the truth, and to share my energies with you so that you can begin the transformation of your mind and, therefore, the transformation of your heart and your world. It is in the misteachings that have been associated with my name that much death and pain has been caused and that much guilt and self-recrimination has been expressed. That was not my purpose; that was not my lesson.

I came to live a life and express love, to express creativity and my own individuality, and to encourage all of you to do the same. My name has been used in vain. My name has been used for other purposes, and it is for these clarifications that I arrive now with assistance from other nonphysical beings who have paved the way for this communication to take place, who have paved the way in helping clarify this channeling by removing the last dregs of interference from its ability to speak my words and offer up my energies so that you might engage with them, discuss things with me, and talk these matters over with me in person. This is going to be part of our journey. Part of your journey will be dialoguing with me and talking about what I truly experienced.

Come to this book with no judgment. If you cannot come to this book without judgment, put it aside until you have disciplined your mind to be at peace, for you will not hear the words if your mind is aligned with that of criticism and judgment and unloving thoughts. The words will fall on deaf ears, and you will not be able to integrate them into your mind. So if you are reading these pages with judgment, hatred, and self-righteousness in your heart, we say put it down. You are not ready to read these words, and you are not ready to hear these words, for it is in the peaceful, kind heart and the quiet mind that knowledge can penetrate. It cannot penetrate through the battle armor of the ego and the narrow focus of the conditioned mind.

If you are able to continue reading, if you feel excited about this material, and open in your heart and mind to hear what I have to say through this particular form, then we look forward to sharing these many pages and these many stories with you. We are happy that you are with us. There is much information contained within these pages, and there are many tales of my excursions into the physical world. There are also paragraphs about how things work and why they work that way. These sections have wider margins and are set off by subheads that introduce lessons, reminders, and special topics Jesus would like us to take note of. As a whole, this is a wonderful blend of story, information, and structural ideas that will assist you in more fully living your life and understanding the history of your religious structures so that you may create a free and self-expressive life of your own, connected to Source in all ways, without the need for intermediaries, rules, or regulations that have nothing to do with the teachings of truth.

There are beings who will look at this production and claim that it is far too casual and far too "nondivine" in its presentation, that I would not speak this way, that I would have an accent, or that I would speak a different language. But these are the small thoughts of the ego. The transmission of information through consciousness does not require language; it does not require anything that is normally required within your three-dimensional world in terms of communication. It is done by thought only. Language and dialect and these sorts of things merely interfere with communication. When you are in the nonphysical, communication is very easy through the thought processes and into the mind that is open to it.

This particular situation offers us an opportunity to speak casually about who I am and what I did. It gives us the opportunity to allow the truth of my life as an ordinary human being to come through in the descriptions I give of the events and the people and the places I visited during my lifetime.

This lifetime is not as significant as you think it is. You have, in your society, made it a very important thing. You have made it a very important storyline in your culture's development, and it is interwoven throughout all of your institutions. It is interwoven throughout all of your beliefs about many different subjects. So it is very important to unravel this story from your culture, and that is what this book is about.

We are transmitting the true life so you can begin to see that many of the stories that your institutions tell you are efforts to control, to repress, to organize, and to intimidate. My life was not what they say it was, and I was not what they say I was. This is why I am engaging in this format — in a casual, conversational way.

People will note that I am speaking ordinary words. There are no choirs singing in the background. I am an ordinary consciousness — if a little more elevated.

The time is ripe. The need for a spiritual revolution is here. The foundation blocks have been set in your New Age philosophies, but it is time to deconstruct the old structures that have kept you in prison for so long. It is time to take down the walls, brick by brick, that have hidden your vision from the freedom and joy that is yours to express. It is time to take down the barbed wire of judgment and narrow-mindedness that many religions have erected to keep you contained within the concentration camp of your own mind, limited by false rules and false doctrines that do not convey the truth.

I am pleased to be communicating with you once again. I am the one you call Jesus. I am the one who was referred to as the son of God, but I am not more the son of God than you. You are too. You are all the sons and the daughters of God, and we are all equal. Some are just further along the road; that is all. We often turn back to grasp the hand of somebody who is sitting on the side, tired and disillusioned.

That is our purpose: to assist each other along the road to awakening.

A Clarification of Terms

THIS WILL BECOME A DEFINING TEXT IN YOUR SOCIETY. IT WILL BECOME something of controversy. It will become something of hot debate. That is a delicious idea in our mind, and it is a delicious idea in the mind of that which you call God. Delicious debate and passionate expression — these are things that are the force behind the creative experience that you have, but if you do not understand this, if you do not understand how things manifest and you think that they come about all by themselves, then you are working at a tremendous disadvantage.

So let us speak about some words we use in this text so that you understand exactly what they mean and can bring the correct definition into your mind and do not labor under any misperceptions, misunderstandings, or untruths.

Ego

Ego is the word that is at the front and center of your society at this time. It is given a bad rap. It is given the attacker's definition. But the ego mind is a very creative device. It is what you have brought with you into the separation experience. You have a fragmented mind. There is a much bigger piece of you, let us say — the part that is connected to Oneness, the part that is connected to God, the Divine Mind, that is a much greater part of you. But the ego mind is the part that you have brought down with you into separation, and so the ego mind is, by definition, focused on separation because that is what you have wanted it for.

The ego mind is relentlessly separation focused. That means, given an opportunity to communicate with another — if you are in the ego mind without knowing what it does or understanding its function — the ego will seek reasons to separate from that being. It will not seek reasons to join that being. You can already see how this contributes to many, many problems in your relationships and causes much of the difficulty in your society. You must understand what the ego mind is, and you must understand why you have brought it with you to experience. Then you can use it without its taking over your consciousness.

Ego mind is associated with the physical body. It is designed to keep you safe. It is the consciousness process that you have incorporated into your consciousness experience here. You decided to come into separation, into individuality, to follow some of your desires, and you brought this focusing device with you. It is a survival mechanism. Its purpose is to keep you safe in your physical vehicle so that you can experience that which you seek to experience. Now, if you look at it this way, it is a very positive thing. It has your personal protection as its goal. But also you can see that if the ego mind is not balanced with spiritual practice — if it is not balanced with an understanding and comprehension of its process and its principles — then it can become an aggressive, self-centered concept, and that is what most of you suffer from.

You have an ego mind at play trying to keep you safe, trying to keep money in the bank, trying to keep a roof over your head and food in your fridge and in your belly, but when you do not balance it with spiritual practice and the greater understanding of what you are, it causes you pain. So when we use the word ego mind, that is what you are experiencing.

The ego is not your enemy, but it must be understood. It must be treated with respect and discipline. It is a large, powerful, and empowered energy because you give it all of your thought. As a divine aspect of Creative Mind, you have tremendous power, so when you feed your energy into something, it becomes stronger to such a degree that it is all-powerful and all-creative. For many of you, the ego mind — with its fear of death, its association with the body, and its limited ability to see (remember it is only looking at the present environment, interpreting the present environment) — is what your space-time continuum requires of you. That is what your ego is for.

You need to balance it with an intense spiritual practice. Why? Because everything that you see and every aspect of yourself represents the idea of separation. If you do not balance this, you will be completely taken over; this is the suicidal person, or the warmonger, or the addict. These are beings whose minds have had the ego run riot without any balance and without any self-understanding or self-discipline.

You have the ability to implement the procedures in your life so that you might, indeed, balance the ego mind. Your television watching is something that is very important to cut back on and control. Inputting violence or pornography into the mind is food for the ego, and those things are very low in vibration. They cause trouble by lowering your vibration and allowing the mind to pick up other frequencies of a low kind.

When you read a spiritual book, when you read a divinely inspired book, the vibration of that mind has been transmitted. So just as watching a violent show about murder will lower your vibration, reading or listening to divinely inspired material will raise your vibration and allow you to tap into another frequency. The ego mind is a receiver; it is acting in the physical body, but its information is being picked up from a level of frequency, and that is what you are experiencing.

It is not what you think it is. The ego mind is a vibration that you are picking up, and your physical body is a demonstration of a particular mindset. It is in the training of the mind and in the expression of the spiritual nature of yourself that you will find balance with the ego mind. You are ensconced in the ego in your world. Everything that you see and the experiences in your body are things that are ego-driven, and it is important for you to understand the magnitude of the ego mind. It is within your power, however, to influence how you experience this as you travel through your incarnation.

Love

Love is the natural state of you. It is the vibration of that which you call God or All That Is, the benevolent force that imbues everything with life and energy.

The forms you see are not reality. They are your interpretations through the sensory device that is called your body, the ego mind. And so you see things that represent separation, but beneath that form, there is an energy, a force, and it is a force of love. It is a force of extension, which is the ever-expressing nature of creativity. So love is that.

Love has qualities. It has qualities of kindness and of expression. It has qualities of creativity, extension, and giving. It is not limited; it is expansive in its vibration. The love that many of you experience — or what you call love on your plane — is not that. It is the ego mind possessing, controlling, limiting, and restricting. So what we want you to understand is the real defini-tion of love. It is always positive, it always feels good, and it always expands and extends. It is unlimited. When you feel the desire to possess somebody or restrict them to keep them yours, this is the ego mind trying to control; this is not love.

So this is a very important distinction for you to understand here: The love that we refer to as the Universal Love, God Love, All That Is, this love is the love that is calling you Home. You have separated yourself from this love vol-untarily to experience individuality and separation, so love is very overwhelm-ing for the ego mind because it is counter to it. This is another reason that it is very important for you to study spiritual material and practice the principles of forgiveness, loving kindness, compassion, and nonjudgment. These are all aspects of a similar quality that reduce your separation from each other and therefore your separation from love.

Love does not discriminate. Love does not separate. Love does not attack in any way. It is a peaceful extension of All That Is. In your separation from this principle, you feel alone, isolated, and fearful. And through the practice of forgiveness, which we will define next, you will return to love and remove the ideas, thoughts, and blocks in the mind that prevent you from the awareness of love's presence.

Love is always there. That benevolent force is always there, calling you Home, but judgments and fears prevent you from experiencing that love. The purpose of my teaching is to remove the barriers to your awareness of love's presence. It is always there, but when you are small and when you are focused on judgment, limitation, fear, and attacking, love cannot reside in that vibra-tion. Love is a high vibration. It is a frequency to which you must elevate yourself, and it is through practicing these principles that you will elevate your vibration high enough that you can experience love.

If you look at your relationships and do not see love there but you see that you are watching violence on television, eating poorly, and perhaps drinking alcohol or taking drugs, know that these cause your vibration to lower, and they keep you out of the realm of love's frequency. So it is in cleaning up your diet, cleaning up your mind, and cleaning up your thinking that you will raise your vibration, and you will indeed step into the realms in which love can be felt, creativity can be felt, health can be felt, and abundance can be felt.

This is all science. It is not spirituality in the sense that you have been taught — that God dispenses good things to good people and bad things to bad people. You can see clearly that this is not the case; your world does not make sense given that belief. But when you realize that your frequency allows you to tap into certain experiences, then you can see that when you feel better, you are able to extend yourself in a state of love toward others, and you will receive much abundance, much give-and-take in that vibrational frequency.

Forgiveness

Next, we ask you to think about forgiveness. This is the path that is prescribed as the resolution to your problem. The problem is separation from Oneness. Your awareness of it has gone. You are still, in your greater self, connected to love, connected to All That Is. You have not been cast adrift by yourself, but you have taken an aspect of yourself on a very intense and at times terrifying journey.

Through this practice of forgiveness, you can return Home. This is not a death process. This is not something you understand. The awakening process is returning Home. You do not escape this life through death when you are in the incarnational cycle. Death leads to rebirth and more and more lifetimes until you begin to understand what is really going on here. Your mind is the Creator. Your mind is the Divine Creator of your world, but you do not know that that is what you are doing, and so your fears and the untruths in your mind bring unpleasant experiences into your existence.

You do not need to have unpleasant experiences to learn. This is a fiction — that humans must suffer. Many beings suffer until they are tired of it and start to look for a new way of doing things. But you do not need to suffer. You can make a choice in this moment to practice forgiveness, to study *A Course in Miracles*, and to read this book. Contained in these books is the truth that you need to understand how life works, how creativity works, and how you can get back in touch with that loving consciousness that is what you call God, or All That Is. It is reaching out to you, but it is of a high frequency, and you must step up to that level because it will not come down to your level. It cannot do that; that is not its nature. So it is up high. You must raise yourself up high. That is what I did in my lifetime, and I am very pleased to bring you all of the information that you need to raise yourself up in your lifetime. You do not need to wait until you pass over, when it is too late to do the work in the incarnation. You must then be reborn and try again, and of course, as you know, you do not remember.

So let us take this opportunity now to begin the waking process, to begin to implement the wonderful, wonderful lessons here. You are not abandoned. You have abandoned God yourself, but we have decided it is time for a concerted effort from the nonphysical to get these teachings into as many hands as possible. We want to right the wrongs of your erroneous history and bring forth the truth so that you can begin functioning as your own communication device with God. You do not need an intermediary, but we can help you. We are offering our services as teachers and instructors, but you can do it yourself. In fact, you must do it yourself. Nobody can do it for you.

PART ONE

The Early Years

CHAPTER ONE

How It All Began

WE WISH TO START AT THE BEGINNING. WE WISH TO START WITH MY BIRTH. My mother was informed in a dream that she would have me. She had a discussion in a very vivid and lively dream that told her that she would become pregnant, that she would have a child who would bring light to the world, and that the spirit of this child would come into this unborn baby and would live its life out as her son. She was told in this dream that she would be responsible for providing the foundational environment in which this being would live. She was told to teach it the Jewish ways, but she was also told to be very gentle and kind with this baby. She was told to love it unconditionally, to love it with all her heart, for it would need her love, and it would have a challenging life at times because of its personality and its nature.

This being who came to her in a dream is what you call an archangel, a being from a higher realm who has responsibilities to Earth, who has chosen this, who is born into this job, so to speak. Archangels have assignments they are in charge of and beings they are in charge of. This archangel was in charge of my life, my transformation, and my education. I have spent much time with this being since passing over so many years ago. Back in that day, this being was able to communicate with my mother in a dream. My mother told my father about the dream, and he pooh-poohed it a little bit, for he was in the male world of reason, judgment, and action.

My mother was an intuitive and kind woman who was open to these other realms, as most women are. This is why you see more women in spiritual transformation groups than you do in other meetings, for women are more open to the nonphysical. They are more receptive in nature; they are more fluid in nature. This is an important fact to bring to mind at this point — that my mother, not my father, was the one with whom communications could be made more easily.

Deconstructing Myths

This is the beginning of the deconstruction of the idea that men play a more important role in the spiritual/cultural interface. This is not the case. Generally, women play a much more important role in the transmission of information — the transmission of new information in particular — for they do not become so attached to the structures, the power, or the politics as men do. So this is my first insertion of blasphemy in this story. There will be many, we assure you.

My mother spoke to this being and was told that she would be giving birth to this child who would shine light on this world and transform things. My mother was prepared somewhat, but the tale of how three wise men were told of my coming did not come about in the sense of the story told in the Bible, this book that you study so much and believe is the word of God. There were indeed shamans and esoteric students of spirituality who got this information, just as any psychic would get such information. It was not unusual in that sense, for there are many beings who always receive spiritual information. So there was some knowledge in the villages and fields around where I was born and people who knew that someone would be born, but there was not a great fanfare at all. There was not a great shaking up of society at that point. It was merely a small news story that traveled through the spiritual realms. I was not important at that point.

The conception was not as is told. Of course, there was a normal marital relationship going on between my mother and father, and they created me as any baby is created. But my mother always felt that there was a special energy contained within her as she carried me, and indeed this was the case. There was much shepherding that began very early on in my physical experience of the spiritual side, of energies and of information to be disseminated and to be imparted to me through my mother's body. She was raised in vibration to assist in my physical development, for I would need a strong, muscular, and flexible masculine form in which to grow, so this body — this child's body that was incubating within her — was given particular attention from the nonphysical realms.

Energies can be shifted in, chemical systems can be assisted in, and light and love and information can be infused into a being that is created within the female form. It manifests out of spirit; it does not grow for no reason. The physical form, the body at the time of conception, is stimulated by the desire of the spirit that wishes to live a life, so it is being stimulated from the nonphysical.

Here I will go into this idea of much controversy in your culture, the question of when the spirit enters the body. When is it human? When is it alive? When is it a sacred being? Well, it is a sacred being before it is born; it requires not the physical body. We will comment on your subject of abortion — which comes up at this point, does it not? You will wish to know when I became this being known as Jesus, for it will be used in arguments on your Earth about when termination of pregnancy can take place, if at all. We say that the spirit always has a choice to be in the body or not in the body, and there is no final decision ever made when the spirit is in the body. A spirit can leave a body at any age, whether it is before birth or after birth. You might decide to leave your body when you are three years old. You might decide to leave your body when you are twenty years old. You might decide to leave your body when you are sixty years old. You might decide to leave your body when you are two weeks old, within the womb, changing positions, or changing ideas.

We bring your attention to this subject — that the physical body is the gift to the world of the spirit, and you are not taking anything from it if you decide that you do not wish it to be born, for a spirit that wishes to be born does not want to come into a home that hates it or resents it. This is not going to be a wonderful place for a spirit to grow and learn and express itself. It understands if the mother terminates the physical expression that is the fetus, this unborn, physically undeveloped being who cannot survive of its own volition at that point. It will create another body — perhaps in the same woman, perhaps in a different one — depending on the circumstances and what it wishes to do.

You do not need to think that you have prevented a soul's birth. That is not the case. You are not that powerful. The soul will create another body in another time in that same woman or in the body of a different woman. It has many choices, and it has no restrictions based on your destruction of a physical structure. It has compassion and knowing, and it will have understanding that if a woman decides that she cannot have a child, this is her free will. This is her decision, and it is up to her whether she feels that she can handle such a large undertaking. It is nobody else's business whether she does or does not choose to do this.

That is our comment on this particular subject. Clearly, we are pro-life. We love life, and we love living, but you all have free will, and there is no judgment or punishment on this side for what you do. If a woman decides she is unable to bring a pregnancy to term with love, she is free to do as she chooses and will not be punished in any way for that decision. The spirit that wishes to be born will not be thwarted so easily. Unborn spirits are very determined in their ability to create bodies, and there are many receptive sites for this to take place.

Ordinary Beginnings

I was born in a normal way, as a normal baby, not really demonstrating anything unusual in my physicality or in my energetic system. But planted within me was a seed of transformation, a seed of rebelliousness. I was born to change the world. I was born to change the restrictive and oppressive society full of misteachings and unnecessary and violent rituals. I was born to bring a light into the world — not through destruction but through enlightenment, through the dissemination of truths. Yet as a small babe, I was as ordinary as any of you, and my mother loved me as any mother would love a babe.

We lived an ordinary life for those first few years. I was a spirited and healthy child. I was happy to be in my body. Some part of me knew that I was destined for great things. I had this feeling all my life: I knew that I would be unusual, and I knew that I would be participating in great events. I did not have an understanding of what they were, but there was always this feeling, this inkling. Many of you have had this feeling that you are destined for something special, and it is true! I was no different from you in that sense. You each are born with a map of sorts that is contained within you, and it is felt as a feeling. It is felt as passion. It is felt as interest, and that is what I felt as a small child growing up. I knew that I was different. I knew that I would be different.

I would like to say here, for those of you who recognize this quality in your own childhood, that this is part of the idea that you are not different from me. You are the same. You are born with a desire for a life that looks a certain way. You are born with an interest in certain subjects, and you are born with a passion to do certain things. Some of you are studious and intellectual and care not for running about and playing; some of you are intensely physical in your expression and care not for books. One is not better than the other. There is no value judgment on the spirit side as to what you choose to do. Your passion is your purpose. That is another subject we will go into in more detail, but we would like to mention it here, just in passing, as I am speaking about my childhood. My passion was my purpose; it was talking to people, helping the underdog, offering assistance to those who needed it, and standing up to bullies and to those who demonstrated cruelty or intolerance to someone of lesser strength.

This was a topic I got embroiled in many times in my youth, and I was often brought before authorities at school for defending underdogs; yet I stood there, firm in my conviction that I was doing the right thing, *knowing* that I was doing the right thing. Perhaps I went at it a little too enthusiastically sometimes, but I always felt the need to do it, the need to assist, the need to be loving and caring.

I grew in my family. I had brothers and sisters. I was not an only child. There is a feeling in this book that you call the Bible that I was a solitary being with no family and friends, but I was an ordinary boy. I had four brothers and sisters, and we would play and argue and fight, these kinds of things, the normal kinds of things that a family would do. But I was always a bit more assertive. I was always a bit more out of the pack, so to speak. They were often looking for me. I would be off exploring nature or with a group of children discussing why things were happening and the meaning of things, even at a young age of ten or eleven or twelve years old.

I was very curious about how the world functioned and why people did what they did, and I could not understand people's cruelty. I could not understand people's mistreatment of each other, so I would stand up in church and I would question the rabbis. I would ask them, "If there is a loving God, then why are we cruel to each other?" I would stand up and ask these kinds of questions, and they would get very perturbed with me. They would get very perturbed that I was contradicting them. They would get perturbed that I was not taking this medicine without argument. That is where my reputation as an argumentative and trouble-making religious student came from.

I was not satisfied with their explanations. They would often say that that is just the way it is, and that did not satisfy me. I had a curious and inquisitive mind. I was always reading the spiritual texts that we had available to us, and I found interpretations that could have been made in a different way. I would bring these observations to the teachers, and they would get quite agitated with me for questioning them, for suggesting that perhaps they were doing it the wrong way. But I knew I was right. I knew I was right in my heart and my soul.

A Rebellious Teen

I continued on an inquisitive path into my teens. By the time I was sixteen or seventeen, I was tired of convention. I was tired of the rules, and I began to break away from what were considered the structures of respected society at that time. I began to venture off into my own world of exploration in nature. I pursued recreational activities that were normal for a teenager (even in your time you would see it as such): arguing with my parents, taking off for periods without telling anybody where I was going. I was annoyed with the strictures and the rules, and I began to hang out with less-than-reputable people. I began to drink a little, to carouse a little. I began to explore my maleness with women, and I began to fight a little and get involved with the edges of society.

This is not what your churches wish to hear. They do not wish to hear that I was a teenager who was a troublemaker. But this is the case for many of the trouble-making teenagers in your society. They are telling you that they are not interested in conforming to your rules, for they look at you with your addictions, your sadness and depression, your financial problems, and your family problems, and they tell you they are not interested in living the same way, so you call them bad. You call them delinquent, but they are merely expressing their truth, which is that they are not inclined to live the way you have, and they have free will. All beings have free will. All beings are given their own guidance systems, which are directed by their desires and their senses of self, and they have the right to express their dissatisfaction with your living in that way.

Of course, as you enter into this time in your history, there are many young people who wish to not follow in your footsteps. They do not wish to kill their planet with pollution and war, yet you call them delinquent. You say they behave badly. But the truth of the matter is that it is you who are badly behaved with your gas-guzzling cars, your poisonous food production methods, and your political and economic systems that are overwhelmingly in favor of the wealthy and the powerful. They do not wish to join in your lifestyles of slavery to a mortgage or a job that you hate. They are far more concerned with expressing themselves and living in freedom and joy, and I support them wholeheartedly in that.

When you look on young people who you consider to be misbehaving, understand that I misbehaved too, for I did not wish to be restricted and imprisoned by the culture that I was living in. I could see that people were unhappy. I could see that they were oppressed and living in jails of cultural creation, and I would not step in there. I would not follow the rules, and I would not behave in the way that religion, culture, and time dictated. So I was a delinquent. I was a rebel. I caused waves, and I ruffled feathers.

I expressed an energy that was powerful; I expressed an energy that was outspoken; and I expressed an energy that was curious about experience. And I enjoyed myself immensely despite the upsets of my mother — who was very concerned and worried about me and thought that I would go off the proverbial rails. But she did not understand that I was collecting information and asserting my independence, and it was a most important aspect of that time in my life. For in that time and place, beings were married young and indoctrinated into the cultural prison very early, and I would not participate in this. I would not settle down and get married young, start a family, and get caught in that restricted and limiting form of life. I wanted more; I wanted much more, and I set about getting it.

We rebelled against the powers that be, the religious and political powers in that time and place. There were many restrictions on the actions of young people, and there were many requirements that society told us we must comply with. Women were told to be very modest, to cover their bodies, and to marry the first man who showed them any attention of any kind, as long as he was from a reputable family. Young men were told to behave in religious ways that complied with the dogma of sacrifices, paying homage to certain people, places, and things that were deemed of high value politically, economically, and religiously.

I was truly a free spirit in this regulated and oppressive society. You must understand that these were small communities. These were small, isolated towns and villages in remote areas, and if you did not comply with the requirements of the powers that be, you were ostracized, you were chastised, and you were often cast out in a form of social blacklisting. You are familiar with this idea of being "sent to Coventry" and not being spoken to, not being accepted into the group. This, of course, was a powerful form of punishment in that time and place. The idea of being kicked out of your village social structure was very frightening for people, but I of course was not afraid of this because of my connection to the nonphysical.

In my teenage years, I was already beginning to receive information. It was before my enlightenment and awakening, but I was getting information through intuition and my guidance system, which was very antagonistic toward authority. I was quite confrontational and had many arguments with rabbis, parents, and teachers, these kinds of organizational forces within my community. I began to bump up against these situations as I was heading into young adulthood. This is when the constraints really began to be exerted on young people in my culture. This was when I really began to rebel.

Meeting Mary Magdalene

There was a group of us who began to hang around together, and we began to function on the outskirts of society. My dear Mary was one of us. She was in there not because of her rebellious nature per se but because her family had fallen on hard times. Her mother had had to take in laundry and deal with the more disreputable elements of our society, so she was given the name of "loose woman." Indeed, she was not this. She was a poor woman who needed to do the work that she needed to do to keep her family alive. Her husband was not with her. He had died, so she was forced to support her family herself. And so this bad name was laid also on her daughter, Mary.

Mary was lonely, and we were a happy and delightful bunch of people. There were several other women in the group. There were eight or ten of us, all told. We would carouse a little bit. We would hike up into the hills and engage in raucous behavior compared to the rest of society but nothing compared with what you are doing these days. There were no drugs. There was a little wine that was procured occasionally, and we would get a little tipsy, but that was the extent of our misbehaving. The worst crime we committed was being men and women, unchaperoned, off by ourselves without the oppressive eye of the ruling elite on us.

That was when Mary and I began to fall in love with each other. We got to spend time together sitting on rocky outcrops with beautiful views and chatting about spiritual life and what we wanted for ourselves. She and I shared many ideals, many ideas, and we began to talk about philosophical principles. We began to talk about the teachings we had grown up with. We began to talk about our dislike of the restrictions, the regulations, the rules, and the arbitrariness of all of these things. We began to see that if there was indeed a God in heaven, then surely there would not be things that went against our nature. We would have long discussions about this concept — that if you were born with a kind of affinity for particular things in your natural makeup, why would the "right" thing to do be the opposite of this? Of course, this is a logical argument, and the argument I will make for you as beings on a spiritual journey.

You are reading this, so you are indeed seeking guidance. You are indeed wondering how you will find your way, and of course, this is the way. Your natural tendency is toward certain subjects. Your natural tendency is toward certain interests and certain kinds of people. It is illogical to think that you are meant to do something else. Yet your parents, your schools, your religions, and your political leaders will tell you this thing that they are telling you to do is the right thing to do. But the logic of this must sit with you. There is no way in heaven or on earth that the divine nature of this universe would push you to do something that goes against your natural inclination. You must understand this; it is illogical.

Think about something or someone you feel passionately about. Think of how you feel when you have a strong desire to do something. It consumes your entire body. You are, in fact, not easily able to override it. It takes a lot of practice to override your guidance system, and of course this is what school systems, family indoctrination, and weekly study does: It overrides your natural guidance system, and you are taught to do the opposite. So your life becomes something that is not your own, a representation of other beings' principles and ideas. This is what Mary and I discussed on our many long afternoons, and we began to fall in love because we saw that we shared a similar sense of being, a similar sense of desire for freedom and self-expression.

I was working in carpentry. This is a truth about me. I was involved in this form of creativity, and she enjoyed sewing and cooking, these feminine tasks, but I did not see them as less valuable than mine. I understood that was what she had been taught and that she enjoyed this form of creativity. And so we shared these activities. I would often make her small things for her home. Her mother was very busy doing the work that was required for the family to survive, and so Mary and I had very little interference from her in terms of our relationship. I would go over to her house at times, and she would cook me meals. I would share meals with her family. They liked me very much; I was very entertaining, telling stories, mimicking and making fun of the powers that be in our culture at that time. I was a very good comedian. I had good timing and keen observation skills, and I was very good at copying the ways people walked and spoke. At dinner I often regaled Mary and her family with tales of rabbis and Roman centurions, and this entertained them immensely. I was full of it. I was very full of it!

But I was in tune with myself. I did not believe the lies that if I did not do this, that, or the other, I would be condemned. I did not believe this. I knew that I was in tune with something far greater than me, and it was coming in the form of intuition, it was coming in the form of dreams, and it was coming in the form of voices in my mind that were clearly not my own but were very loving and authoritative. I knew that many prophecies and many sources of information from the past had been communicated in this way, and I did not doubt myself. I did not doubt that I was receiving divine communications. There were many references to texts of religious material that we were reading at the time.

You must understand it was not called the Bible at that time. It was the Torah; it was the Old Testament, which of course it was not called then. It was the Testament. It was the doctrine that was read in the churches and synagogues of the time. Being well versed in it, I was familiar with these passages. I was familiar with these things, and much of the information that I was given from the nonphysical was about this material, about real interpretations of it and what it really meant, what the Garden of Eden was, these kinds of things. I studied this material a great deal of the time. This was my main recreation, studying these religious texts and doctrines. I was very well read in them, and I was very good at analyzing, studying, and comprehending these materials. This is what I did with my spare time in my early twenties.

Mary and I spent a lot of time together over the years, and eventually we married. At the ripe old age of twenty-seven, I married Mary, and we set up our own home. But we had been friends and even lovers for many years. We had become intimate in our long and wonderful times together. We did not seek sanction by the authorities for the very reason that I have stated: We were not living a life that was condoned by them, and we did not feel, in our hearts, that we needed their blessing. We felt that we had Spirit's blessing because of our desires for each other, our knowledge of each other, and our love for each other.

So we came to know ourselves in the physical sense before we were married, but this was not something we really struggled with. Our passions were healthy and based in a loving and committed relationship. We knew that we would be together, and we knew that we would marry and have a house together. This was something that we eventually decided to do, for Mary wished to have a child. This was something that I also wished. So we knew that if we were going to bring a child into the world, then we would need to be married. This is why, of course, I chose to take that path. But I'm jumping ahead a little bit. I still wish to speak about my twenties.

Early Teachings and Travels

I was holding classes, informal classes, discussing these materials with young people who were disenfranchised and disillusioned with the powers that be.

Some of them were very upset with me when I gave a different interpretation of a scripture or proposed that perhaps the scripture was being taught in the wrong way in the churches that these beings went to. But this did not bother me. I was always open for a healthy discussion or argument. I was always open to hearing somebody else's point of view, but I was very well educated in the principles of spiritual connection to the nonphysical and in the texts of the Old Testament, as you call it. Some of my discussions became heated, but I often won the argument because of my superior knowledge of the material.

My role as teacher was not new after my enlightenment. I already had a following of sorts in my twenties. I would roam around with this group of young men and women that I was associated with. We would travel hither and yon to other villages and other towns — not as a gang of marauding delinquents as it sounds. (The channel is indeed visualizing it this way.) That is not what it was at all. We were merely exploring the environment. We were exploring and going on adventures to find new communicators, new areas of interest. We would travel to port towns and meet people from overseas and other lands, and this was very exciting at the time.

It was on these excursions that we came to realize — the few of us who were brave enough to step out of our cultural conditioning and participate in these kinds of activities — that there were many other religions and that there were many other places one could go. It was then that I began to find interest in other societies and other cultures, particularly east of where I was living in the Mediterranean area. There were many travelers from India, Central Asia, and Southeast Asia who were coming through that area of the world, so there were many tales of other religions and other areas that piqued my interest and, indeed, came to affect me greatly.

I had a great desire to travel to these areas and investigate their religions to find out about their cultures, to find out about their ways, to find out about what they were up to. Indeed, I decided to go on a journey to these places after a trip to a port town. Mary had stayed at home. This was when she was still living with her mother, before we were a married couple.

I went home and told her that I wished to go on a journey, that I was going on a trek into a different part of the world, and that I would be leaving her behind for a little while. This caused a great rift between us. She was very angry with me and would not talk to me for quite some time. But I bided my time and waited until she had calmed down. It took several weeks. In fact, she was very distressed that I was leaving her and thought that I would not come back, that I would not return to her. This was not the case. I fully intended to return. I simply knew that there was something inside of me that had to go on a walkabout, as you say this term of the Australian Aborigine. But of course it was not called that then; it was called bad behavior in my time.

I received censure from many people around me as I decided to do this, for I decided to do it without any compatriots from the group in which I had been hanging around. At this time, I was twenty-four years of age, and I had reached manhood. I was strong, powerful, and independent. I knew that I needed more information. I was hungry for information, and my internal workings were telling me that I needed to do this. As I listened to tales of the Far East, India, and such places, I felt an overwhelming desire to go, and I could not stop myself.

I told Mary this, and she ran from the room crying and upset, knowing that I would be gone for some time, for the journey was some considerable distance. I did not even really understand how far it was or how long it would take, but she must have known in her heart that it was going to be some time indeed for this journey to transpire.

CHAPTER TWO

The Journey

WE RETURN TO THE PLACE IN THE STORY WHERE I TOLD MARY THAT I WAS GOING on a journey. At the time, I had become friends with a captain of a ship at one of the ports I had visited. We traveled there a few times, my group of friends and I, and we repeatedly encountered this being who had a boat. We had become fast friends over a year's time, so this was not something that I leaped into without thought. This boat captain spoke the same dialect as I did. In fact, he spoke many languages, and I found this fascinating. I found it quite intriguing that he could converse with so many different kinds of people.

It was this relationship that prompted me to venture on a trip abroad, so to speak. He agreed that I could travel with him for a certain amount of time and visit some lands that were not familiar to me, that were not familiar to anyone I knew except him. I spoke to him about his destinations and about his experiences. I was indeed intrigued, particularly by the experiences that related to religious and spiritual practices, for that was my specialty and my passion.

On the day that I left, Mary was very upset. In fact, she did not come to say goodbye to me. I had packed a few items of clothing, a little bit of money, and some food, all wrapped up for the trek to the port town, but she remained in her room, crying. Despite my efforts, she did not allow me to see her. I told her I loved her and I was doing this for the higher good of my life. I wanted her to understand that I would come back with information that would change how we did things, change how we experienced our life together, and add to our experience together, but she could not see this. Of course, in those times, women were not free to travel as they are in your day. They were not free from these cultural constraints. Despite our unconventional ways, she still lived within the confines of a small town as a woman, and this was her ultimate prison. We were able to negotiate our way through some rules, but the overall structure of society did not allow her to come with me. She would have been ostracized completely and forever from her family, from the area of the town in which we lived, in which she lived.

I decided to go alone on this journey not through any joy of leaving her but through my love for her. I would have loved nothing more than to have her with me, but I did not know what territories I was going to venture in, and I did not wish her to come home to people who would not talk to her, to people who would not see her as a decent woman.

Understand: the Myths of Sacrifice and Suffering

You might say that I was selfish in going on my adventure, and you would be correct. In the beginning of your spiritual practices, when you are venturing into this new world of understanding, you must indeed be selfish to a certain degree. This is one of the great teachings that is misused and associated with my name in a very definitive way — the idea of sacrifice and the idea of suffering. Somehow, the crucifixion, the form of my death as you perceive it in the Bible, was given this metaphor for all lives, and it was particularly laid on women, this idea that if you suffer and sacrifice, you will go to heaven. That is not the message of the crucifixion at all! That is not what the story meant. There is no such association, in truth, with my name, and there certainly is no association of suffering, torment, and martyrdom with going to heaven. They have nothing to do with it. This is a complete and utter fabrication.

Here I wish to say that those of you on a spiritual path already — or perhaps those who venture on a spiritual path after reading this material — will need to focus on your own minds, will need to focus on yourselves. The fact of doing this is going to make you a much more valuable, more powerful, and nicer person. You could say that not focusing on yourself but focusing on others is of high value, but that is not the case for most of you. In reality, most of you become very bitter when you sacrifice. Most of you become very resentful when you sacrifice. When you are separated from your passion and your joy, you become sick and depressed, and it serves nobody. You end up being a burden to other beings, an albatross about their necks, and in fact, you end up not being of any benefit whatsoever. These are more blasphemous statements that I wish to make: Sacrifice is not required! Suffering is not required! Martyrdom is not required!

This has nothing to do with achieving the state of mind that will bring you into a heavenly, peaceful place. None of these things are required, and it is the religious structures in your society that have, over time, played out that story to achieve their own ends and to achieve the result of beings who are removed from their passions and their own source of strength, which is their connection through joy to Spirit. They have used these principles for their own gains and their own benefit.

That is why I recount this aspect of the story. I knew in my heart, from the guidance system I had been listening to for many years and from the spirits I had been listening to for many years (for they continued to talk to me in my dreams; they continued to dialogue with me in my mind) that I was being pushed to go on this adventure. So this is what I did.

I left the town with a heavy heart and a bowed head, worrying about Mary. But she had a good family who loved her, she had work that she enjoyed, and she was going to be okay. I knew that in my heart. I had to go on this journey; there was something deep inside me pushing me to do this work, pushing me to go on this extremely unusual trek into lands that I had never known and that I had never seen before.

The Port Town

It took me two days to get to the port where I would embark on this boat, and then I had to wait a few more for my friend to arrive with his ship. He regularly arrived at this port every two or three months. We had arranged to meet at a particular time, and he was a little bit late but not distressingly so. I was nervous enough to go on this journey, and I enjoyed being in the port town. I enjoyed speaking to people from different places. Many of them could speak my language. I was less adept at speaking theirs, but I tried to learn different tongues. I recognized certain languages that I encountered repeatedly, and I thought that I would try to understand some words and learn some phrases.

I stayed in a boarding house that was quite raucous and loud, but at that time, I was eager to forget the suffering of my dear Mary, so I joined in the festivities.

I was faithful to Mary at that point. There were, of course, women of ill-repute in port towns, and I talked to them, for there was no judgment of these women in my mind. I knew that they were put upon by society, that many of them had no choice, and I had an understanding of this conditioning. I had been studying it for many years. This idea that beings behave badly because they have no choice, given the constraints of their mind and of their teachings, had been a subject of my deep and reasoned contemplation.

You must understand that I was always being instructed from the non-physical on these principles. The enlightenment and the complete and utter waking that I received later in my life were merely the finale to a process that was going on through my entire youth and young adulthood. I was given more and more information all the time — much as this channel is given information all the time that is shifting her consciousness and her ability to perceive the truth of each human she encounters.

Remember: Approach People in Kindness

The truth is that all humans function in this idea of the ego. It is through this conditioning process — operating from the small and narrow constraints of linear time, believing in the past, and fearing the future — that you become less-than-lovable beings. But when you focus on people behind the behavior, when you focus on people beyond what they do for their livings and get into conversations with them and hear their stories and their truths, you find a commonality in all beings.

This is something I wish you to think about as you read this story. Do not think about me as some special being who is higher and better and more evolved than you. Think of me as a man on a journey who was given the information that you are now receiving. I was no different. I was given information about a world that I was observing. I was given information about a world that I could see, taste, touch, and feel, and I applied it as I encountered beings. I saw that if I was loving and kind to them, I could access a part of their minds and hearts that was not always easily accessible. If I came at them with grasping hands or judgmental thoughts, they had armor around them that was very difficult to penetrate, and I would almost lose contact with what that being truly was. So this is what I had been studying. This is what we, as young people, had been talking about in our desert meetings for so long.

I applied these principles on my journey, and I never lacked for communication with strangers, for I knew how to approach them. I asked them about their families, and I asked them about their passions. There was nothing simpler than to see a man's heart open, and that is the truth. That is what I applied on this journey, and I never suffered for anything. I never suffered for food or drink or good companionship, and I was shown the way to go. I was given communication assistance from the nonphysical in the sense that I was given directives, intuitions, and promptings on where to go, what road to take, what houses to stay in, and which ones to avoid.

You too are given all of this information, but when you are immersed in the ego mind, you cannot hear it, so you become lost. You become confused by the information that is coming from the ego mind, which is easily affected by others' opinions, easily offended by others' statements, and easily confused by the information coming in from the material world. There are many opinions in the material world, and there are many roads to take in the material world. If you listen to the material world, you will be confused. You will indeed become lost and not know which way to go.

Spreading a Message of Self-Love and Self-Awareness

I spoke to the young women who worked the dock area. They were confused because I did not wish to purchase their services, but I was very nice to them and told them some of the things that I had learned. I hoped that these stories, these ideas of self-love and self-awareness, would help them find ways to make their livings that were less dangerous and less detrimental to their health, for it is very serious business, selling the body for sexual purposes. There are many diseases associated with it, and there are dangerous and drunken men. These women put their lives on the line every night, and I wished to assist them in any way I could. But I did not purchase their services. I had committed myself to Mary many, many years ago, and this journey was not one of searching for sexual freedom. It was one of searching for spiritual understanding. It was one of adventure; it was one of seeking comprehension of the human state and seeking comprehension of the spiritual adventure that every human goes on as they travel on this plane that you call Earth. Of course, I had no idea what I was in for. I had no real idea where I was going or what I would learn. The few days that I was there, I befriended them, and they me. This was something that was normal for me, in the sense that I did not judge people's value by what they did. I had come to this understanding through my years of study of the Torah, of religious scriptures, and of the downloads of information through the nonphysical contact I had. I was given the message that all beings are equal in the eyes of God, all beings are creative in the eyes of God, and all beings are equally valued in the eyes of God.

I was also told that God is not a person, as we had been taught, not a being with an ego that attacks and destroys but a force that reflects everything we think, everything we say, and everything we do and magnifies it back unto us. This is something that I have been taught many, many times through my meditations, dreams, and psychic connection to the nonphysical. So for me to sit down and talk to these women of ill repute was normal in my value system. I was not demeaned by it. There was no judgment in my mind at all, not one single ounce of it; my heart was full of compassion for these women who were forced into this terrible way of making their living. I understood that they could not leave it unless they were given the tools to do so, and this was what I spent my few days there doing: talking to them about their minds, their focuses, and their conditionings.

The patriarchal structure at that time was very powerful, and these women had very little influence, so there were limits to what they could do. But teaching them that their creative source was their minds, their thoughts, and their ideas gave them some power, as much as anyone has power in this world. You have the power to transform your world by what you focus on. So this is what I did as my service to these women.

When my friend arrived a few days later, he was full of jokes and fun, for my new friends whooped and hollered as I walked past them in the evening hours. He assumed that I was a patron, but that was not the case. Mary was dear to my heart at that time, and I was faithful to her. I was faithful to her for many reasons: I loved her heart, body, mind, and soul; she trusted me, and I wished to look her in the eye when I returned home and know that I had not betrayed that trust; and I could honestly, with all my existence, tell her the truth with an open expression. Of course I knew on some level that my destiny lay with her, and I did not wish to change that. I wanted to go home, I wanted to create a life with her, and I wanted to be with her in her existence. I knew that I could not traipse around the world with her. But I knew that I had to go on this journey. I knew that I had to have my own experience as an individual and as a man — it was a rite of passage, if you will. Many cultures go through this. Ours was no different, but I chose an extreme form of it. My mother had also been quite upset with me, but she was used to me going off on my own. She had emotionally parted from me many years before because of my wandering and unconventional ways, so she was less concerned. However, a mother is always concerned for her child, and she was no different.

Sailing to Africa

We embarked on our journey, my friend and I. We stood on the prow of the ship as it left the dock on a beautiful warm spring day, and we headed out into the ocean. We were, indeed, heading toward that place you call Africa. The northern coast is where we were headed, so we went south, and the weather was beautiful. Of course, it is always sunny in that part of the world, or at least it was in my time. Your climate is changing. It is getting harsher in that particular zone now, and it's not such a lovely place to live, but in my day, it was much milder. The heat was less brutal, and the vegetation — the fruits and vegetables and things that could be grown in that area — was very lush. It was really the Garden of Eden in that sense.

I began to talk with my friend about his adventures, and he told me that he had been to many places. He had traveled with caravans across the desert to the land you call India. He would seek out sources of spices and other materials he wished to sell, and he had done that for many years. He was working as a captain on a ship because his contacts were made, and his contacts were the things that I was very interested in. Of course, he had names and locations of trusted friends that he had made over years. He assured me that if I connected with these beings, I would be given a welcome response, hospitality, and information that I needed to be safe in the area of the world in which I found myself.

I took copious notes. I was a good penman, and I wrote pages and pages of names, places, and destinations. He told me which places to go to experience the religious and philosophical centers that I was interested in. He had come across these in his journeys and had been a student of spiritual matters himself. So it was with this advice that I stepped off the boat some three days later and began my trek across the northern end of Africa.

He had dropped me off in the eastern portion of the country you call

Egypt, and I began my voyage with a caravan of beings he knew who had been waiting for him. They had transferred goods and services to him. By services, I mean he was transporting beings who would be sold as slaves. Of course, this was abhorrent to me, but it was the business, and I was not trying to change the world at that point. That is my job now; I am trying to change the world now. But at that time, I was merely a young man on an expedition.

The captain took on these beings and goods, and we parted ways. I was sad to see him go, for when I stepped off his ship, I once again felt alone, even though I had my nonphysical companions with me. You must understand that I speak of these beings as companions, for that is what they were. I had come to know them. In a sense, I was channeling as much as this being who speaks for me here. They communicated with me in ways that were very tangible, and a relationship had developed over the years. I was indeed doing this. I did not broadcast it around my hometown, for it would have been considered some evil possession, but this is what was happening. These beings gave me information that was of high vibration and helped me always in my life. This prevented me from feeling truly alone.

Before I began the journey with the caravan, I was given more suitable clothing by my kind friend. He had access to many possessions, of course. He asked me not to pay him for the trip, for he said that our friendship had provided him with much information and that my wisdom, even at such a young age, had provided him with a source and content that was, as he called it, valuable. So he gave me some clothing that was suitable for a trek across the hot desert: long and draped fabric, head coverings, and these kinds of things. He provided me with a beautiful leather bag full of succulent dried fruits and clear water. He also gave me things to exchange on my way and some gold coins. He gave me valuable jewels, glittering objects that I did not really need, but he insisted. This made him feel good. I knew that to receive these gifts with gratitude and grace would make him feel even better. He was trying to repay me for benefits he had received from our relationship, and I knew that to refuse them was to prevent him from receiving something more, which was the ability to repay a debt. This is something that I will talk to you about at this time.

A Quick Lesson: the Gift of Receiving

It is wonderful to do things for people. It is a great joy to give gifts; it is a great joy to offer wisdom to beings, and it is a great joy to share your possessions with them. But it is very important for you to understand that it is just as important to receive. This is something that many of you have difficulty with. You have difficulty being in this receptive place. There is a part of the ego that does not like to receive, that sees it as weak in some way, that sees it as a lessening of the strength of character somehow, but this is not the case. The opposite is the truth.

The universe — this wonderful, benevolent force that is always offering you abundance — is working in many ways, and one of the ways that it works is through the beings in your life. If your culture teaches you to provide for yourself only, to work hard, and to always look after yourself without any reception of gift, you prevent the universe from giving in one way that it is most able to give, and that is through the beings you meet on your path, the beings who are in your life, the beings who you work with, and your friends and family.

So I say to you, allow beings to give you things, and receive them with gratitude and grace, for this is a way to increase your abundance and to increase your connection with the universe. If you refuse her gifts, if you refuse the opportunities and material things that come your way or that appear to come your way through serendipitous means, you are indeed cutting off the flow of abundance from the universe, and this will not serve you. This will not bring you what you wish. The universe is always stepping up. She is always offering you more and more and more, and the more you receive, the more you understand this principle and the more you will be able to take into your heart and into your experience everything that is your due, everything that is your dream, and everything that is your desire.

You might not realize it, but if somebody offers you some small thing, then to refuse that thing cuts the flow of energy to you. You will be offered another small thing, and if you refuse that small thing, the energy is cut down one more time. What you must understand is this: All of your wishes and dreams, all of those things that you think about, and all of those things that you desire in your mind but think of as big things that are beyond your comprehension to manifest and beyond your ability to understand begin to come to you in small increments. If you cannot accept those small increments, the larger things will not come to you. But if you accept the small increments with gratitude and grace, you will indeed begin to receive the larger things, the larger objects, and the larger experiences that your heart's desire is showing you.

This is a principle that is very important to understand. I knew this at that time, so I received all of the gifts with great gratitude and grace and was very handsomely adorned and outfitted by the time I stepped onto my desert trek, which was a camel train that had ten or fifteen camels in it. I forget the exact number.

Facts Fade and Feelings Remain

I know that many of you will not like these vagaries, but I am not here to prove this experience to you. This is not something that I am trying to do. I am trying to speak to those of you with open minds and open hearts who are interested in this story and in the principles. I am not here to prove locations, times, latitudes, and longitudes to those who are skeptics. If you are a skeptic, close this book. Do not worry about it. Go off into your day and experience your life, and come back to this book when you are tired of living your life as a skeptic with its down-and-outs, its negativities, and its accidents. I am willing to speak to those who have reached the understanding that it is in the comprehension of the universe's principles that they will make the lives they wish to make. So that is why I do not go into the details of names of places and locations: It is of no consequence in this story. The details of where I am going, the details of my experiences, and the details of my lessons and teachings — these are what I wish you to grasp. The inaccuracies that the ego mind is going to pick apart in this story are of no consequence to me. I care not for them. I will discuss anything that you wish to discuss, but I will not go into these.

In fact, when you recount stories from so many centuries ago, the details do in fact fade. They are not what you remember when you go into the nonphysical; that is not what you recall when you go into the nonphysical. You recall the love, you recall the relationships, and you recall the general principles and feel of events. You remember what you learned, you remember where you were incorrect, you remember where you made a poor choice, and you remember where you encountered beings that you connected with. These are the recollections from the nonphysical. So these tales will be too vague for those who seek proof and who seek evidence. They can go to encyclopedias for that. This story will not satisfy them, and I do not mind. This is not a statement made in anger. It is merely a statement of fact.

✳   ✳   ✳

So I joined this train of merchants and merchants' workers. Of course, you must understand that there was a leader, and he was quite a wealthy and noble man. He and I began to discuss principles, for once again, these traders, these leaders, and these men who travel from country to country spoke many languages. For the many weeks that we traveled across the desert — for this was no small trek that we were undertaking — I studied a language he told me would serve me well, and I began to work daily with him, learning the words. He was happy for the company, and he was happy to be engaged with somebody who had such a voracious desire for understanding and knowledge.

This trek began, and we bounced, if you will, from oasis to oasis. We went through quite harsh desert environments where there was little water other than at these oases.

CHAPTER THREE

Sanctuaries in the Desert

IT HAS BEEN SOME TIME SINCE I HAVE SPOKEN USING A PHYSICAL BODY, it is true. I have been using the astral form for many of my teachings in the last little while. I have, indeed, been showing up in locations around the globe. Do not think that I have disappeared. One reason this subject of Jesus's teachings seems so unusual or so fantastical is you have, in your culture, the idea that I have been gone for 2,000 years, but this, of course, is not the case. I have been working from this side with many beings over the centuries. I have been working with many beings, assisting them with their lives and their communications with the world. This is an example of how the narrowness of your culture's beliefs about me, about my name and what it means, have perpetrated an untruth.

The idea that I have been gone for 2,000 years and suddenly I pop up in this form of a voice, in a woman on the west coast of Canada, seems unbelievable, but this is because you have believed untruths, so it seems improbable. Given your belief system, it is improbable. However, this is not what has been happening. I have been very active and continue to be active through many different beings on the planet, offering them inspiration, offering them healing, and offering communications.

Understand: Physical Attributes of Historical Jesus

Many of you assume that I only work in your culture and that if anyone encountered me they would know who I am. This, of course, is not the case. There are many beings who have no clue what I look like. You have your religious paintings of an Anglo-Saxon, bearded fellow with blue eyes, but of course that is not the physical form I took in the desert life we write about. I had black, curly hair. I had quite dark skin, especially in the summer months, and I was not predisposed to wearing my hair very long. It was unruly. I was often outside, and I kept it a little shorter than your images of me portray. So even if I met you today, you would not recognize me as this being that you consider Jesus. I may show up in your dreams in that form merely to give you the message that it is me, but when I choose to project my astral form into the physical world, I am not usually recognized as the being that I am, which suits me just fine.

So we continue with our story, the tale that I am weaving of my life, my real life (not the fantasy life that is veiled in mystery), including all of the years of it that you have no writings about. Of course, I was living my life fully and in an exciting way.

The Caravan Owner

We have reached the point where I traveled with a caravan across the desert of northern Africa, heading southeast, I believe. This is something that was in the hands of the captain of the group in which I was traveling. I was indeed walking with this group. We would occasionally ride on a camel, but those of us who were traveling with the caravan were mostly on foot. I assisted in tending to a particular camel I found very fascinating. It was a cantankerous creature, but I appreciated its hard work and its willingness to walk in a long line carrying heavy supplies and materials to a part of the world that I was so excited to see.

As I said, I was becoming quite friendly with the owner of the caravan, for in those days, these people owned all these animals, and there was a proprietary ownership of the trail itself in some cases. This was not the case in this particular instance. This being was using what would be considered a highway, although it was a line in the sand, nothing more. But these beings knew every twist and turn of these roads. They knew exactly where the water was, and they knew exactly where the dangers were, in terms of bandits and these sorts of things. We seemed to have a relaxed and wonderful time of it.

The captain of the caravan was a very handsome, dark man with a beard and very dark, black eyes. He wore a turban, and he was charming and intelligent. He would regale me with tales of his exploits with women and money, and I gathered he was quite wealthy. However, how does one define wealth? This is something that I would speak about at this time.

His life was one of freedom and choice, and he was very happy indeed. He had all of his needs met in terms of food, companionship, and adventure, yet perhaps some who might have seen him sleeping in the desert in a tent at night would have said he was poor. But if you spent some time with him, you would see that he was very wealthy indeed. He would not have traded his life for anything. He would not have traded his life for a sedentary existence in a home with all of those domestic chores.

A Quick Lesson: the Pursuit of Material Wealth

This is something that more of you need to think about. In your Western world, you are convinced that home ownership is your salvation, and yet many of you are overburdened with your homes. Many of you are overburdened with your possessions to such a degree that there is no space for "time out;" there is no space for freedom. Your lawns need mowing, your gutters need cleaning, your kitchen floors need scrubbing, and you have these massive edifices to the Western mind. They are albatrosses around your necks, keeping you from the adventures your hearts wish you to participate in.

For that is what I was on: a heart's journey. I did not know where I was going or what I would encounter, but I knew it would be good. I knew I would learn something new. This is why so many of you are bored. You are in prisons of materialism. You are in prisons of television, and you think this is living, and indeed, it is not. You get up and go to work on a Monday morning only to repeat your week again. On Friday night, you fall into your alcoholic unconsciousness, watching television shows. And on the weekend, you run around doing work of a different sort. And yet the recreations you have are limited, and your joy is often very limited. It is a joyless culture in which you live. You see images of people on their boats, mountain climbing, or these sorts of things, but for many of you, your overwhelming responsibilities cloud these experiences. To be truly free is something that you have no comprehension of.

Not only is your physical world taken up with massive

responsibilities, but your mind is also taken up with the worries and fears of loss of the objects of your desire. So this is something that I wish you to think about as you imagine my trek across the desert with no destination in particular and no particular possessions — I was merely experiencing that which I saw every day.

This is something that many of you should think about doing. You should think about selling your material possessions, for if you are not happy in your home, why would you keep it? Divest yourself of these responsibilities, liquidate assets, and have an adventure. You will find your life is much more exciting, and for many of you, the kinds of monies you may realize on liquidating your assets would provide you with the life of a king in some countries. It is certainly something you should ponder. It is certainly something you should think about when your blood pressure is high and your waistline is expanding, for your body is telling you that you are not living a healthy life, and your blood pressure is a heart about to burst with sadness; that is what it is.

The Oases

We trekked through the desert for what I would consider seven to ten days. We were making good time, but it was a slog, as you call it. The desert itself was not as slippery as you might imagine. The ground was hard packed, and there were dunes around us often, but the trail was well established, and fast time was made in terms of walking speed.

We would arise at dawn. Sometimes, if there was a full moon, we would trek during the night to rest during the hotter parts of the day, for a moon that is close to full provides a beautiful light, and the coolness of the nighttime was much appreciated. We sometimes had to travel during the day, it is true. But we chose to travel early in the morning if this was the case, and often we were set up within tents by noon. If there were an oasis, there would be water and shade from trees. This was greatly, greatly appreciated by the travelers.

There were several of us, six travelers, all men of course. Women were not really allowed to do that sort of thing in those days, and it is not so much their tendency, it is true. You have women these days in your world who enjoy adventure, so I do not wish to demean them in any way. Your culture has at least given women more freedom, and for this, you should be grateful. Women who are imprisoned and restricted in male-dominated cultures are a resource that you lose. You are not controlling anything; you are merely losing one of the most powerful, benevolent, and creative forces on the planet. A free woman who is able to express herself the way she chooses is a gift from God, and all men who are reading this book must surely see that your culture at this time is missing so much of this feminine energy.

People have become very out of balance, and of course, this is one of the lessons I am writing about. Men must begin to look at the women in their lives with more respect, for women can offer many riches in terms of spiritual information. They are more open to the nonphysical than men, for their focus is less narrow and more easy; they will receive downloads of information with much more ease than men who focus intently on the material world and the physical realms.

Our first oasis arose out of the desert four days into our journey. I am guessing here. I did not keep an exact diary of this journey. It was a long one. But I kept a journal. My captain friend had given me a wonderful, leather-bound journal, and I wrote the stories of the travels and experiences I was engaged in.

We arrived at this oasis, and indeed an entire town was built in this place. It was not an oasis of six or ten palm trees around a little well. This was a massive community of beings around a considerable body of water, a small lake that was fed by many springs. You could see them rising out of the desert, bubbling up with clear, beautiful water. In fact, it was cool when it first came out.

There were many tents — I am guessing fifty or so permanent erections that were beautifully decorated with goods from the camel caravans that traveled through. Whenever a caravan would arrive, the payment would be in objects such as carpets, fabrics, and things called saris that were new to me. These beautiful lengths of fabric intrigued me, and I was told that they, indeed, came from India. These tents were draped; their ceilings were draped with saris of gold and other beautiful colors. They blew in the breeze. There were tassels adorning the doors. There were bells and weavings of all descriptions, and on the floors, cushions. It was the most magnificent sight. I had never seen anything like it. My home was a modest one of mud and wood and some bricks that were sunbaked. It was quite plain in nature and much unadorned, I would say. (When I returned home after this trip, I became much more creative in the decorations I used. I brought a few things home with me.)

It was, indeed, a magnificent sight, this group of palm trees in the desert around this body of water, the busyness there, and the children playing. Swimming was not permitted because the water was considered such a valuable resource. Anybody who wished to wash needed to pull water from the lake. They did not allow all and sundry to go into it, and for this I was very grateful, as I drank this water. I could see that if they had not respected the body of water, it could have become contaminated or dirty. But as it was, it was pristine in nature, crystal clear and wonderfully cool to the touch if you managed to fill a bucket from an area where the spring was rising. It must have come from deep in the earth. That is all I knew.

We spent several days there resting. The break was as much for recreation as it was for rest. The man who ran the caravan was very social, and he had a woman in the camp that he enjoyed spending time with, so we spent three days there. I was very intrigued by the entire thing, and I began to try to learn the language, but in three days, one cannot do much. I learned a few words by pointing at things and saying the word that I knew for them, as you might do when you are in a foreign country. I found this quite intriguing. Their language was difficult. It was very guttural (in the back of the throat), and I found it very difficult to speak.

The women were not allowed to commune with the rest of us. They were covered, and they spent much of their time indoors, but there was an area of the compound, I would say, that was more for the women. But I cannot blame these people for protecting the women from such itinerant travelers as we were. We were pretty dirty when we showed up after four days of sleeping in the desert with the dust and wind and these sorts of things. But by the time we left, we were cleaned up. Our clothes had been cleansed somewhat. We took them off and beat them. We were able to rinse them out and hang them up, and we were provided with clothing to replace them so that we were modest in our apparel. There was considerable concern about keeping the body covered.

After three days we left, short a few baubles and objects we used as payment. We could see that these things provided a very nice life for those beings. Not only were they adorned in beautiful clothes and their homes adorned with wonderful things, but they had also received quite exotic foods. My dear friend the camel owner had a basket of particularly delicious foods set aside for these beings. So it was a wonderful way to make a living, although the people there were quite restricted in movement, in having to stay in that particular location. I would not have liked to live there too long; three days was fine for me. I was happy to get back on the road and to continue on my journey.

As we traveled for the rest of that ten-day trip (we were ten days on the road, not including our three days at the first oasis), we stopped at another oasis two days before the end of our journey. And indeed, it was very similar in design — although you could see a different tinge to the culture. The colors were a little different, and the decorations were a little different. There was not so much color expressed. It was more of a similar palette with less varied colors. There were more reds and blues in this one. The other one was a cacophony of color, I would say.

We did not spend so long a time at the second oasis. The owner of the caravan was intent on reaching his destination, so we stayed overnight, again paying with products and coin. I handed over a gold coin for being able to stay and refresh myself there. It was not a payment I resented at all; it was the most magnificent joy to rest in these places, these shady cool places, after trekking across the desert for such a long time. I did not know how the caravan owner did it day after day, but it was a wonderful adventure when I was involved in it.

Another Seaport

At the end of our trek, we came to another port town. It was clear we had traveled across the desert, and we were on the coast one more time. I do not know where, on your modern map, the location of this place would be. It does not matter. We were received in a yard where the camels were tended to and the goods were unloaded. I parted ways with the captain of the caravan, as I called him, and we agreed that when I traveled home, I would come back to this place. He gave me a rough indication of the times of year that he would be there. He was there so often that I felt I could show up at any time, and he would not be too far away. This trek that he made across the desert took him three or four weeks, so he was there and back each month of the year.

He said he did not rest too often. Occasionally he took some time off, and when he did, it was in this place. So if he were resting, I would find him. He had a small home there where he would stay with a woman of his acquaintance who lived there and was his maid and his companion, I believe. (I did not delve into their personal relationship. It was none of my business.) The town was a medium-sized one, I would say, for the time in which I lived. It was not a large city, but it was, again, a bustling port.

I was ready to move on to the next phase of my journey. I made my way down to the waterfront with my bag and my few possessions. I was certainly not carrying much then. I had decided that I would trust in the ability of the universe, or the ability of the world, to provide for me. I still had gold coins, and I was not worried. I knew that I would be provided for. This was an awareness that I had: that if I stepped into the world, I would be cared for.

As I approached the waterfront, I again saw more boats, so I decided to see whether I could achieve the same effect that I had in my previous port encounter — that is, to befriend a captain who traveled to the places I wished to see. However, at the time I did not know what I wished to see. I was on an adventure, experiencing the world and experiencing everything new about the culture, for the culture was very different. There were many different beings in this port town, not dissimilar from the previous one I had spent time in. But I could tell I was in a different part of the world: The clothes were very different. There were longer, more elaborate costumes, and there were many headdresses. The women were completely covered, which was not the case in my area of the world where women were modestly dressed but not covered to the same degree that they were in this place.

Many exotic animals were loaded and unloaded in this place. There were animals I had never seen before, animals that you would consider very unusual. I will not go into great detail of what they were, but there were leopards and lions, these kinds of things, that were being loaded and unloaded. I do not know what they were for; gaming, perhaps. The slaughter of the Roman Empire was well known, so I can imagine that was the destination for many of those poor beasts. They were stressed out, growling or laying down in lassitude, wishing they were wild and free again. It broke my heart to see them in such distress, but there was nothing I could do. It was an illustration of humanity and its cruelty.

CHAPTER FOUR

India

IT IS A GREAT JOY FOR ME TO TELL MY STORY, KNOWING THAT IT WILL BE SHARED and that it will finally be discussed. You have wondered about my life before I was deemed a celebrity, you would say. So we will continue on with the elaboration of that portion of my life because many beings are curious about what I was up to in my youth.

This is a time in my life when I had the most wonderful experiences that continued to open up my mind to other realms, to forgiveness, and to the practice of acceptance of others. You must remember, I was raised in a small town; I was raised in an area of the world that was very proscribed at the time. The culture was very judgmental, and so it was as if I had been in a cage despite my connections to the nonphysical. To escape that small environment and the judgmental eyes of beings who had known me all my life was a tremendous burst of freedom for me, and the information that I gleaned, the experiences I had, and the teachings that I encountered all assisted me when I returned home to my beloved.

This, of course, was the draw for me. I could easily have stayed away, but my family and my dear Mary called to me through my heart, and I knew that this was where I would teach — not because it was the best place in the world, necessarily (although it was quite a bustling and central location), but because it was the place that needed the assistance the most. That is the rationale for the trip and the return.

I had arrived at this new port town, and it was a beautiful city of white walls and citadels. It was on the edge of the sea, a beautiful whitewashed town, and the port's access was another international connection. I knew I would not stay here too long. I could feel it in my inner self that this was a temporary stop, but I decided to stay for some weeks to do some work and to earn some money. I decided that I would assist in loading and unloading some of the bags, barrels, and supplies that were transported by the ships. Clearly, there was a need for assistance and strong bodies. I was young and very strong at that time and was very able to assist in this work.

I befriended some dockworkers and began to work. I rented a room in what you would consider a tavern, which was too loud for my liking, but I immersed myself in the experience. I did not wish to keep things the same, as many of you do when you travel. The point is to experience something new so that you can take home new information and an expanded view of the world. So that is what I was doing: I was expanding my view of the world and taking on tasks that I had not done before.

Listening to Others

I had not hung out in the kinds of environments where there was drinking and carousing to such a degree. I had never seen, really, the kind of depravity into which humans could sink. I had sipped some wine here and there with my friends in the desert and become a little tipsy, but that was all. I was basically a straight-laced and well-raised young man, so extreme drunkenness, promiscuity, and prostitution were very interesting things for me to observe. I was very interested in the states of mind of the beings who exhibited these behaviors, and I could see that consuming large quantities of alcohol was not beneficial to the human mind or body. I could observe the damage that was done, the ravages of this kind of lifestyle, and it was clear to me that the human body required a different kind of attention. So I kept to my healthy ways, but I assisted beings whenever I could with my counseling. This is something that I did regardless of where I was or what I was doing.

I chatted with fellow workers as we unloaded bags of grain or pots of oil, and we would discuss their unhappiness, their dissatisfaction with life, or whatever it was that was troubling them. I offered them some counsel from the teachings that I had gleaned from my religious studies and from my spiritual connection to the nonphysical. I was always receiving information. I was always downloading truth from the nonphysical. I had a wonderful connection to it, a connection that was clear and uncluttered, and as long as I stayed in a place of total acceptance and nonjudgment, the channel stayed open.

This was the information I was working on. I was not working on ordinary mind information. I was working on information that had been coming to me for many years. Despite my youth, I was mature beyond my physical years, and many people commented on this, on how mature I was, on how wise I was, and so on. Not to blow my own horn, but that was the case. I had been receiving information from the nonphysical for a long time, and I knew much about truth. I knew much about the principles of the mind and how it works. That was one way in which I engaged and connected with people, for when you connect with the mind — when you see past the conditioned ego mind and understand that within each person there is a gem of truth, there is a clarity and purpose that is merely hidden by bad behavior and bad teachings — you become able to relate to people in a completely different way. You are able to speak to the lowest of the low, knowing that they have become so far removed from the truth that they are dying of it. It is easy to offer a compassionate voice or a helping hand to beings in this state; it is not difficult at all. So this is what I did to bide my time as I earned some money.

I had somewhat depleted my money in the months since I had received the gold. I had begun with a little bit of my own, but that was long gone on food and supplies. Now I was replenishing my coffers, so this dock work was what I did for several weeks until I connected with another being who was a trader and had a boat. This time, the boat was doing shorter trips across the sea off the port. This being would make week-long trips out and return with new goods and services for the town. I decided that this would be the boat that I would board.

Reaching a New Shore

I paid some money and was indeed booked, so to speak, on a trip that would take me across the sea to the next section of land. I hopped aboard this trading ship, offering my services as a deck hand even though I had paid a small amount to travel across the waters to another area of the desert. I was still in desert lands, and I was intrigued to see the shifts in environment. I had gone from quite a lush and verdant homeland that was warm but temperate to what you would consider a hot and difficult climate with desert landscape. It seemed relentless at times, and I was not eager to stay in it. It was not in my nature to stay in such a harsh environment, so I kept moving. And at the other end of my ocean trip with this particular trader, I found a person traveling with a group of mules. It was not camels this time. The trek was less arduous, and we traveled along the coastline, where the temperature was more agreeable. I assumed that was why the trader took that route.

This trader was not as amenable and friendly as the other one, and I decided to remove myself from his company after only a few days on the voyage. It was not fun. He was a drunkard and a mean-spirited person, and I did not enjoy it at all. I became lonely. I had left the home I knew, and now I was traveling through desolate lands — lands that did not appeal to me in any way — and yet I knew I had set myself on this task. So this was what I did for several weeks, verging on several months: I connected with beings who were traveling together, for it was not safe to walk alone, and I walked or I rented the use of a mule or camel, depending on what was serviceable and what was available. In most instances, I had no choice; if I wished to move along, I had to take whatever was available. I continued to head east.

The direction in which I was heading was an intuitive, guided decision, and as the landscape's fertility and population increased, I became happier and much more engaged with the people and the teachings. I observed the shifts in environment, and I observed the shifts in crops and activities that people participated in. In the desert areas, many people participated in trade, as their harsh environment was not conducive to growing much fruit or food of any kind. However, as I ventured east, I reached landscapes that were moister and more verdant, providing the locals the opportunity to grow crops in their own backyards, so to speak. This was how I continued on for some time. I planned on being gone for two or three years. I knew that I wanted to travel for one year away from my home.

I decided that I would be brave. This was a once-in-a-lifetime opportunity, and I would not turn around until I had gleaned some understanding of the world and of myself. As I traveled in this way, I met many different kinds of people. I ventured into lands where language was a problem, so I often communicated with local beings through signs and signals.

The Fishing Village

When I arrived in what you consider the western regions of India (this is indeed where I found myself after several months of travel), I realized I had traveled continuously and was quite exhausted. I decided to settle down in a delightful village on the ocean, and this was where I stopped for some time to rest and to recuperate. I had lost quite a lot of weight through my travels and was not doing so well in the sense of feeling strong.

I found myself in a wonderful village on the beach inhabited by fishermen who farmed in a subsistence manner, so I was able to offer my services as a fisherman. Of course, fishing was something that I did in my home area, and it had a language of its own that required no translation whatsoever. I was able to assist fishers on the oceanfront, and of course, this provided me with not only my own food but also something to trade for other goods. I chose to live in a small and beautifully situated hut on the beach that was much to my liking. I spent many hours there when I was not working. I spent many hours there reading. I spent many hours there writing. I spent many hours there learning the language and meditating on my life and on the communications that I was receiving.

The language was what you would consider a dialect of the Indian subcontinent, but it was a language that seemed to permeate throughout that region, so I began to learn the words for "house," "boat," and "food," these kinds of things. Before long I was able to communicate in primitive but understandable sentences, and this made my life much easier. I was able to smile and have tea with people and communicate a little bit about their lives. Of course, this improved rapidly once I started using the language information, and I was able to have more in-depth conversations with people.

At this time, I began to talk to the local shaman. He was not a priest, but more of a medicine man, and I began to understand the principles on which the local people based their lives, the principles on which they based their religious practices. I made notes and began to observe this as a form of study, because this was my fascination. My fascination was with the consciousness of man, the effect that negative beliefs have on the mind and the body, and the effect that positive and uplifting ideas have on the mind and the body.

I saw that no matter where I went on this trek of mine, the same information showed up time and time again. When people became angry and judgmental and when they lost their connections to love, they became vicious. I could see that it caused them great consternation and great suffering when they attacked their fellow beings. Of course, this was something that became clear to me: It was a pervasive problem with the human mind.

So this was something that I made note of and began to observe in many, many different circumstances, as you do now when you walk around your planet. You see that it is battles over partners, battles over property lines, and battles over ideas and concepts that cause wars, that cause divorces, and that cause fractious human relationships. It was clear to me that there was a better way, and I was intent on finding it, refining it, and teaching this to human beings. This was my work and my destiny, and I could feel it. It was what always drew me, what always attracted me, this idea of communication of truth. So that is what I did, along with living an ordinary life. These spiritual pursuits were my passion, and this is what I did with most of my time.

Of course, in this village I began to develop relationships and friendships with people, but any idea that I was involved with a woman is not accurate. I was celibate during this time of my travels. This was not a difficult thing for me at all. I had met the woman I loved, and I would go home to her. I was not on the road for any other purpose than to educate myself, to experience different worlds, and to come to some understanding of humanity's relationship to spiritual matters. This was my passion, this was my joy, and this was what drove me every day to continue to work, travel, and explore the environment.

Becoming a Pupil in Kashmir

I continued on in this way for a year, I would say. This is an approximation. I did not mark it with such accuracy as you do these days with your technological monitoring. In those days, things were done more by season. I continued walking eastward into the depths of what you call India, and I found myself in the northern realms in this place you call Kashmir, these foothills of the Himalayas. I was drawn to this place, and it was here that I settled for one year to prepare myself for the return home.

This was not at the forefront of my mind, but I knew that I would return home and that I was in Kashmir for a limited time. This was how I structured my journey to get to the extent of my comfort zone, if you want to call it that. There was no boundary, and I could have gone on forever were it not for my family and my beloved back home. But I continued exploring the environment and some of the spiritual practices in that area.

It was an interesting time and an interesting place, and there was much to learn. I will not go into great specifics, but I wish you to know that I was constantly immersed with the beings of that area in the exploration of themselves and the exploration of their minds. I took several excursions into the mountainous regions, and there were monks and ascetics there who practiced rituals and ideas of prayer and meditation that I had not encountered before. I ventured from the village into the mountains frequently when the weather permitted.

Of course, in the winter months this was difficult, but I would go during the summer months when the snows receded and the weather became quite pleasant in the foothills and the lower realms of the mountain ranges in that area of the world. The mountains there are spectacular indeed, and there is a clarity of thought and a clarity of mind that occurs in that part of the world that I enjoyed greatly.

For the time that I was there, I studied with many you might consider to be gurus who meditated for extensive periods, practiced yoga, and these sorts of Eastern practices that are calming in nature and illuminating in their energies. This was something that I found quite fascinating. I did not study with one person in particular. It was something of an honor to be allowed to spend some time with one of these beings. They were particularly solitary, and so I engaged with them in an international form of sign language. I also used the few words I knew in their language and picked up a few more so that I could communicate with them.

Leaving in Gratitude

I traveled hither and yon and, indeed, learned much about myself. I learned about my ability to survive in the physical environment. I learned about my ability to engage people, even though the languages were not completely shared. It did not take too long to learn the few words that I needed to communicate basic living with most humans. I kept my journal, and I kept counsel with myself. I did not make fast friends. Of course, when you are on the road, you have short, sweet encounters with beings. You may work with someone for a few days or a few weeks. This was the gist of my journey. It was a trek. It seemed never ending, but there came a point when I wished to go home. I had been gone twenty months, verging on two years, and I wished to return home. This was what I did.

I said my goodbyes to those beautiful mountains in which I spent some time and would return to in the future, not in different incarnations but in a different form — let us say in an astral form, a body that was not physical in the sense that you know the body to be physical, but a body that is reformed and reshaped through the ascension process. (I discuss this much later.) This part of the world held a great attraction for me. I was very glad that I had gone on the journey and very glad that I had observed these spiritual practices. I was very glad indeed that I had ventured into a part of the world that was so different from where I had grown up, so different from where I had lived.

So I traveled to India in my youth, but it was not through some divine intervention. It was merely through the adventurous spirit of a young man who knew there was something over the horizon that he wished to see but did not know what it was. Eventually I came to the end of my journey, and I wish I could convey to you the joy with which this experience filled me. I knew that all of the experiences I had, all of the beings that I met, all of the labors that I underwent, and all of the transformations of mind that I experienced would add to my ability to assist human beings on their journeys toward peace and joy and away from suffering.

I saw that suffering was pervasive, and I saw that the more judgment was involved, the less happiness was apparent in people's lives. I saw this; I saw that angry and judgmental beings were often alone. I saw that the kind and gentle souls were always welcomed into other people's homes regardless of where this took place. And it became evident to me that this was one of the most important principles to teach people: that being kind and generous, kind and loving, kind and openhearted, and kind and considerate of others is the path toward happiness and joy.

— CHAPTER FIVE —

Returning Home

WHEN I DECIDED THAT I HAD GONE FAR ENOUGH AND SPENT ENOUGH time in the place you call Tibet, this place in the northern realms of India in the Himalaya Mountains, I was twenty-six years old. It was time to return home, and I began that long journey back. I knew I could find my way. I had indelibly imprinted each part of my journey in my mind and would return quickly, stopping less frequently and for shorter periods. The trip home is always half as long as the trip out; I was eager to return. This is not unusual on a trip. You have experienced this yourself: There is a wonderful, invigorating feeling when you leave your home and you feel as if you could drive or walk forever. Then there comes a time when you have slept on enough rough floors and you have slept on enough strange beaches, and you wish to go home. It is natural for humans to want to be where they were born or with the group of people to whom they are attached. And so I will speak about this a little bit, for many of you in the Western world have this idea of relentless travel as a way to entertain yourselves, and it is detrimental in some ways that you are using it.

Take Note: Travel to Overcome Your Cultural Mindset

Let us talk a little about the rite-of-passage journey. This is the kind of journey you take after you leave school or university, when you leave the financial security of your parents' safe nest and the faces you have known for many years and go, perhaps, to a part of the world where you have never been. Many of you have done this or are doing this now. These kinds of journeys are magnificent for the mind, for you do not realize what your conditioning has done to you until you step into a town where people have a completely different set of values or until you see people living below standards that you are used to or above standards that you are used to in some cases (although Westerners generally do not experience this). It is not until you encounter these diverse manifestations of life experiences that you begin to see where you fit in the puzzle. And many beings who stay in their Western world, tucked into their expensive houses with nice cars, do not understand how they are conditioned.

You may be reading this book not realizing how you have been conditioned in your culture, in your town, in your family. People believe that what they know is right, and this causes narrow-mindedness, self-righteous judgment of others, and fear of expansion on the consciousness level. The trek I undertook in the early years of my life showed me where I had become limited, where I did not understand the true magnitude of the planet on which I lived, and what the true magnitude was of the range of experiences that were available to me.

I had spent time with yogis who were capable of things that ordinary beings were not capable of. They were capable of manifesting objects; they were capable of living, in mostly unclothed states, in conditions that would have caused anybody else to freeze. I began in that time and place and on that adventurous excursion, to understand the human mind even more. In fact, it is true that I wished to spend the rest of my life in that place, but as I said in the beginning of this section, there is a reason people wish to be with family and friends and in the place where they were born. They were born in that location for a reason, and they were born unto those people for a reason.

Your prebirth plan — your karmic makeup, if you will — brought you into that particular family, into that particular region, and into that particular value system, so this is why you are always drawn to go back to what you know. It is not until you have done the work and come to understand what that life was designed to give you that you are truly free to move on. Some of you will leave your natal family filled with desire to get away from them because of their poisonous ways or their ignorant acts, and yet you will always be reacting to them, even when you go to a new place and create a new life. Your family of origin will always affect you either in the things you do or in the things that are abhorrent to you.

This is not freedom. This is freedom of the body, but this is not freedom of the mind, and this is what I seek to convey in these texts. It does not matter where your body is; it matters where your mind is. If your mind is free, if your mind is in alignment with love, and if your mind is aware of what you are — a spiritual being having a physical experience — then you have freedom. But you must grasp this principle, and it is a long road; there is no doubt about it. Reading one book will not do it. In fact, reading rarely does it. Reading is not how you learn; it is through experience that you learn. However, you must learn the principles to apply to your life from wisdom that is not yours, for most of you are not living in a wise way. Most of you are not living within wisdom; you are living within ignorance and conditioning.

A trek, an excursion into the unknown, is a wonderful way to begin to understand your limitations and your conditioned mind, for you will come up against beings who have completely different views of the world and completely different value systems, and you will begin to understand that yours is merely one choice among many. The more you travel, the farther you go, and the more cultures you are introduced to, the more you realize that your culture is not real in that sense. Your experience as a human is real, as the experiences of humans around your planet are real. This is what I wish to explain to you: that it is not the accouterments of your culture — the cars, the houses, the jobs, and the careers that you are so obsessed with in the Western world — that are of significance. That significance is in the human experiences of love, creativity, joy, and compassion, with appreciation for those experiences thrown into the mix.

Now, these might not seem like very intellectual things. Your Western mind appreciates the intellect, the masculine side of the mind, but that is because your culture is deceptively out of balance, and you do not realize it. You think that this is normal. There is destruction of the environment. There is a lack of appreciation for children and women, even though they are given legal rights within your society. There is still a lack of truly honoring and appreciating these sectors of society. There is a refusal to provide equality for people of color. These are some of the areas in your society that need to be looked at, and these are some of the areas about which I speak in this book so that you might understand the life that I led and implications on the life that you are leading.

Many of you think that I have nothing to do with your lives, but you are wrong. Your entire society is built on lies about what and who I am and what my life meant, so I must deconstruct this for you. I must assist in the clarification of your mind. This is something that I feel drawn to do, for many of you are laboring under severe misconceptions. Wherever you live now is where you are supposed to be, and if you feel that you are unable to make shifts or changes, if you feel that you are caught in a web of conditioning that is beyond your control to change or beyond your control to shift, I suggest you go on a trip. Now, this might have to be a limited trip if you support a lot of people with your labors. Nevertheless, I suggest you take a trip to somewhere you have always wanted to go — not as a tourist, not as a five-star-seeking Western tourist as many of you try. Go on a trip to somewhere that interests you. Go on a trip to somewhere that has always drawn you. Perhaps you are attracted to a different culture, perhaps to a particular city, perhaps to a particular form of expression — an artistic community, something like this — or perhaps to an ashram or a religious community. Regardless, step out of your life for one month.

Arrange it however you must. You will not be able to explain it to those beings who live life with you. They will just have to deal with their lives without you, and this is also a benefit at times for beings who have become so attached to each other that they have no freedom. If you have financial dependents, do the best you can to support them for that month. You may have to postpone your bills for a little while and tell people that you have to take some mental health time, but I suggest you do this.

You will immediately hear voices screaming out that this cannot be done, but you will be surprised at the effect of this journey. You will be surprised at the effect of this separation from beings who perhaps take you for granted. Perhaps this is why you are struggling: You know that you are not seen, not even by yourself. This is something I recommend thinking about for those who are stuck, for those who read this book and who begin to get some inkling that they are conditioned and not seeing themselves clearly. They might wonder why I went on a journey such as this. It was for self-illumination, and it was also to realize the call of home, the call of the tribe into which I was born, for that was where my lessons lay.

I had to do my work in that particular environment, and many of you must do your work in your family environments, even though your Western families are dispersed around the planet at times. You can do the work of forgiveness and the work of transcendence in the mind. I go into this more later on, but this is a note to get you to begin to think about it. Begin to think about why you are in the place where you are and what lessons are in front of you. What do you have to learn in the tribe that you are born into, the tribe that you have created through your own family?

Homeward Bound

I did, indeed, venture back through the villages and towns and on the roads and byways I had previously encountered on my journey, but the trip was much quicker. I did not sit and observe so much. I traveled with a purpose, and that was to get home. So this trek was much shorter. I had accumulated some funds through various activities that I had performed when I was settled for brief periods. I had worked hard, and I had studied hard, and I had meditated hard. But I had also worked for money at times, and I had always chosen to take payment in an international currency of gold or silver, so I had a little supply of funds to get me home and did not have to spend the weeks working that I previously had to fund my trip. I was heading back with a little nest egg, and I dispersed it very sparingly. As a result, by the time I reached the port on what you consider the Persian Gulf, I was quite emaciated, and I decided to spend a little time there.

This port was a beautiful one, as I said earlier, and I decided to set up a small rest spot there. The weather was hot, so I needed some shelter. I began to work for a carpenter in that place. I was talented in these skills, and he began to allow me to work with him. Over a two-month period, I rested and spent some money on food to build up my strength, for I did not wish to arrive home as emaciated and drawn as I was. I looked like one of those Indian ascetics: My hair had grown long and unruly, and my beard was long and thick. I began to groom myself a little more in accordance with how beings were used to seeing me, and I began to put on a little weight.

My structure was naturally lean and muscular, so I did not easily put on weight, but I worked quite hard moving wood and wielding a hammer, so I built muscle. I felt good for this. It was good to stop; it was good to do ordinary work, and it was good to come back into the world, if you will. To a great degree, I had been on a journey of the mind and consciousness, and now I felt I needed to come back into my physical body, into my world, because I knew that I would have physical work to do at home. I knew that I needed to be grounded on Earth and in the ordinary lives of beings. So this was the beginning journey back into the body and back into my ordinary mind, my ordinary consciousness (although my consciousness had changed considerably on this journey). I had learned practices and principles that were different from what I had come to understand in my youth, and I was intending to bring these back to assist people in their self-understanding.

I continued on my journey after my two-month respite in this wonderful port town. I got back in the camel train that I had once traveled with. The man who I originally traveled with in that caravan was not leading this time. He was doing something else at the other end of the trail, so his son led it, and we formed a similar friendship. This family was obviously of an elevated nature, intellectual and broad in understanding because of their travels, and the son was as much a joy as the father had been.

We stopped at the oases again. Now, this was not in my control, so the days we spent there were the same as before — three or four days spent in each one. I came to realize that this was the family and social life of the caravan traveler. He had a wife in one of these spots, so it was natural for him to want to be there and not work all of the time. I enjoyed these places once again. It was a returning home of sorts, coming back to these familiar environments and seeing that people's lives had continued on in an identical way. I took this in. I took this into my mind, understanding that people's lives stayed the same unless a drastic change was forced on them.

Remember: Shift Mindsets to Ease Suffering

When you look at your life, you must understand that you cannot shift it without a great effort of the mind. You might change your physical location, and you might change your clothes, and you might change your job, and you might change your partner, but unless you change the internal process of perception, you cannot change the outside, for the outside reflects who you are on the inside. This is why most people's lives stay the same even though they might be very irritated with how things are going or with all of the lessons that keep returning. Until you understand this principle (that your life is an outer reflection of your inner condition, and if you wish to change your it, you must change yourself. You must change your perceptions and your judgments, and you must change your hatreds and your fears), you will not change the outside manifestation. This was something that also dawned on me as I ventured home through these places.

I realized that because I insisted on changing my mind, I was able to change my life. There were few beings I encountered along the way who truly comprehended this. Of course, the wise men of the East did, and they taught me more profound things than that. They understood this principle, yet they were completely happy with their lives, for they knew that given a choice, they could change it in any way they wished. They were happy with where they were, studying their spiritual concepts and practices.

The ordinary lives of the beings I witnessed on the way home differed from the wise men in that most were not content. Most were embittered with petty rivalries within their families or with their neighbors. I witnessed a lot of arguments and fighting and unhappiness and a lot of sadness and suffering. I took a note to myself to reinforce the belief I had that I could assist people out of their sadness, out of their restriction, and out of their limited ways of thinking. This was the project I was planning when I returned home, so it was always on my mind. I always focused on this particular reality, this particular form of expression and suffering. I knew that people were not enjoying themselves, and I knew that I could shift that. I knew that I could assist them on that journey.

I returned to the port of call, and I was greeted most warmly within a few days when my friend arrived. He had wondered what had happened to me, and our meeting was one of brothers long parted. He stood back, held my shoulders, and commented on how I had turned into a man. I had been a young man when he had seen me last, but my long trek, which was about two and a half years in duration, had transformed me. He saw the wisdom in my eyes and the strength that I had developed in my body on the long, physical, and traumatic trip. I did not go much into the story of the trials and tribulations, but walking and traveling for that amount of time through such difficult terrains — hot deserts and mountainous territories — had developed structure and musculature that were quite impressive by the time I returned. Despite my thin nature, the underlying structure was strong. I was a changed man, and he could see this as we connected once again.

We spent two days together doing what brothers would upon reuniting: eating. I told him about the things I had learned. He had always enjoyed my take on the world and was enthralled with these things, these yogic practices that I had come to understand. He paid great attention and was rapt as I described all of the things I had learned and all of the places I had been. He had considered himself well traveled until I returned from my trek, and then he realized that I was a very, very well-traveled being and that he was sedentary in comparison. We joked about this a little bit.

I was getting nervous at this point, wondering whether Mary had abandoned me, whether she had taken up with some other man. I had some visions in my mind of her meeting me with a babe on her hip and a toddler at her hand. But I knew that these were merely fantasies of the fears that were manifesting in my mind, so I disciplined myself not to go to that place.

CHAPTER SIX

The Homecoming

WE WERE NEARING OUR HOME AGAIN. THE SHIP'S CAPTAIN, WHOM I had spent a couple of days with talking about what I had learned and what had transpired on my excursion, was a most agreeable companion. We were as if never parted, and the three-day journey back to the port town near my place of residence was one of great joy and communication. We continued to discuss what I had learned about the mind and discipline and what they can achieve. I learned a lot more about him and his journeys through the world, and as I had been on some excursions myself, I truly appreciated his long travels to organize his sources and supplies of goods and services.

These were long and difficult arrangements to make in those days. There were no telephones. People had to travel to various locations and develop relationships with others they could trust, for there was much money involved in these transactions. The "highways" that were the lines along which goods traveled were dangerous and often raided by marauding villains and thieves. It was interesting to me, after having traveled the distance that I had and having visited the places that I had, and I had a much deeper admiration for his work. I did not see him as some playboy who merely liked to ride a boat. I had come to an understanding of his deep and committed relationship to his work.

When I alighted in the port town that I had visited many times as a young man, I was very, very happy and at the same time, nervous to be home. You can imagine that with no communications — no letters, no telephone calls — my mind wished to make up a story about what might have transpired and what my reception would be like. But because of my lessons, because I had learned so much about disciplining the mind, I could recognize a story developing and quickly stop it, quickly prevent it from causing me any anxiety or fear.

A Quick Lesson: Train Your Mind

This is the case, dear ones: You create your own fears. You create your own hell on this plane you call Earth through the undisciplined nature of your mind. It is this galloping, wild horse that you try to ride. You keep being thrown and getting back on, and it takes you to places you do not wish to go. It is as if you are trying to live your life on an animal that has a will of its own, yet it is not so! Your mind is completely trainable. Your mind is completely focusable. It is very important for you to understand this, because it is your mind that is the creative force in your life. It is your mind that creates passion and emotion, and it is emotion that creates physical objects.

When you think of something in a dispassionate way with no energy behind it, it does not do too much, but when you think about something with passion and desire or with intense fear and hatred, you add fuel to the fire. This is what you must understand: Your hatreds and fears that are generated by an undisciplined mind are manifesting all the time in your life as disruptive elements such as people you do not like who attack you, places you do not wish to go to (your work or your home in a bad neighborhood, perhaps), and things you wish to avoid (diseases, unfortunate conversations, or combative relationships). These are created by your thoughts, your beliefs, and your emotions all working together. This is something I go over many times in this book to impress the importance of it in your mind, for you must truly understand that this is where your suffering comes from.

You think suffering comes from your sicknesses, but your sicknesses come from your fearful thoughts manifested over decades. You think it comes from your bad relationships and your obnoxious partners, but these beings reflect your own vibration, which is caused by your fearful thoughts and your anxious ideas. You think it is caused by labor that you think is exhausting, that you feel is not up to your own standards, and that depletes you of your physical energy. These experiences are brought to you by your lack of self-love, your lack of self-value. You are unable to create work that is beautiful, meaningful, creative, and a joy to accomplish when you do not see yourself as deserving of such or when you do not see yourself as able to achieve that kind of goal. So you see that many of your underlying belief systems are manifested in your world.

As I stepped off the boat, I knew these things beyond a shadow of a doubt. I had studied and immersed my mind in them, and this knowledge allowed me to step into every environment where I went, knowing that I would be fine because I was in charge of my own mind. I was in charge of my own thought processes. Now, this might seem confusing if you believe the stories of how my life came to an end, but this will become clearer as we delve further into this story. You will understand the process that I was involved in toward the end of my life. But we will not jump ahead to that now.

Reunion

I alighted from the boat onto familiar territory, and this was a great joy to my heart. I saw a few of my friends, the young women who were working the docks, and they were very happy to see me, for I had made an impression on them as a loving being who did not judge them for their ways or their work, and I spent an hour or two chatting with them about the changes that had been made. Some of them had, indeed, shifted their "careers" (I use that word lightly, of course) to other realms. They said that it was a direct result of some of the conversations that I had had with them, and I was grateful to hear that someone's life had been affected; someone's life had shifted in a better direction because of some of the information I had shared. This made me very happy, and it made me even more determined to assist people in shifting what they were and what they could accomplish in life.

As I climbed the hill out of the town, I turned back and looked. I could see the landscape, the town situated at the side of the water and the dusty hills in the distance, and I could see the concentration of humanity in that area. I thought for a little while how interesting it was that humans put themselves in such concentrated numbers despite the surrounding environment. It was clear that humans needed to be together, that they thrived in some way by being close to one another. Yet their ability to live together was deeply compromised by their fractious ways and their attacking minds, which caused attacking behavior. I had this thought as I turned around and looked, and I saw that they could be spread apart so that they would not have to deal with others, but humans do not do this. They will pack themselves into a very small space so that they do not have to be alone, for another aspect of the mind that is very powerful is this belief that we are alone.

Of course, that is not the case. But this will be a lecture I give much later on, when I tell you about how I became enlightened. At this point, I was not enlightened. I was somebody who had merely educated himself well on the state of the human mind and human thought processes and had seen, through observation and personal practices, how thoughts create different lives and how behavior comes from thoughts. This was something that fascinated me endlessly, and of course, the unlimited number of permutations and patterns of this manifesting in the world are always fascinating to see. I always mulled it over in my mind and listened to the voices that continued to disseminate information to me.

Now, you must understand that this was not a frightening thing. I had become used to it. It had built in frequency and quality over time, and I was able to walk along and hear a voice in my mind that would speak about a particular subject or a particular principle. So as I was walking along, it might have looked as if I were doing nothing, but in fact I was being educated from the nonphysical by the nonphysical; I was receiving information. Of course, this is the kind of thing that anyone who observed me did not know, so they were surprised to hear some of the things that came out of my mouth and wondered where I got the information, for it was not always information that was available in this time and place. It certainly went against a lot of the doctrines of the church that was in charge of the lands at that time. You must also remember the Roman aspect in that time and place. There were military installations around. Forces were not in huge numbers, but we were indeed occupied by soldiers, by gangsters, if you will (that is how a lot of them behaved toward the ordinary people of this area). But I digress.

I walked very slowly through the landscape, paying attention to this dear and wonderful place that I had been away from for three years. This was not a trip I had taken lightly, and now, as I stepped toward my hometown, I became concerned. I am thankful that I knew that only through remaining in the present moment, by focusing on that which I wished to create, would I remain at peace. If I went where my mind desired to take me, I would have become very anxious and nervous about what I was to encounter.

I approached my village very cautiously. I did not know if I would see Mary married to another man, and I did not know what would happen. As I approached her family's home, I saw her outside doing some laundry. Of course, you remember that I had grown stronger, I had grown bigger, and I had taken great care of myself over the previous months to present a handsome and strong visage for her to see. As she lifted her head and recognized my walk — she obviously saw me coming from some distance — she dropped what she was doing, and as many of your movies portray such a scene, she ran toward me very happy indeed.

I was ecstatic to receive such a welcome. I had anticipated anger, but all I received was joy and love, and as we embraced, we did not care whether people were looking. We did not care whether gossip was generated (for that was one of the main activities of the community in that time and place). We simply embraced each other long and hard, and the emotions that arose were powerful indeed. I was moved to ask her to marry me. I was moved to ask her to become my wife, for I was now a man capable of the kind of commitment that this bonding required. She was overcome with emotion and tears, so she could not answer me, but I had come home to her, and she knew that I had completely surrendered myself to our relationship and our bonding. It was a magnificent moment — there is no doubt about it — one that stands out in my memory above many of the events of my life.

A Stranger in a Familiar Land

It was magnificent to be home, to be in the arms of my beloved, and to see familiar faces again. After being away for some time, I found the adventure of seeing new faces faded, and I wished to see some old familiar ones, so it was quite reassuring to see people sitting in the same places. It was reassuring to see beings doing the same work. It was reassuring to see houses that were familiar in form.

However, my journey had changed me, and I was no longer one of these people. I had become something different. I had become something of a guru, in a sense. I had become somebody who wished to teach, somebody who wished to impart knowledge to others. I felt, deep in my heart, that this would be the path I would take.

Mary and I walked into her house. Her mother was much cooler to me than Mary had been. She remembered all of the tears and heartbreak Mary endured when I departed and I'm sure for some time afterward. You might know what this is like, this feeling of being abandoned by the love of your life. Many of you have been through this, and it is a painful experience. You do not believe that person will return. You do not believe that love will come back to you.

But I wish you to understand this: If you bond with somebody in the heart and the mind and the soul, then there is very little that can take it apart except hatred and judgment, unforgiveness and fear. These are qualities that undermine relationships. These are the ego's way of tearing apart that which is sacred, that which is joyful. And this is also one of the reasons why those of you reading this book need to understand the importance of its teachings, for these teachings will keep your relationships of love alive. These teachings will allow you to make bonds that are lifelong and strong — not the fragile and precarious ones you make in these times. This is important information, and I go into it more later on. But as I recount this story, it is important for you to understand that my ever-loving thoughts of Mary, my ever-loving trust in her, and my ever-loving faith in our relationship had kept it alive. If I had spent those three years telling myself stories of infidelity and fear, if I had spent those three years projecting onto her everything that I did not wish to happen, then I can assure you that the story would have been different when I arrived home. She would have felt those ideas, and she would have reflected back to me that which I focused on. Because I focused only on her love and our commitment to each other, everything worked out well. And so that is the story of my return to Mary.

I then had to return to my parents, to my mother. They were overjoyed to see me, I have to say. They also performed dramatic motions of love, running toward me and embracing me as a group — my brothers and sisters, too, were at home when I walked up the road that led to my parents' house. They all came to me. There was some hesitance between my brothers and sisters and I, for they had been younger, but they remembered me well, and it was not long before I was sitting at a table with all of the beings whom I loved so much, eating and drinking.

I began to regale them with tales of my journey, and this took some time. We spent several days working together to come to an understanding and a reconnection of the relationships that we had and wished to maintain. I could not stop telling them about the places I had been, the things I had seen, and the people I had met. It was a great joy for me to recount these stories.

Getting to Work

It was hard for my mother to understand that my stories were true. There were times when she looked at me and did not quite believe that I had traveled as far as I had, both in the world and within myself. I noticed that she had great difficulty with these internal theories, and as I was speaking to her, I came up with some ideas of how to communicate them. If I was going to share this information with beings, then I needed to translate it into stories that they could understand; I needed to translate it into a language they would comprehend. Over the next months, I began to develop what you call parables, stories about different things that related the principles but were easily digested. The minds of these beings around whom I lived — they had lived simple lives with little adventure — could not understand these concepts, so I started to take some time each day to fabricate stories about principles that are quite sophisticated, and I had to turn them into everyday language with symbols ordinary beings would understand.

I returned to work. At times I worked with my father doing carpentry. I also wanted more freedom and more action after my travels, so I started fishing a little bit. This was something that I enjoyed greatly: going out into the water, communing with nature, and feeling a sense of the freedom I had had when I was on my travels. This was something I cultivated over that three-year period, and I needed it. I needed to get away from the confines of village life, and I needed to get away from the confines of women — not in the sense of judgment, for indeed I loved the women in my life with great emotion and great strength, but there was something about the way that they spoke about their daily activities and how they seemed to talk all the time that I found difficult after my solitary journey. The men in my life were much more taciturn. They did not chatter quite so much, but they were shut off and difficult to approach, so the time I spent fishing became very valuable to me not only because it procured food and goods for trade and sale but also because it allowed me to be with myself, to be with my own consciousness, to commune with the consciousnesses that I was tapping into in the nonphysical.

Settling Down

I became quite popular as a teacher. I had gone from being a delinquent, radical, undisciplined young man with a bit of a chip on his shoulder to being something of a wise man, even though I was still very young. I spent the next little while enjoying my return home and enjoying my relationship with Mary. And of course, it was this time, over the year following my return from my trip, that we married in the traditional Jewish way and moved in together.

Before we wed, we went through the normal preparations for marriage that took place at that time, and we were very happy. We were excited to wed. We had always had a very close physical relationship, and we were eager to be together after our long and difficult separation. We did not wish to be apart from each other. We fell in love with each other all over again, and there was a great deal of sexual energy available to us. We wished to be married so that we could enjoy that energy.

Now, this is the part of the story that your Bible does not tell, for it was removed from the scriptures about me. This information was available and had been written down by many of the people who had observed my life, but it was removed after my death — after I vacated the physical plane in a way that you could discern and see — for it proved that I was an ordinary man, and this the Church would not allow. They needed to create in me something divine, something unattainable for the ordinary being. This was their purpose. They knew that if I was an ordinary being, I would be a model for people's behavior in a way that was achievable. They felt that this would have given people hope and would have given people a belief in themselves that would have empowered them.

Of course, that is what I seek to do in this book. I want to tell the truth of the matter: I was an ordinary being who merely applied his mind to the truths of reality. Not the reality that you see now, that you think of as real in your culture. It is not real. These are layers of misperception and untruths that are taught to you and that you believe are real. When I say "real," I mean the truths of the universe and the way it works. The way creation works is reality. That is the way I use the word "reality" — the reality of the creative mind, the reality of love, the reality of God's word. This is a subject, of course, that gets me quite upset, because I do not like my name being associated with untruths. I do not like my name being associated with things that hurt people, so this is why I am telling this story, recounting these tales.

We approach the time of my enlightenment in the next section, and I begin to get into the stories that you have read in your Bible. I tell you what my experience really was of those things. I hope I can cover the things that you are interested in, and I hope you accept this story at face value and take it to your heart, for it is indeed the truth. I am indeed speaking through this being, this channel, but these ideas and these concepts are the recollections I have of my life on your plane 2,000 years ago. I have many new ones that I will speak about as well, at some point in the future, but for now, we are clarifying the past. For now, we are clarifying the teachings you have read and the distortions you have taken under your wing and that have caused much consternation in your lives.

PART TWO

Enlightenment and Ministry

CHAPTER SEVEN

A Reminder of Purpose

WE ARE HAPPY THAT YOU ARE WITH US TODAY. WE UNDERSTAND THE constraints of humanity and the body and the requirements of work. We have enough experience in that department ourselves to recall quite well how days can get away from you and how it is challenging at times to dedicate yourself to your spiritual practice because it is seemingly less important. However, it is far more important because it allows you access to the realms of energy that truly control your life. Your small mind thinks that it is in charge and that it can wield the reins of control, but that is not the case.

The Spiritual Mind vs. the Ego Mind

This is one of the things that humans must understand as they study this material: that they have split minds. Indeed, you have minds that you believe are integrated, but they are not. The human mind has accomplished a great vision in an attempt to achieve a level of peace that it can live with. It is not a level of peace for most of you, of course. You project outside of yourselves all those things that you do not associate with the "good self." You project outside of yourselves all of the things that you dislike, all of the things that are out of alignment with truth, and you call them "the world."

This is a massive concept to understand. It is not a concept you have been taught in Western culture. It is not a concept you have any understanding for whatsoever in reality or in your daily awareness. You have some idea that perhaps you influence the outside world by being more positive or negative — a little more negative, perhaps, than positive in the sense that you see negative people getting sick or you see negative people having negative experiences. There are those beings who are very positive and seem to create a great magnetic field around them that attracts abundance to them. This is the extent of your understanding. But there is an underlying principle at play here, and it is that you are not your true self. You are the physical manifestation of the errors of your mind. You are a physical manifestation of that which is not connected to Source, and so you are here in this three-dimensional plane experiencing things, experiencing concepts and ideas. But this is not who you truly are, and this is why you do not recall your home in the place that you call heaven. This is why you do not understand all of the ramifications of your past lives. It is because you still believe in illusion, you still believe in hatred, you still believe in separation, and you believe in your own power to create your world.

Now, we seem to be saying a paradox here: that you are the creator of your world yet you are not the creator of the world. We will clarify this before we go on.

Your understanding of how the world works causes you to function from an aspect of your mind that is quite primitive — this would be the ego mind. The ego mind has two aspects to it. It has the part that is contained within the physical body, the programming that keeps your body running: digestion, breathing, and these kinds of things. Also of the ego mind is the stream of consciousness that you tap into when you are functioning in the lower realms of thought, those below a certain vibration. It is as if you have two realms to choose from — the spiritual and the physical.

When you focus on the physical — on the body, on food, and on money in the sense that you believe it is your god, your destiny, your controller, and your idol, if you will — when you believe these things, then you have access to this ego-mind stream of consciousness. It will feed your fears, your narrowness of mind, and your control issues. When you raise your vibration and consider the spiritual, you can see yourself as a being who is manifested only partially in this physical world and understands the true concept of your reality, which is that most of you is not manifested here. You reside in a physical body, but it is not who you are. You can see that if you are kind to people, you will receive a kind of abundance in return that is not of the physical world; that if you are creative, you will tap into higher realms and these sorts of ideas, these sorts of concepts. If you understand that meditation connects you to a higher source of energy, then when you focus on these realities — that you are all connected, that love is all there is — you will tap into the spiritual mind and into the higher realms, and you will begin to get more information from there. So you see, it is about what you believe. What you believe is true makes your world different. This is the underlying aspect of the teachings that I am bringing you, and I can clarify all of these subjects in much more detail, of course. This is the information I was given in my enlightenment.

When you believe that you are in a physical, three-dimensional world and that you are a body and that you die, you are not in touch with reality. You are in an illusion — a very convincing illusion, but it is an illusion nonetheless. You are seeing only your attachment to the physical structure that you appear to be living, appear to *be*, for you are not that.

That is the story of my life, in the sense that I overcame death. This is where some of my words in the Bible have been misunderstood, for the writings of the Bible are not accurate at all. There are snippets of truth that remain, but the stories woven about my life are indeed for the purposes of political aggrandizement — to hold powerful influence over beings, keeping them in the cage of ignorance — and of manipulation in terms of monarchy and power over the general populace in that sense. These are all agendas that have been woven into the Bible over the years, and as they have been preached as the "word of God," the truths have been lost among the lies.

I do not wish humans to go around now believing in lies that are woven through my name. I wish to unravel my name from the lies and clearly place it next to the truth. For the truth will set you free. You have heard before some of these phrases I am using, but I wish you to understand that the truth is this is not your natural home, this world that you find yourself in. It is full of trials and tribulations because it is the manifestation of your lower mind. It can be shifted. It can be made into a heaven on earth. It has been such a place in the past, but humans in their very nature do not understand how the mind works, and they do not understand how creation works, and they do not understand how my life worked and what it was for. You have been fed these stories.

So this is why I remind you why I am writing this story. I will continue to remind you.

Your "reality," as you call it, is not reality. It is a dream you are living, a dream you are expressing so that you can live within your own mind. You see, your conflicts are so great that when you actually bring them into your awareness, you become fearful because the balance is lost and your peace is lost, and you cannot live with the conflicts. These are the fears and terrors of your life. And so you place the conflicts outside of your mind in a further iteration of the dream.

Embrace Equality

You create enemies in foreign countries. You create "bad" people in your life so that you can focus all of your guilt and shame and anger on them, and you remain the "good" person, the person free of sin. This is why everyone you speak to has enemies. This is why everyone you speak to has judgments and sounds as if he or she is the one who is good. People have their own moral structures that keep them safe and keep them at peace in their own minds. You will see that everyone's behavior in your world is motivated by these structures.

It seems as if there are good people and bad people, but if you speak to the "bad people," you will learn that they too have bad people in their lives. You are in a group of beings who share a similar aspect of the illusion, so you kind of agree on who is bad and who is not. You have these pockets. Yet if you travel to other parts of your seemingly existing world, there will be other pockets that think you are bad. They will see you as the infidel; they will see you as the white being who acts superior, if that is what you are and they are oppressed by you and your desires and your economic structures.

So there is no peace in your world. That lack of peace is manifested externally in battles, conflicts, wars, and arguments. You do not have any internal peace, either, when you believe in the material world, for the battles of judgment cause great rifts of pain within your own heart and mind. You tear yourself asunder from that which you truly are when you judge, when you attack another, and when you act in an arrogant way. This is what I meant by "the meek shall inherit the Earth": When you truly comprehend who you are — that you are equal to all other beings on the planet and you are all as mistaken as each other — you do not go around in arrogance and self-righteous anger. You become more powerful, but you become humbler; you become more aware of your shortcomings in the sense that you see where you are not what you think you are, or what the ego thinks it is. You become much less showy, much less demonstrative of your grandiosity — and your true grandeur comes through.

So this is the structure of your world. You have separated yourself from your true nature, and you have a sense of fear because of it. This is what you cannot live with. You are terrified. You are scared of what you have created in your own mind.

There is an aspect of you that knows you are not at home. It is that feeling all of you have that there has been a terrible mistake, that you were put in the wrong family, that you are not understood, that you are alone. This is the fear that I have come to help undo, for you unknowingly create it yourself. You do it by perpetuating these ideas of separation, and it is through the practice of forgiveness — not in the sense that you believe in the sin but in the sense that you understand that the sin is not at all real — that you have created the sin in your own mind to bring yourself peace. Allowing yourself to attack another brings you some sense of relief from your inner conflicts.

That is the underlying principle of this book. It is a complicated principle when you have never heard it before. But the book I penned called A Course in Miracles covers this information. It is written in a language and in a way that is very powerful. It is written in a language and a way that will change your internal structures in a gentle and deliberate systematic way. So when you read it, it is hard to understand if you come at it from your ordinarily trained Western mind. It requires some discipline, and it requires some faith in the sense that you might not understand what it is talking about or understand what it is doing to the mind. You think that if only someone had written it more clearly — if only someone had written it in a different language — that it would be easier for you to comprehend. The truth is, it is written that way for a purpose! It is written in that way to undo the teaching and the conditioning of the Judeo-Christian principles of the world in which you find yourself. It is explained too, in other texts, and these I shall refer to at a later point.

However, I am clarifying it here; I am clarifying it now. If you wish to begin to truly access peace, if you wish to begin to truly transform the thoughts and processes of your mind and come to a deep and profound understanding of that which is the truth, A Course in Miracles is the book that you will wish to read in concert with this book I am penning through this channel at this time. For if you understand my true life story, in combination with this book, you will have a complete understanding of what has transpired, what is transpiring, and how to achieve levels of communication with Spirit and levels of peace that are beyond your comprehension at this time.

A Course in Miracles came to your planet several decades ago, and there are many beings who have picked it up, who have it on their shelves, and who have heard of its teachings. But this book, my autobiography, is the companion text to it, for there are many of you coming to this book with misconceptions so profound about who and what I am and what I stand for that it is imperative that you have this information also. You are laboring under a misconception that I am the only son of God, that I am the Christ who you read about in the Bible, and this is not the case; that is not who I am.

Choosing Your Path

I am redefining who I am. I am telling you who I am here, and this will assist you on your journey to transformation, for you cannot truly understand your own divinity if you think I am more divine than you. I am further up the ladder, but the ladder is one. It is from hell to heaven. I am further along the road, but there is only one road: You are either walking in the direction toward heaven, toward the light, or facing in the incorrect direction and taking steps toward the darkness.

You must understand these concepts and principles. We are all together. Some are further along the trek than others but can come back to assist you in your journey. They can come back to hold your hand and to help you over the difficult parts of the road. They can call down to you from higher up the ladder, telling you that it is okay that you are tired, and that you can take a little rest; it is all right but keep climbing. It is beautiful up here. You can see so much more clearly, and the light is so much brighter. You are not alone; there are beings all the way up the ladder, and they are all welcoming you and calling you, calling you to continue this apparently difficult trek.

There are times when the trek is clouded by mists of the mind and you are confused and wish to stop, but you cannot go back down easily. It is not a good feeling to go back down, for it is an endless ladder, so there is no relief in going down: You only go back through all the old issues and fears of the past and the things that are driving you. If you continue up into the light, you are relieved of your burdens, and your journey gets easier and easier.

So I would like you to think about these two images as you read this book. I would like you to think about which way you are walking on the road, for you only have two choices. Your world appears to make so many different choices available to you, but the truth is that if you are immersed in the physical — believing you are a body and believing in death — then you are going down the ladder and walking on the road toward hell. If you believe in your divine nature, your creativity, your heart, your openness, your kindness, your connection to others, and your ability to transform and create your own world, then you are on the right track. You are in alignment with truth, and your remaining few illusions (for you all have them; otherwise you would not be on the Earth plane) will come into your mind as you step further toward heaven. For untruth is not compatible with heaven, and you cannot get there from a place where you believe in untruth. The ladder requires you to become lighter and lighter; you cannot step into the higher realms when you carry baggage that is unnecessary.

— CHAPTER EIGHT —

Enlightenment

MARY AND I WERE TRADITIONAL HUSBAND AND WIFE IN THAT TIME AND PLACE. We had decided to do this because Mary wished to have children, and it was time. I had gone on my way and had known not to marry before the excursion I went on. It was not part of our relationship. It was something I needed to do for myself, for my consciousness, and I knew this.

That is why the marriage was postponed for so many years. In those days, marriage was undertaken very young. For that particular time and place, we were inordinately old, and getting married at twenty-four and twenty-seven was unheard of. However, I was not a conforming young man, and Mary had taken up with me for that very reason. As much as our families were troubled by it at times, we stuck by our beliefs, and we continued our relationship regardless of the fact that we were not married as young as most beings would have preferred. Now, many of you in modern society will say that this is untrue, that I would never have done such a thing. But you must understand that I was not an ordinary being. I was not a man subjected to the rules of society in that sense. I was making my own way, and my decisions and my actions were not in conformity with tradition. You can look at many events described in your Bible and know that I did not behave myself, so do not be surprised that before those events were documented, I was not behaving myself either.

After our wedding, Mary became pregnant quite quickly, and this was a great joy to me. This was a wonderful, wonderful experience. I will not go into the details of the children, what their names were and who they were. It is irrelevant; that is not why I am telling this tale. I am telling this tale to sort out your version of my life. And so I will leave it at that — that we had two children quite close in age, and we were working and living as a happily married couple with young children. Anyone who knows what that experience is like will know that it was a busy time and a joyful time. The deliveries of the children were without difficulty, and it was just a wonderful, idyllic time of my life, I have to say. It was one of the most ordinary times of my life because the duties of being a father, a husband, and a working person were demanding. But I kept up my teaching practice.

Partnering with Mary

There were many women in my life, so stories that have been interpreted through the eyes of men who did not like women, did not respect women, and did not value women are very circumspect. I am retelling the story from the events as they transpired from my point of view. I want humans to know what happened, and I want this to be the foundation, for I cannot dialogue with anybody in a real sense until they have an idea of what and who I am and why I am here. If I come at beings with the stories in their heads about what I am now, they do not hear me clearly, and they do not see me clearly. So this is a very important thing to understand. I am not doing this to show off. I am doing this to help you understand who I am, what I am about, and what my real purpose is.

In that time and place, Mary was on the edges of what you consider polite society, but when we married, there was a properness returned to her. I was not in favor of the arbitrary decisions that people made about other people's value and these sorts of things based on their own moral decisions and their judgmental, self-righteous opinions of what people's lives meant.

I knew innately that Mary was one of the most gracious and intelligent spiritual people I had ever met, and I had met quite a few at that point. She held a very special place in my heart, and I wish here to state that the stories that are told about her are blatantly untrue and that she was indeed an equal partner with me in my ministry. We worked together discussing itineraries, actions, philosophy, and the spiritual principles that were streaming into my mind as I approached my enlightenment. We studied spiritual material very closely together, we read the Torah together, we prayed together, and we meditated together.

After I returned from my trek in the Far East, we began a steady and intense meditation practice, and this allowed us to connect in a way that we had never connected before. It allowed us to open up our minds together in a way that we had never shared, and her spiritual development was incredible after my return. She was voracious in her desire for understanding. She was voracious in her desire for the comprehension that comes with steady spiritual practice. We spent many hours each day [on this], whenever we could between work tasks. We felt very strongly that work interrupted our true purpose, which was to study and teach.

We had informal meetings with people, beings who were my friends, about this material. Of course, these beings were somewhat inclined to disagree with the powers that be on religious and moral matters. So we had informal meetings, but I did not mistake myself for some kind of spiritual teacher. All I knew was that I saw very clearly what people were doing in their lives. I saw very clearly how they were stressing out over things that had not happened yet. I saw very clearly how someone else's behavior, based on his or her own system of belief, could offend somebody else so deeply and profoundly that the relationship was destroyed for a lifetime. This fascinated me, and I worked through the spiritual text of the Torah, picking out areas where I saw this ego at play and where I saw true spiritual principles at play. I began to write down those things that spoke to me. I began to write down all of the lessons that I had learned on my journey to the Far East, and I also began to think about what I wanted to do with the rest of my life.

I was not impressed with the structures in which I saw people living. I saw people being put upon by religious organizations that insisted they behave a certain way or devote a certain amount of their money to keeping officials in the manner in which they desired and keeping the working people in a poor state. This upset me very much, and I did not appreciate it. I understood the oppression that was coming through the belief in the texts that the religious structures were teaching, and this bothered me very much, so I decided that I would assist people in understanding what was happening and try to help them free themselves from the tyranny of taxation and the requirement from the Church to provide a certain style of living for the beings at the head of the organization.

So this is what we did for the period following my return. I worked with my father as a carpenter part of the time, and I fished part of the time. I enjoyed this. As I said previously, the water became a real place of contemplation for me. We were not far from the water, you understand. It was very easy to get there. So Mary and I agreed that this would be how I would make my living, that I would be in the village for a certain amount of time working on carpentry projects, helping people build their homes and furniture and these kinds of things. I enjoyed this work very much, but I found the restriction of my physicality challenging, so I needed a more physical job to balance this out.

I had been on this long trek, and I had enjoyed fishing very much when I did this along the way. It had not been new to me, of course, but when I came back, I understood the connection with nature and how it nurtured me and how it made me feel balanced and strong. And I enjoyed the effect on my body. I enjoyed the movement. I enjoyed the ability I had to sit quietly with the water lapping and the sun beaming down on me, and I could take a lot of time for contemplation, self-reflection, mulling over principles and also receiving information.

This is something that continued to happen, and it did indeed fill up many hours in a week, this experience of information coming to me, of teachings coming to me. I really did not understand the implications of it at the time. I did not know that I was going to be woken up. I did not know that there was an enlightenment process going on. But I wish to say here that there is a scientific approach to the awakening process. It is a vibrational experience. It does not happen randomly. It is dispensed not only to those beings who are good and divine from an objective point of view but also to beings who raise their vibration through practices that clarify the mind and bring it into a state of peace.

This is what I did on a daily basis. I observed my inner thoughts and my desires, and I saw how things would upset me if they did not come to me when I thought I needed them. I began this internal discipline by listening to the material that was being downloaded to me at the time through channeled information, and I began to monitor my internal processes very carefully. I began to truly integrate the teachings I had learned in the East with the information that I was learning in the channeled material that was coming to me.

I worked with Mary on this, but she did not quite have the same focused discipline that I had. I think I had developed this ability on my trek. The trek had opened up aspects of my mind and had opened up aspects of my awareness that she had not experienced. But I did not see this as detriment. What I saw was that we had a partnership, a partnership of support. In fact, when one person is deeply immersed in the transformation of mind, it is good to have a practical and more solidly grounded being in partnership, for one person must pay attention to what is going on in the world. One person must keep an eye on things, so to speak, in the ordinary realms so that the being who is more occupied with the nonphysical can stay safe and feel comfortable.

We agreed that this was the way our partnership would look because she enjoyed her spiritual studies very much and was a very spiritual person, but she understood my deep and driving desire for transformation. She was very supportive and understood many things that I did that perhaps other wives would not. We had a wonderful relationship in those years, and we came to be in a place of great partnership and great understanding with each other. So we continued in our relationship. We saved a little money here and there, but we were not too worried about accruing material possessions. My understanding was that my wealth lay in my peace of mind. My wealth lay in my ability to assist others, so that was my focus. As the years passed, I became more and more interested in this.

I was indeed involved in educating young beings. I was indeed involved in discussing the principles of mind, culture, and religion whenever given the opportunity. This was something that was very important to me and was my purpose in being. My purpose was not to make money and live an ordinary life. My purpose was to teach and to assist beings in their waking processes; however, I did not see it as that at the time. What I saw it as was to develop lessons that would assist them in living, lessons that would assist them in relieving suffering. This is what happened over those few years after my return home and when my children were young. It was a time of consolidation. It was a time of ordinary things, ordinary activities. But my curiosity about religious life and my curiosity about spiritual awakening was never ending and was always increasing.

John the Baptist

There were rumblings in society about John the Baptist, who was a relative of mine. He was indeed baptizing beings and involved in discussions with me about religion and God and these types of things. His point of view was radical, unorthodox, and at times quite wild in a sense. His lifestyle was very wild, but I was drawn to him because of his passion and because of his understanding of principles. He did not pull any punches. He did not translate his teachings for beings. He hurled them full strength at humans, and it was an intense experience to be in his company.

It was with this deep and powerful interest that I listened to stories of John the Baptist, and I spent some days, I would say, watching him baptize people in the river. I was not one to leap into such an event myself, for it was a more traditional approach to religious indoctrination, but I was fascinated by what drove people to go there and by the things he was saying. He was indeed a powerful orator, but his ability to tap into nonphysical realms overrode his ability to articulate the material, and there was some rambling and disconnection in what he spoke about. He spoke about the nonphysical in a very passionate way. His God was much more judgmental than mine was, so I had some hesitation in becoming one of these beings in the river.

But one evening as I meditated, I was given a download of information that stated that I was, indeed, to go the next day to be baptized in the river. This was quite a surprise to me. At the time I was not expecting it. I was somewhat judgmental of the words and speeches he was making. There was some controversy about him: He was not always fully clothed, and this upset people and caused a little bit of a ruckus around the town, so to speak, but his motivations were clear and highly intentioned as far as I was concerned. He merely made me a little uneasy at times. On that evening, I was meditating by myself when this information came to me. It was quite clear, so I did not really question it.

I had been having a long and fulfilling relationship with whatever beings were communicating with me. I did not know their names, and I did not care. I was merely intrigued with the information. I was intrigued with the accuracy and truth of what was being disseminated through my mind. So the following morning I went with two other friends to the river to participate in this baptism. My friends were not so keen, so I said that they did not need to take part. This was not the purpose of my visit, to insist that they follow in my footsteps. That was not the point at all. I was following the guidance that I had been following for many years.

I took my place in the line. There were twenty or so beings lined up at that point, and it gave me some time to reflect on the environment, to reflect on the beauty of the place. The sun was shining. It was early in the morning, and it was not hot yet. It was a beautiful, clear blue day. The hills were covered with short trees — some, olive trees — and bushes, and some flowers were in bloom. The river was blue, beautifully calm in its flow, and inviting, so as it swirled around my knees, getting my robes wet, I was just enjoying myself. I was in a very calm and happy place. I did not have any resistance to this event, and I reflected on that too, surprised that I was so easy in my manner as I approached this being who was so volatile and on the edge of society, so to speak.

He was speaking in tongues and preaching as he baptized people, which he did quite quickly, so it did not take long for my turn to come along.

The Transformation

As we stood in front of each other, John the Baptist looked into my eyes and asked me if I was ready to join the realms of the angelic and to connect with God in a divine way. Of course I said yes, not really understanding the consequences of this action. He dipped me into the water, and in the instant that I hit the water, something tremendous happened: I was infused with an energy that is incomparable. It is hard to explain. I was shot through with a force of power that is impossible for you to understand unless you have experienced it. My body flailed and jerked. I came up out of the water completely out of control. I looked like I was having a fit; I have no doubt about it.

There was a continuing stream of energy coming down through the top of my head, coursing through my limbs and through my torso, and I was in an ecstatic state. But I am sure from the outside it looked as if I was in great pain. I was in the state of what you call extreme bliss, connected to everything. I had a moment — I can only say a moment, for it came in that short a time — of complete comprehension, of complete understanding of everything! I understood everything, and it is very difficult to impart this experience to those of you that have not had it. Some of you out there have had it, this moment of complete and utter understanding of the movement of the stars and the organization of the universe. These were the things that came to my mind.

I staggered into the nearby trees. The river valley was very beautiful in a time of year when there was much activity going on in nature. I found myself sitting under a tree after this experience. In fact, the experience continued on for many hours after the initial blow of energy entered my mind, entered my consciousness. So I staggered into the woods desperately trying to find somewhere to rest while this transformation of my consciousness was occurring. It felt like a long way in this state of mind, which was blissful and ecstatic, yet it was very difficult to control my body as the shocking, massive wave of energy infiltrated my physicality, my mind, and my consciousness.

I sat down and merely observed the transformation of my vision, the transformation of my consciousness from an objective point of view. I was sitting up above myself, a separate being, if you will; that is what it felt like. The "old" Jesus was observing what was happening, and I was observing a transformation of vision that was magnificent indeed. I began to see that the world was not solid. I began to see that the world was made up of energies; it was made up of light. It was made of a pulsing and ever-vibrating and moving force within it. Now, this is hard to explain because I had two levels of vision. I had my physical vision that you are familiar with, in which you see objects in perspective and know where they are within your spatial field. But my vision was also enhanced with another aspect after this immense event. What I began to realize was that if I focused in a particular way — using my heart and my mind in concert to seek out that which you would call God, to seek out that which you would call the Divine — my vision would change, and I would see the interior nature of whatever it was I was looking at.

As I was inundated with this energy, I could see that as I looked on things, they changed and shifted. It was very clear to me very quickly that when I was in fear (which I was at times, as this event was happening to me over those few hours and, indeed, into the next few days. You can imagine that I did not really know what was happening), I would see things differently than when I was at peace. This peace and fear ebbed and flowed in some kind of a wave nature, ups and downs, this state of mind, this state of being.

So over that time, I observed the shifts and changes in objects as I was watching them. If I concentrated, I could see clearly into an object, a tree or a rock or a plant. This happened not only with what you consider live things but also with the entire landscape. The entire content of my reality was made up of this ever-changing, ever-shifting "soup" of information, light, and energy.

Wandering in the Desert

I stayed out in the natural environment, and as the days wore on, I wandered for quite some time. I did not wish to be around people, and there was a part of my mind that knew Mary would be worried about me, for I had gone up into the wilderness for a day or so to seek out John the Baptist and to seek out this environment and investigate it. I had not really planned on being baptized. Part of my mind knew that she would be worried, but the massive part of my mind was overtaken with this influx of information.

This was not only information that was shifting my ability to see; I was also given information and understanding that I had never had before. I was given the true comprehension of our oneness. I was given the true comprehension of the conditioning that human minds were laboring under and the restrictions it was causing in our abilities to create. I was given the information that all of us were holy, that we were all connected to the divine Creator. That it was only through human thinking processes and the learning of lies and misteachings that we became disconnected from this natural state of wondrous and absolute divine creation.

Now this sounds all very flowery, but you must understand that I came to these conclusions over a considerable period of time. I did not come to these conclusions in five minutes. This was a process of several weeks of self-analysis, several weeks of paying attention to what was happening in my body, in my mind, and in my heart. And your stories in the Bible of the temptation in the desert were no more than my explanations of what went on in that time. For I was going back and forth between complete understanding and my ordinary consciousness — that of the man, that of the ordinary being living in the ordinary world — and in those moments, I was frightened at times. I was worried that I would lose everything I had gained in my life. I was worried that I'd lose my connection to my family, my connection to my Mary. I was, in fact, scared for my life at times, as I was almost removed from my physical body, taken off into realms of light and love that I had never encountered before. At times I thought I would die. This was the temptation in the desert that you read about in your biblical texts. It was not truly in the desert, for there were many trees and plants, and it was not as desolate and difficult as it sounds. I merely described it as a desert in the sense that I was alone; I was not able to get assistance from anybody else in this process. I had to fight with my conditioned, ordinary human mind, and I had to integrate the inundation of information and awareness that had been given to me over these several hours after my baptism.

As I walked through these woods, as I continued to explore what was happening to me, I began to integrate this into my mind. This was obviously happening to me for some kind of purpose. I had enough awareness, and I had had enough connection with nonphysical ideas and concepts to understand that I was being given tremendous information. I knew from the blissful and ecstatic feelings that were associated with this transition I was going through that this was a divine event. I knew that with all my heart and soul. But I tried to integrate it and to come to terms with what this would look like in my ordinary life.

There was no way to continue living the way I had lived with this information. I could feel a dawning reality in my mind that there was, indeed, an imperative force pushing me toward sharing this information. For it was clear and simple: Humans were thinking things that were keeping them from their true destiny. They were thinking things that were causing them tremendous suffering and sickness. They were thinking things that were interfering with their ability to live with each other and to have a profound understanding of the nature of reality.

This is what I was given. I was given a comprehension of the nature of reality, and indeed, it was as if a large bucket of water had been dumped over my head. You have seen the shock on the faces of beings when this is done to them. This was a spiritual version of that kind of event. It was overwhelming and terrifying at times, and it was a curious experience. At times I wondered what I could do with this knowledge. I knew that I could do whatever I wanted with this knowledge. There was a part of my mind that understood that I could manipulate things to suit me and that I could change things to suit me.

Now, you must understand that this is exactly what is meant by the temptation of the Devil. I used language when I taught about this time in my life that the beings who I was speaking to could understand, and they understood the concept of evil. They understood the concepts of self-centeredness and greed and these kinds of behaviors. So this was the language I used to describe my transformation in that time of isolation. I used words that were often metaphorical, and I used situations and descriptions that beings of ordinary existence could understand.

You see, I was teaching beings who were farmers and simple workers in the fields, simple people. There were merchants and professionals who came to listen to me after some time, but my concern when I was teaching about these kinds of events was the ordinary being who was stuck in conflict with his neighbor, the ordinary woman who was overwhelmed with her domestic life, these kinds of beings. These were the ones I wanted to help. They had no cushion of financial abundance. They had no support system of maids or servants to assist them in their ordinary lives. They were stuck in the realities of their minds' creations. These were the beings I had in mind when I chose my words.

And so for a period of five weeks I was out in nature. It was a time of year when there were no problems with the weather. There were no cold winds or rains or any of those things that make life unpleasant when you sleep outside. I suffered a little, for I did not eat very much. I was ragged around the edges when I decided it was finally time to return home. My hair was messy and matted; my beard was disheveled and longer than I usually had it. I had not really paid much attention to myself. I had not really paid much attention to my physical body, for the things that were going on in my consciousness were far beyond this.

Returning from the Wilderness

I ventured back toward town, and I intuitively went to my mother's home first. When she saw me, she was horrified, for she had heard that I had gone missing. She brought me into the house. I did not go to Mary first, for I knew that there is this special bond between a man and a woman, and I needed the nurturing of my mother; I needed to speak to her first. I needed to reestablish relationships.

This rebirth I had gone through, this second lifetime that was starting — that is what I intuitively knew this was. I knew that I had been born again. I knew that I had transformed into a completely different being. The consciousness of the man Jesus was still there, I knew my mother and where to find her, but I knew that I needed to be brought back to myself somehow. I knew that I needed to be held in arms that were unconditionally loving, for I could not explain as a wife needs to be explained to. A mother is much more understanding at times and will see her son falling apart or having difficulty and will merely gather him to her chest and love him. A wife, perhaps, asks a few more questions that were impossible at that time for me to answer. I needed some time again. I had taken much time in the desert, in the wilderness, to integrate this information into my being, but now I had to integrate myself back into the situation of my family, the situation of my culture, the situation of my being human. That is why I ventured back to my mother's house.

She was not particularly pleased with me — there is no doubt about it — but as mothers do, she took me in and bathed me and cleansed me and chided me for being too thin, all of these motherly things. I have to say it was music to my ears after being alone for so long. I stayed with my mother for a week. My brothers and sisters were around and confused, a little bewildered, for they had given up on me for quite some time because of my unusual ways and the focus of my life. My long trek away from the family had confused them. They did not understand my motivation for doing such a thing as that. It was a difficult time for them, but it was within this week that I began to realize I could affect humans very strongly by the new sight, the new vision, that I had been endowed with.

I would sit in a room and speak to somebody, and if I shifted my consciousness a little bit, if I focused in a different way, I would begin to see that person's body as an energetic system. I would begin to see the physical self as a vibrant and shifting and morphing essence. I could see where there were problems. I could see where there were joints that were stiff. I could see a lack of movement, a lack of vibrancy in the very structure of the energetic field. Perhaps this is what you would call the aura these days, but in my vision it was less transparent. It was quite a visceral and solid vision that I had.

I also associated feelings with this. I would feel the energetic emotion around whatever it was that was causing somebody difficulty. I would understand, for example, that it was a liver problem, but it was about anger; it was about holding on to old judgments. If it was a broken heart, I could see that it would cause some difficulty in that area, but I knew it was about unforgiveness regarding a past relationship. These sentiments, these intuitions would come with the vision, and so I began to work very quietly and carefully with my family, for I could immediately see where their thoughts, their anger, and their resentments would affect their physical bodies.

This was quite a fascinating experience to have. Initially I would say it was like in your superhero movies when somebody is transformed with the qualities of another creature. I was given a vision that I had not had before, an understanding that I had not had before, and I quietly worked with my family members the week that I was with them to assist in their understanding and to try to give them some comprehension of what had happened to me.

It was in this week that I realized I could not explain what this was, this experience, this complete and absolute shift of consciousness and vision. I began to understand that I needed to edit what I was saying. People could not believe or could not comprehend what I truly experienced. I needed to find some other words for it. So I began to speak in these concepts — these ideas of "reaping what you sow," these concepts of your thoughts being very powerful so that even if you think about something, you have accomplished it because your body reacts as if it is true. I was also gifted with this true understanding that if you focus on something, you bring it to you, regardless of whether it is good or bad. It does not matter. If you resent somebody, there is a magnetic force that is set up, a magnetic attraction that is started, and if you are full of passion about your hatred, then there is much more energy in it, more focus and intention in it. Indeed, I was given this awareness that beings attract to them that which they think about, that which they energize through their thoughts, words, and deeds.

Now, this awareness came to me over quite considerable time, and I received this information when I was by myself. But in the week that I spent with my family, I could see very clearly some of the things that I was now able to do, and I was overwhelmed; I knew it would take some time for me to be able to comprehend what was truly happening to me. You must understand that now my connection to the nonphysical was profound indeed, and I needed to spend time each day away from humans and in communion with the energy, with the consciousness, for it was clearly communicating to me.

I understood it to be this being of God, but that was not really what it was. It was a loving force of awareness; it was a loving consciousness that was not chiding me or judging me as the God that I had understood was described. It was the most unconditionally loving force, and when I was by myself — when I was able to go into meditation as I had learned when I had journeyed into the realms of the mountains of India — I came into direct contact with this consciousness. I was given information, I was given knowing, I was given understanding, and I was given a profound and deep comprehension of all I was being taught and all I was being shown.

It was a magnificent time indeed, although it did frighten the smaller self that was now contained within this larger self. And yet I was also given the comprehension that this was my life's work now. This was what I was designed to do. This was what my life had been leading up to. This was the understanding that was given to me: that I had, in fact, been in a massive training session for the thirty years of my life and that I was now ready to step into the role that I had taken on myself in this lifetime.

It is very difficult to truly give you a concept of the massive amounts of information that I was being given. But these were not coming in lines of text or these kinds of things; they were coming in concepts that were complete and pervasive and overwhelming at times.

I had a hard time integrating back into the family, and they were somewhat annoyed with me because I required times of solitude. After a week of eating my mother's fare and gaining my strength a little bit, I knew it was time to head back to Mary. We lived in a different town at that time, so I had a few hours to walk to get to our home, so it was a time of contemplation and preparation.

Those of you men who are married can imagine what was going through my mind, for we were an ordinary couple in that sense. Our relationship was filled with much love and compassion and communication, but I knew that this event — my disappearing for what amounted to six weeks — was unacceptable from a wife's point of view, so I was preparing myself for the worst. But knowing her wisdom, knowing her intelligence, and knowing her spiritual and aware nature, I knew there would be relief on her part also.

CHAPTER NINE

A Second Reunion

I WALKED ON THE ROAD FROM MY PARENTS' HOUSE TO MARY AFTER MY long and interesting sojourn in the wilderness. I had learned much, and after a week with my parents, with my family, my appearance had recovered from the weeks in the desert.

You must understand that when the human body is transmitting and receiving higher energies, it can lose its connection to the physical world, so a person forgets to eat. The body will drink to keep itself alive, but even that becomes unnecessary when the higher vibrations of extreme light are transmitted into the physical structure. Sometimes this will actually kill beings who have this experience, but they do not care, for they are in such a state of ecstasy, such a state of bliss, and such a state of connection to Source energy that they are not even aware of their deaths. For death is a psychological state; it is not a physical state.

You think that when you die it is painful; you think that it is distressing, but it is only your ideas about death that cause the destruction and difficulty of transition. When you are in touch with reality — which is that you are not a physical being, that your consciousness is who you are, and that your consciousness is your connection to Source, not your physicality — then you are able to leave the body as easily as breathing, as it is not a difficult thing at all.

Husband and Wife Reunited

As I was walking to Mary, I could see that I had recovered somewhat; I was trimmed and cleaned. I was still quite underweight compared to what I had been before, but it had only been a few weeks of not eating much at all, so it was what you call a diet.

I approached my home with some trepidation, as all married men would under these circumstances. As I opened the door, Mary rushed into my arms and flung herself at me with such ferocity and a voracious anger and passion that it was quite a delight, I have to say. She was angry, but she was so relieved. She had heard that I had been at my family home, but she had chosen not to go there. She had discerned, in her own wise way, that I was there for a purpose, and she knew that I would not do this without a reason. After a few thumps on the chest and some passionate kissing, we sat down. She sat on my lap, and I held her tightly, and I began to tell her the story of what had happened to me.

She had heard from those who witnessed my baptism and the transmission of energies that I had disappeared into the woods afterwards. They had seen light, and they had seen my body reacting in a way that clearly was not my normal self, so the story had spread quickly. She knew something had happened, but because it was associated with a baptism and it was associated with my desire to have this experience, her wisdom allowed her to understand that it was a spiritual event. She had been worrying in the normal realms of the human mind, the wifely mind, but there was also an aspect of her as my partner in spiritual studies that knew something large was going on. As we sat with each other those first few hours, I explained to her what had happened, and I began to explain to her what my experience of the past few weeks had been. And the new powers, the new awareness, the new understandings I was experiencing — I began to speak to her about those. She knew from my demeanor and my conversation that a massive awakening had happened, that a massive spiritual transformation had happened in my mind and body complex.

We spent the next few days bonding again, communing again with each other, and speaking about these experiences. I began to methodically go through with her what I experienced. We came up with a plan to begin sharing this wisdom with other beings, for we knew that it was a gift from heaven, if you will. We knew it was a transmutation of consciousness that was profound, and we knew that I receiving information that other beings were not receiving. I was seeing within beings, and I was seeing within the structure of the world on an energetic level in a way that I had never experienced before.

I was able to dip in and out of this awareness; all I had to do was change my focus, and I was able to see the aspects and the functioning of the inner structure of whatever it was I was looking at. And I could see how I could affect it and change it. Indeed, we began to do some basic experiments with plants and these kinds of things. It was clear that I could make a plant thrive if I chose, and it was clear that I could make a plant die almost instantaneously if I chose.

This was somewhat intimidating initially, because I realized that I was wielding tremendous power. I took it upon myself to meditate for several hours each day in communion with this new connection I was experiencing. I was experiencing direct, vocal communications from Spirit, and I was receiving direct teachings from Spirit. I understood that my life had changed — that these preparations, these years of studying spiritual texts, this journey that I had been on, and this new transformation was all planned and part of my life's purpose.

Mary and I discussed these transformations and began to truly understand the magnitude of what was happening to us. For we saw it, I saw it, as something that was happening to us — the physical shifts and the consciousness shifts had happened in *my* body-mind, but Mary was my partner in all ways. This is an important point for you to get in this story. She was not included in your biblical transcriptions because your book does not go into detail about this part of my life. It does not go into detail about this because there was no one there to witness it; there was no one there to understand it. All the descriptions of my life, all the descriptions of my story, were laid upon it after my enlightenment, were laid upon the world many years after my experience happened. So I am telling you the truth of my experience as a man, as I experienced this in the three-dimensional world.

Remember: You Control Your Transition

Now, I was not under any illusions about my divinity; I was not under any illusions about being the son of God. This is something that was laid upon my life story many, many years after my death. I wish you to understand this: My transformation is a transition that all human beings are capable of going through. Your transition of mind, of consciousness, is related to your own divine nature, not my divine nature. I am no more or less divine than you.

I have continued in the pursuit of light with a voracious hunger and with the assistance of all the prayers and attention of the consciousness of the planet. You must understand that as this untruth that

I was a divine being was perpetrated on the population of your world, all of these beings began to pray to me, for me, about me, and with me so that this energy became something I could access because I was focused on the relief of suffering, the further enlightenment of myself, and the assistance of other beings. There is unlimited potential growth in the consciousness of the mind, and the energy that then focused on me for centuries has shifted my level of development into high, high realms of light and love. This is the process that I have undergone.

That might appear to be contradictory and sound as if I have become special in some way. That is not the case. This has merely accelerated my growth and awareness programs, and you too can accelerate your growth and awareness programs. By coming to a profound and true understanding of your connection to the Divine (your aspect of creation is required by the Divine), it is the Divine expressing itself through you.

You are taught in the Bible that the creative process, this thing you call creation, was done in a week, and this, of course, is ridiculous; this is not the case. Divine nature is creating itself all the time through each of you, through each of your mind's expressing, creating, loving, exploring, changing, undoing, and doing. These are all experiences that add to the Divine Mind, and they are reflected back to you in your world. As you shift your consciousness, your ability to create your world shifts, and all the elements of your world shift within it. As you raise your vibration, those areas of your mind that are incompatible with that vibration come into the forefront for healing, and they will come into your awareness as negative events manifested in front of you. This is a very important awareness for you to have.

You see your world as this objective thing that is happening to you; it is not. It is a responsive system that shows where you are in your own consciousness. The world is your world. The world is your mind reflected back to you. So you see that there are many things that need to be shifted, and there are many things that need to be changed. When you are ensconced in the physicality of the material world, it gives you an idea of where your vibration is.

Now, I am not coming at this from a judgmental point of view, for I was an ordinary man, so you must understand that I have gone through this journey. It was my studies in my twenties, the elevation of my thoughts, and my focusing on the healing of suffering and pain of my fellow humans that began to raise my vibration into higher realms. As I raised myself out of the conditioned mind of the culture into which I had been born, I became freer and I became wiser, and I could access more and more spiritual information.

You see, the conditioned mind of your culture keeps you narrow. It keeps you boxed in, it keeps you limited, and it keeps you from growing into that which you truly are, which is a divine, aware, enlightened being who is able to affect many different things in your experience.

Your biblical stories are edited and manipulated. I hate to tell you this — or I love to tell you this in fact, I should say. It is a great joy to tell you the truth. It is a great joy to explain to you what really happened, for now is the first time, really, in your history when this kind of transmission can transpire as a dialogue, as an ongoing communication.

With the technologies you have now, the freedom of thought you have now, and the state of mind your general population has reached, there is a crack in the armor of conditioning; there is a crack in the armor of religious persecution and repression that can be opened up now. The dam is cracking, and there is going to be such an influx of information and material coming through this channel that you will be able to awaken very quickly. This is our purpose. So this is a great joy to participate in this book.

This is an important text, for the beliefs that you have about divinity and the beliefs you have about guilt, suffering, and surrender are some of the many concepts that you have very mistaken ideas about because of the Bible, because of the religious teachings for centuries in your culture, and because of the underlying structures of thought that have developed in your culture. We must take it apart from the base upward, which is what this autobiography is about. It is about deconstructing your beliefs about what is good, what is right, what is divine, what is evil, what is correct, and what is incorrect. It is about learning how to get from where you are down in the depths of your consciousness so that you can understand that your nature is divine, that your desires are honest and true. But there must be a clarification of consciousness first; there must be a deconstruction of the conditioning that you have been through, and you must truly understand that your culture is built on large untruths, misperceptions, and in some cases, blatant lies.

CHAPTER TEN

Teaching

WE HAVE REACHED THE POINT WHERE MARY AND I COMMUNICATED ABOUT what to do with this information. You must understand that we lived relatively ordinary lives after my return from my trek. We had settled down. We were a happily married couple, even though we were older than most newlyweds, for we were in our late twenties when we married. As my awakening came upon us, I was thirty years old, and this was considered too old to have children after that. People began reproducing at a very young age in that time and place. But I will save the specifics of that installment for a little later on.

Translating the Message

We sat together, wondering what we should do with this information. It was a magnificent event, this awakening that had happened, and we began to speak about sharing the wisdom and information coming to me and through me.

The way it felt was that information was coming to me, and I was required to share it. We discussed this idea of thought creating and that the world reflected back to us exactly what we were doing. So I began to come up with parables, stories that human beings living simple lives could understand, for I was dealing with downloaded information that was pure and uncontaminated but somewhat sophisticated in its concepts. In that time and place, we dealt with ordinary working people, uneducated in most senses. They were people who struggled to survive and who worked in fields, in stores, as laborers, and as mothers and fathers. So we dealt with people who were not necessarily spiritually educated.

You must understand I was a serious student of spiritual texts for my entire life; this was my passion. I was very well read — I was very well educated in that sense — and I had spent years and years connecting to nonphysical energies that had been informing me of truths and principles, so I was relatively sophisticated in this area of study. Mary was not quite so, for she had not received the direct downloads I had. Yet she was very sophisticated too, because we had spent much time together studying material, discussing material, and conferring on what this meant, what that meant, and what the implications were. We also saw the rigid structures within the Jewish society that we lived in. There were many rules, and there were fears about breaking these rules that were deeply embedded in the minds of the people. It was with this in mind that I began to design ideas and stories to help teach them.

I knew I must word it all in ways that fit into their belief systems or it would raise too many fears. If I began telling them to abandon that which they practiced because it was useless — a ritual that meant nothing, a ritual that actually harmed them — they would not have been able to integrate the information. I was not able to go into their culture with these ideas, so I began coming up with stories that would allow them to integrate these truths within their lives and would bring an understanding into their minds of what they were doing to themselves. For this was the biggest realization: that all of the human suffering they witnessed — the poverty, the sickness, the embattled relationships, the family feuds — was fueled by judgment; it was fueled by the misunderstanding that they were separate from each other and that the world would not respond to their thoughts or ideas or emotions.

This is the basic premise of suffering, this idea that your connection to Source is already broken and that you have no help; you are alone on this planet. This is the basic mindset of the human being and particularly the human being in the Western world now. But in that time and place, there was a separation through the belief that God was punishing and that God had many requirements that one had to fulfill. If you did not fulfill them, then you would be assaulted in some way in either the present or the future by some punishing, angry, and vengeful God.

People walked around in fear of this, and they walked around in judgment of their neighbors because they did not understand that their judgments were indeed inflicting pain on themselves. So I had to come up with stories that could fit into their belief system. We knew, through this process I had gone through, that we had to work within the mind, as it existed in that moment, to teach it that most of what it believed it knew was untrue. This is a tricky system, to work within a mind filled with lies and misperceptions and untruths that it fully believes are all true, all just, and all inviolable. To begin to shift that consciousness little by little is a tricky subject. So this is what we discussed. We began to invite friends over. We had our friends from our past, when we had been ranging over the countryside, discontented with the status quo, and so these were the people that we first sat down with and shared this experience with.

Gathering Shepherds

I emphasize again that Mary was my equal partner in this. I needed her support and love; I did not wish to be alone in this journey. I had no prejudices around the inequality of women in my mind at all. I had been given the wisdom and the understanding of our absolute equality with each other, so I fully intended, as did she, to include as many women as possible in these teachings. We knew that the women of that time were more connected to intuition and the spirit world through their natural state of receptivity and openness, and they would be the disseminators of information to families and to children, of course. We understood the importance of the feminine influence. We understood the importance of stating the equality between men and women, for this was not the natural state of the culture.

We began to invite beings we knew, friends we knew to come sit with us in the evening several times a week. We would share the stories of what was happening, the information that I was being given, and the opportunities for personal growth and personal expansion of abundance and awareness that these truths bring to the ordinary human being who begins to practice them. This idea of forgiveness, this idea of not reacting to a negative attack from the outside world and instead seeing it as something that you can transform through love and through an open heart and an open mind — these were the teachings.

There was much heated discussion. Ah, the sounds of beings who do not wish to hear that their suffering is caused by their own thoughts and judgments. This is a volatile subject for the human mind, as it is trained and conditioned in violence, in judgment, in hatred, and in separation. This subject is not welcomed at all, this idea of connection, this idea of forgiveness, and this idea of healing through love. This idea of transforming the world through love is not a welcome one, yet there is an aspect of the mind that knows that this is a possibility for what most human beings were doing and what most human beings are doing now — what you are doing.

You realize, on some level, that it is not working when you are not at peace, when you are not in abundance, when you are not in perfect health. You know that there is some terrible error going on, and it is an error of understanding. It is not a punishment by a vengeful God; there is no such thing. These are stories made up by primitive minds that have no understanding of what is going on. They try to make sense of a senseless system, because they do not have the correct information.

This is why this information is coming to you in this form: We wish you to understand that this is a benign universe in the sense that there is no judgment; there is no punishment. Your world reflects your state of being, and when your world does not reflect back to you a state of being that you like or find enjoyable, it is only through shifting your own consciousness, shifting your own focus and your own responses to stimulus from the outside world, that you are able to shift the outside world. You are the creator, you are the maker of all things you see in front of you, you are the most powerful being, and you are divine in nature. This is what we were studying together.

We began to understand, from the discussions we had with our friends — who were, of course, skeptical, happy, open, and fearful; they exhibited all of the range of reactions to this material. They were afraid that a vengeful God would smite them for even entertaining these ideas. They were terrified that their friends and family would ostracize them. Some even refused to come to more than one meeting when they understood what I was speaking about, for they felt the fear of peer rejection and could not face all of the repercussions of the shifts that I was talking about, despite my pleas to come back and try again, to try to find a way of integrating these principles in their lives. Many beings could not do it. They were too frightened, and the material was too far out of their realm of understanding.

From this I learned much about how to teach. I began to back off from the truth of discussing the images I saw, the reaction of these objects to my thoughts, and these sorts of things. I began to merely speak in simple stories. I began to come up with the idea of really, I will use the phrase, "dumbing it down," and I do not mean this in an injurious way. What I mean is that I had to find a way to bring this information into beings' lives in a way that did not scare them. For you must understand that it was an oppressive time, and the

Church wielded great power. There was much fear about being punished by God, so I had to work within those parameters.

So many of my teachings over the years appeared to be contained within the structure as it existed, but that was only because it was the only way for the information to be transmitted. If I had come at it with the truth and simplicity of its true nature, its absolute reference to a loving energy that drives the universe, a loving and caring energy that always shows people where they are wrong and asks them to change themselves so that the world can change, this would have undermined the teachings all together, and my teachings would have been refused — lock, stock, and barrel — by all of the people.

In the core group that came together after some weeks of this kind of discussion, our conclusion was this: It was imperative that we cloak this information in garb that was acceptable to the Jewish structure at the time, to the religious oppressors of the time, and of course, to the militaristic oppressors of the time, the Roman legions and the Roman soldiers who were part and parcel of the oppression of those people.

Healing through Higher Vibration

It was with those ideas that we began to entertain the idea of traveling and working with these energies and with these teachings in a grander scheme. But before I talk about increasing the mobility of the teaching and going on treks, I wish to speak a little bit about the healing capacities that I was then endowed with.

The beings within these groups became very aware of my ability to shift their energies and to shift their focus; they were influenced by my presence. This was the biggest side effect of my awakening. I had been endowed with the ability to infuse a room with energy that I had never experienced before, and this was something that these beings became very aware of. They began to feel better. Small aches and pains that they had been suffering from began to fade from their awareness, and they began to heal from chronic sicknesses and issues that had been dogging them for some time. They knew that it was I; they knew that it was my effect on them, so this increased their willingness, of course, to come to these meetings. They wanted to be well. Humans wish to be well.

There is nothing worse than being sick. It is only in raising your vibration to higher realms — I had it done to me on an ongoing basis throughout my teens and twenties and finally with my enlightenment — but these beings were feeling my vibration raising the vibration of the environments around me. With the teachings, it was also shifting their consciousness, and they were beginning to change their ideas. They were beginning to change their thoughts and consequently their emotions. So they were beginning to feel the effects of being in my presence, and it was clear and unequivocal that I was healing them.

This was a great burden in some ways as an ordinary human. I was only a few months into my enlightenment process, and it was a tiring experience to be around humans that were of a lower vibration. This sounds condescending, but that is not my intention. What I am saying is that I had become a different being in some sense. I was influencing people greatly, and I had to discipline my mind. You must understand that you do not wish to have random thoughts flitting through your mind when they are creative to such a degree. The responsibility weighed heavily on me at times. I was overwhelmed and broke down at times in Mary's arms, wondering why this had happened to me, because it was such an overwhelming responsibility. She, of course, soothed me and cared for me with such love and devotion, and we were deeply bonded, even more so through this process because of her understanding and because of my intense requirement for support.

Your stories in the Bible are of a solitary man who is only connected to God, this vision of an individual in the sky. This is not what my experience was. I was a human, I had become awakened, and there was much to deal with in terms of my relationships to other people and my relationship even to my partner, which was burdened with this heavy responsibility. Yet she rose to the occasion and shared her experience with me in such a loving, supportive, and unconditional way that I could not have done it without her.

Again, this is something I wish you all to know: I could not have practiced my ministry — I could not have gone out and done what I did — without my dear Mary's support, love, and unconditional acceptance of the process. She was part and parcel of my journey and continued to offer her support even when she was not in my presence, which happened over the next few years as we began to venture farther and farther afield from my home as the import and magnificent repercussions of what I was doing began to be felt.

CHAPTER ELEVEN

Spiritual Equality

WHEN I LAST SPOKE TO YOU, I TOLD YOU I HAD RECEIVED MY AWAKENING, and I was indeed hashing that out with my dear Mary. We had begun to teach classes, if you will. These were unstructured gatherings at which the effect of my energetics became quite apparent, and beings began to see that their sicknesses were healed in my presence, that their limitations began to recede, and they began to get in touch with what they had always dreamed they were: more powerful, more energetic, and more loving beings.

This became apparent to Mary and me. I was able to see into the structure of bodies and to see where there were energetic blocks, and I was given information from the nonphysical in what you would consider a download or a transmission of what this particular thought structure was from. All sicknesses are thoughts brought into manifestation as negative, physiological objects. So you would say an ulcer in the stomach is from lack of digestion, but it is not; it is from fear. It is from the lack of absorption of the truth. It is a rejection of the truth that manifests as fear. It is stress related to fear, and that is what causes an ulcer.

So when I was in these evening classes, when beings came by to commune — for they knew that something was afoot and that there was some strange happening — not all were conducive or open to this information. Many listened to me speak and left immediately for fear of retribution from the God they believed in, for I spoke blasphemy as far as traditional Jewish teachings went. I conveyed information about reality that was truly beyond their comprehension, and it was through this process of speaking to few that I realized I must speak in words that were understandable to the common folk. And, of course, I have mentioned this before, but this was the inspiration for how I developed this idea of speaking in parables, of speaking in story form. It was so that the beings of ordinary mind could comprehend what I was saying, and I could also disguise the teachings to prevent persecution by the Church's hierarchy.

It became very clear to me very early on in this experience that there was much disapproval in the Church structures over these messages I was passing along, but if I told a story about sheep or wheat or buildings, I could not get in trouble. I could not be accused of blasphemy. However, when I spoke of God, when I spoke of Spirit, or when I spoke of divinity, I was accused of preaching when I was not qualified to do so. I saw that this was the case, but what I realized was that I needed to pass on the truth to as many beings as I could because this was clearly a message from the Divine. It was clearly a message from that which you would call God, although my definition was drastically changed in those weeks.

I no longer understood God to be a being. I no longer understood God to be an angry man in the sky, as many beings understood him to be. This had been shifting for me over many years, but when my enlightenment took place, I was clearly shown that this is an energy that creates all things and is manifested in all things but can be shifted through thought. So it is not independent, in and of itself; it is something that responds to human thought. I realized that there must be some mistaken definition in that which we called creation, for I was not seeing a hard and fast objective reality; I was seeing a reality that responded to higher-vibration thought. I had obviously been endowed with some energies that were not what you would consider run-of-the-mill, or normal. I was coming to understand that I had been invested with a powerful force of transformation and illumination that was a large responsibility to bear; there was no doubt about it.

Mary and I spent many a night talking over what this meant for us and what this meant for humanity. I was given information on a regular basis — a daily basis and many times a day — from the nonphysical, and I communicated this information to Mary. It was clear to both of us that this was a massive responsibility, that I was given information that was destined for humans to hear and destined for them to understand. We decided that this information would be well served by bringing onboard a set of people to whom I could communicate this openly and honestly without fear of judgment. To speak this material to strangers was not possible because they were not always in alignment with that which I was preaching and often ran to their rabbis or priests to complain that blasphemy was being spoken. It triggered their fears of judgment by a vengeful God.

As you can imagine, I received feedback from all the beings I spoke to early in this process. Some were enthralled and happy, especially those whose health I affected in very positive ways. But there were also beings who ran in terror within a few minutes of my speaking, and I began to see that I needed to be careful. I had my dear Mary, who was pregnant at the time, to consider. [*Channel's Note: In private sessions, Jesus mentioned that Mary had a miscarriage. This explains the mention of more than two pregnancies in the text.*] I was concerned for her health and well-being. I wanted her to be able to live where we were living in peace, happiness, and harmony. I did not wish for her to be attacked because of my outspokenness and my experience. So we decided that I needed to find some compatriots to whom I could teach this material, and that Mary would not participate in this particular aspect of the journey, for she had the babe to consider.

Her belly was growing. It was a wonderful experience for me to think about becoming a father again. But I had this tremendous burden laid upon me, and at that time there was an aspect of me that questioned the validity of what was happening and what my experience was. I was fearful in a way because of what the consequences might be. You did not have to be very smart to realize that this was a dicey business and that there were many forces at play here in the physical world that were against freedom, self-empowerment, self-expression, and love or to know that the forces I promoted undermined their authority and indeed their way of living and their way of controlling.

Traveling Missionary

I spent much time with Mary discussing what we should do. She was completely supportive of my work now. She understood, as a spiritual and intelligent woman, that something magnificent was happening; yet we had to look at our lives as husband and wife and parents. We decided that I would go on some small treks out of the village to prevent the contamination of her living environment. We decided that this would be the best thing, so I went with two or three friends on a journey to begin communicating these teachings and to take them away from our home base, so to speak, so that there was no disturbance. We did not wish to disturb our home, our sanctuary.

We were human, of course. I was human in that sense, when I was incarnated in that life, and I had the ordinary concerns of a husband and father. So you can imagine the dilemma that I was in. It was to follow this teaching, to share this teaching, to relieve the suffering of many, and to explain to people what was happening in their world and why, but I also had this idea of protecting my dear partner.

The Disciples

I began to go off for two or three days at a time, and over several months, I became acquainted with those beings that are referred to in your Bible as my disciples. They were a variety of men who I contacted along my treks as I taught. Some were very interested in what I was preaching and decided to work with me. This was not as it was portrayed in the Bible, where I commanded beings to join me and they dropped their lives. This was not how it was at all. These were beings who I spoke to as equals. These were beings who were interested in what I was saying and could see that I had an effect on the bodies and minds of those who I spoke to. It was direct evidence; this was not some fabricated story I was telling. They could see that I was able to heal people and that I was able to affect people greatly by discussing these ideas.

So we formed a group over several months, and I began to teach. And, of course, with the advent of the healing properties I had been endowed with, the numbers of people who came to see me were ever increasing. All it took was the healing of one person to spread the word throughout the local area, and more and more people began to show up.

Over a yearlong period, I ventured out with this group of men in particular, but as I traveled around, there were also women who came to speak to me who were enthralled by this material as well, so I taught them. The selection of male disciples that is portrayed in your book is indeed out of balance and filtered through the misogynistic mind of the early Church. Women were equally instructed by me; however, they were restricted more by the cultural norms in that area at that time. They were not as free to travel. Their families reacted much more negatively to the idea of them going on the road or following me. They were allowed, within their family structures, to sit and listen in the daytime perhaps, but their duties and their family obligations restricted them much more than the men of that time. I was adamant that women should know this information. I was not buying into the society's demands of that time that women could not know how to free themselves, could not know the truth of life, the truth of creation, the truth of this thing, this being that you call God, and the desires that God had.

I began to see, however, that the belief systems of all beings — not just women but men and women both — were extremely limited by what they had been taught within their narrow education. There had been much fear instilled in their minds through this narrow and focused education to comply to rules and regulations that were meaningless to this energy that I was speaking about, so I had to couch all of my teachings within a language that they could integrate within their mental structures. I was forced, not through any desire of my own, to speak to them in words they could understand. And as they referred to God as a male god, I used that kind of language only so they could comprehend what they were being told.

I felt that the principles of awareness and the understanding of judgment and the perception of what it did to the mind were very important, so I couched the message in language that was available to them within their own minds. I had tried to speak more freely, giving out the truth that I had been given about the nature of reality and about the effect that the human mind has on this reality, but the concepts were so far beyond their materialistic teachings and their religious and psychological parameters that I was forced to find a way to speak a language that fit within their world. I had to show them that their world could change by doing certain things, so I began to speak about sin and the repenting of sin in the way that it was meant for you: to stop judging sin.

The translations that have come from much of what I said were incorrect. I would speak about relinquishing sin — not in the sense of being the sinner, but in the sense of judging the sin of others. This is where the greatest interference comes in the assimilation and understanding of these energies about which I was trying to teach.

So repenting of sin was, in fact, a poor translation. What I was actually saying to beings was that they needed to give up the concept of sin, that there was no sin in the eyes of this energy. There is only a lowering of vibration through narrowness of thought and judgment, which was, of course, stimulated by this concept of sin; this narrowed the energies and restricted the being's ability to connect with higher realms. So this is what I meant by the idea of repenting of sin. The language used in the translation was chosen to pick a word that was similar but was not a correct definition of that principle that I was teaching.

This was one of the most important principles that I taught in my ministry, this idea of nonjudgment, this idea of forgiving that which was only a concept in the mind of the one judging, so to speak. So this was something that I couched in many parables, in many tales, this idea of nonjudgment, this idea of staying out of the business of others and paying attention only to your own.

I also spoke many parables about investing, and this is something that those beings understood in their culture at that time. There was much talk about money and investing it; this was a principle that was well understood, so I would couch parables in this context of investing in yourself to magnify that which you are rather than resting on your laurels and staying as you are, ignorant in your conditioned mind. These were some of the stories that I told about beings who were given money to invest in an attempt to get people to understand that if they invested in themselves, they would multiply their own abilities and their consciousness. You educate yourself; you break out of the narrow mind that you were taught as a child, for many beings never outgrow childish concepts. Their families teach them something, and they merely parrot those teachings throughout their lives. Their churches teach them something, and they merely parrot those teachings throughout their lives. What I was trying to get beings to do was to invest in their own education, to invest in themselves so that they could magnify their rewards on the Earth plane.

But it was a tricky time. There were so many restrictions from the Roman occupation. There were so many restrictions from the religious dogmas that ruled that time and place. Of course, that was why I was given the opportunity to teach the truth; that is why I was put in that time and place, for the minds of the beings there had become so preoccupied with judgment, materialism, militarism, and restriction that an intervention was made. This intervention was not made by a God, sending his son for sacrifice. This is not what happened! I repeat: This is not what happened!

Each being is sent forth with wisdom and the potential to connect with nonphysical and transmit information, and I was a very diligent student of this subject. Over the decades leading up to my enlightenment, I pursued my consciousness-raising efforts so diligently because the passion in me was so strong that I achieved what was very rare and what was very unusual.

This was not so unusual in some of the other places I had visited on my trek, in the Indian ashrams and those kinds of isolated locations in the northern realms of that magnificent country and into Tibet, with its high Himalayan monasteries. This kind of transformation was more common than not, because there was such a dedication to the understanding of the mind and such an understanding of the truth of creation and how it worked and how to master its science. For it is a science; it is not something that is bestowed on you by a god. Let me emphasize that too: It is not bestowed on you by a god. It is a science that you practice, a science of mind and of transforming the mind into a disciplined focuser. This then allows reception of truth to come into the body-mind complex. And it is through this reception of truth, through the body-mind complex, that awareness and awakening occur.

So that is what happened to me, and I was trying to describe it to beings, but they were limited in their ability to understand, so I focused a lot of my attention on the beings who were called my disciples and the other followers who dedicated themselves to my ministry. I had many females in that group. There were many who followed along to the best of their abilities whose husbands, generally speaking, were followers of mine. These men, because of the teachings they learned from me, came to understand that restricting their wives and punishing them for seeking spiritual awakening were, indeed, not in their own best interests. So there were many women who came on board through my ministry via their husbands' interest in my teaching.

You must understand that the restrictions on women were considerable at that time and in that place. You are not faced with that anymore, but do not let the history of the time and place distort your mind into thinking that women were of lesser value in my eyes. They were not. My dear Mary was indeed my most valued disciple. She was a great teacher, and she was a great supporter of my personal, mental, and emotional balance.

Understand: All Are Equal in the Eyes of God

There is no need for women to be restricted in any way, shape, or form from teaching spiritual material, especially anything that relates to my teachings. I ask all religious institutions and I ask all religious groupings to stop this prejudice, for it was only transmitted through the translations and editing of the early spiritual texts that detailed my life, influenced by the male domination of that time and place. It has nothing to do with reality. It has nothing to do with my decision whatsoever. I spoke to men and women equally. I spoke to all beings as my equal. That was information that I was privy to and that I was in complete understanding of.

You are all equal in the eyes of God. You are all equal in the eyes of this benevolent force that responds to your every thought and to your every idea and concept. Now, there are other realms in which nonphysical beings reside, and I will go into that in some detail later on, but at this point, I wish to undo any of these prejudices regarding women and spiritual matters. In fact, I always found, in my teachings, that women were more receptive to new ideas and less obsessed with the material and action-based world. They were more able to integrate these new gentle and kinder concepts into their minds.

So I say here, for the record, that women are equal on the scale of divine nature. There is no differentiation whatsoever in the nonphysical. This is merely an ego-mind trick. It is merely a misperception of the physical world, which is essentially not in touch with truth. There are very few beings that are in touch with truth, but that is why we come now, for there is an egalitarian quality around the world with your new technologies. There is a lessening of the Church's influence and an increase in disillusionment because of your secular and materialistic and scientific ways. Now is the time to set right this historical record, to set right this foundational information on which your society is based and to come to a true understanding of what happened in that time and place — what my purpose was, and what my life was about.

So I end this section here, and I carry on next with more details about my life, about my ministry, about my family and about the effect this was having on my family, because it was profound in its effect, and this story deserves to be told, for they had to live as my wife and as my children, and they had to live with the consequences of the choices I made. They deserve their place in the true story. They deserve to have their story told.

I will continue to tell the story right through until the end of my experience in that incarnation, and then I will go on to further details of my life after my incarnation so you can understand how this system works. You are under many misconceptions about life and how it transits from the physical into the nonphysical, and you do not understand the continuation of one's work, the continuation of one's development and spiritual awakening.

CHAPTER TWELVE

Healing

I AM RETURNED TO CONTINUE ON WITH THE TEACHING. THIS IS AN EXCITING PROJECT for me. I teach often on this plane that you call your world. You do not realize this. It has been proposed by the Church elders that any communications from me, about me, or to me have been quiet for some time except for those blessed few high up in the Church who seem to have a direct line to me and my wisdom, my experience, and my purpose. This is, of course, not the case.

Appearance in Prayers

I communicate all the time with beings who pray to me. I communicate all the time from the nonphysical — with the assistance of many beings who work with me to disseminate wisdom, to disseminate truth, and to disseminate information, such as we are doing here.

I am given to work with people in their dream states, for this allows their conditioned minds to be out of the way so that they can dream about this one they call Jesus, this vision they have of what I looked like — from very inaccurate drawings, as I have said. I was much darker. The brown-haired, blue-eyed Jesus that is portrayed in your biblical illustrations is very inaccurate, but when beings pray to me, they often pray with this image in mind, and so that is the image that appears so they know who I am.

Unfortunately, in many of your psyches these days, if you truly saw what I looked like in that time and place, you would think of me as a terrorist rather than a divine being (of course, I am not more divine than you are).

Healing the Sick and Performing Miracles

I have told you that Mary was with child and that she was not able to travel for obvious reasons and for cultural reasons of that time and place. She would not have been welcomed in these large gatherings, and she would have been ostracized upon her return. It was a mutual decision on our part that I would head off on journeys to do this teaching work and to do this healing work. It became very apparent that my abilities in healing were magnificent and that I had been bestowed with this vision, an ability to see sicknesses within bodies and to see what was causing it. So you must understand that I will describe to you what I was in fact doing.

It is true that the mind creates the body. This is a fact, not supposition. It is the truth. Your thoughts, beliefs, prejudices, fears, desires, hopes, and dreams are all manifested in your physical body as structures. This is where health comes from and where sickness comes from. If you have a repetitive hateful thought about a being, you will create a negative area within the physical body related to that relationship. Let us say you have hateful thoughts about your mother. This might manifest as a problem in the uterus area because that is the area of female reproduction and represents the energy of motherhood. This would be an example of the kind of thing that I was able to perceive.

I was able to look at a human and see his or her energetic body, and I was able to see where the restriction was, and — though this was not apparent to those beings watching me — I was given information from nonphysical beings about the thought processes that were at play with that being. That is what I shifted when I worked on healing people. I was connected to truth; I was connected to love through this connection to nonphysical beings, beings from higher realms. I directed their energies, their wisdom, and their clarity through my body. I channeled their consciousness, and I could then shift in the person the thought processes that were causing the physical manifestation that came through as sickness. This is what was happening when I was healing people. I worked in concert with the nonphysical beings who were my teachers, my guides, my mentors and my gurus, if you will. I had been developing this relationship throughout my life, as I mentioned previously. There were many communications that transpired before my enlightenment.

Enlightenment is this: It is the absolute transformation of mind, removing all the blocks to love's presence — removing all blocks, all fears, and all hatreds — and it is often accomplished when beings have done much work themselves, working with love energies, forgiveness, compassion, and these kinds of things. I had done much work through my teens and twenties and when I was on my trek to remove fears and thoughts from my mind that caused pain and suffering.

Often what happens is the nonphysical beings — what you would call archangels or ascended masters, teachers who have moved on to higher realms where there is complete awareness or a connection to the Divine in an absolute and uninhibited way — are able to communicate with beings who have done much of the work, and they are able, in one motion, to eliminate the thoughts and ideas of limitation. This is what enlightenment is. You then become aware, as a human being, that you are still manifested in the physical body, but you are aware of energies, ideas, concepts, and connection to love and divine nature that most human beings are not.

This is what had transpired with me, so every time I met somebody, if I focused my mind in a particular way, I was able to get this information. I was able to see where his or her sickness was and I was able to ask for intervention from the higher realms, from these ascended masters and these higher beings, to transform his or her mind. And as the mind is transformed absolutely and unequivocally, the body responds.

This is what you call a miracle: It is something that is out of time and out of the normal laws of physics (cause and effect) that you believe to be true. Most of the laws that you believe in can be completely overridden because they are based on belief. And in fact, there are enlightened beings who can override things such as gravity and are able to levitate, bilocate, and do all kinds of things that your physical laws, as you believe them to be true, do not support. This is what happens when the mind is raised up into the realms of truth, the realms of divinity: There are no physical limitations. That is the world I functioned in at that time, and as you can imagine, it was a difficult burden to bear in some ways, for I began to upset the apple cart, so to speak.

Private versus Public Life

This was also one of the reasons why my dear Mary did not travel with me in all these circumstances. I did not wish her to be put in a place of danger. It was clear very early on in my ministry that the powers that be were very upset by what I was doing. I was delighted at this turn of events, of course. I was a rebel. I was a troublemaker. This was my purpose in life: to free humans from the dictates and the unfair rules of oppressive regimes. This is what I was doing, and they did not like it one iota!

It became very clear to us both that this was dangerous territory we were entering into. However, we agreed that there was no turning back, that there was no stepping off this train that was picking up momentum. And Mary — in her wonderful, supporting, and loving way, in her intelligent and spiritual way — understood what we were about. As we were in this together, she gave me her support by wishing me well on my journeys and treks, and I came home frequently.

This is not written in your Bible. It was not apparent because I did not wish it to be apparent. I did not wish Mary to be involved in these processes. I did not want her to be put in danger or at risk in any way, so when I was out and about doing these things that I did, speaking and teaching in this way, I did not mention my wife. I did not mention anything about the life I lived — the private life I lived.

I was very fortunate at that time — it was a different time than you are living in. This is not what humans can do at this time. Your life is public if you go into the public realm, but in that time and place, if you kept your mouth shut, nobody knew what was going on at home, so that was what I did. This is why in your Bible texts you see no mention of my wife, no mention of my children, and no mention of these things — because I made it very clear to those who I worked with that this was the policy, that the private life was to remain so for safety reasons. And of course, everybody realized what shenanigans we were up to, rattling the structures of oppression that were at play at this time. They knew that it was very important to me that my wife and family were kept safe and kept out of most of what was happening. This is why in your texts you do not see mention of this, and you do not see mention of most of my life. Do not be surprised that there were aspects of my private life that were not documented.

You must understand that your biblical texts are very small fragments — in fact, they are minute wisps of information — compared to what my life actually was. I was a human being living twenty-four hours a day, seven days a week, and twelve months a year, as you understand it, and I had many, many experiences and many, many relationships, and many things happened and were not documented.

So you have a book that you consider the word of God, but it is not the word of God. It is a fractured and incomplete text written by men trying to explain things they could not explain. Also there is much information missing from that text. There were gospels and there were sections of writing that included teachings about women, marriage, and sexuality that were removed in the early phases of the Church because they were offensive to some of the men who were in charge.

It was clear after my disappearance from the physical world that the Church was going to be a powerful thing. You could motivate people very quickly with the miracles that I had worked and with the effect that I had had on the populace, with the charisma with which I had affected people. This was the truth. There were beings very early on in the Church who were not enlightened, who were not focused in love, and who were not focused on my teachings, per se. They were focused on what it could bring them as political animals, as beings in offices of authority, and it was used for this purpose.

But I digress. I will return to this time when I began my ministry. I set up relationships with men who in the Bible were called my disciples. They are named, and these are reasonably accurate depictions. But they were beings who chose to travel with me; they were not forced in any way. They were interested in my teachings, and I began dividing my teachings between two particular realms. I was using my parables and simple stories for those beings who were uneducated and who were visiting for a short time. I did this partly so that they did not get in trouble within their own religions and their own structures of culture. I did not wish to disrupt people's lives and cause them problems, but I did wish to instill in them some concepts that would help relieve suffering in their hearts and minds and daily lives. And so these were the stories that I fabricated, the parables that I talked about to people.

Teaching the Disciples How to Heal Others

My closer compatriots, my disciples, as you call them in the Bible, were really my friends. They were people who I had an affinity with and who were very interested in learning the information and techniques that I was participating in. We began meditation exercises together. I explained to them what I was doing. I will answer the question about disseminating information that allowed these beings to heal. It was over a year-or-so-long study period that I began to teach these beings the effects of what you would call bioenergetic feeling — the combination of focusing the mind on love and health and how this can transform the physical body.

These disciples of mine began to practice among themselves doing this work — focused meditation, focused observation of sicknesses — and we began to work together healing people. I would tell them where the sickness was, and they would begin to work, through mental focusing and through certain body movements, to focus the energy field of their own bodies into the bodies of those humans who were sick. They were able to affect considerable healing of their own. So this is what we practiced for some time, for it was a technique that I had been told to teach others. I was told that this ability could be effected by many people if they focused their intention onto healing.

This is not what humans did. They focused their attention on sickness because they did not understand the creative process behind it. When they understood that sickness was created from negative beliefs and negative thoughts repeated over a period of time, then it became clear that focusing positive, loving, and pure thoughts on the same area could affect a reversal of that condition. So that's what started to happen.

There were many women in my groups to whom I taught the specifics of the energy work that I did. Now, I was a much more accomplished practitioner of this, of course. I was provided with such clarity of mind, such clarity of connection to the higher realms, that I was able to effect almost instantaneous transformations of body. The people whom I worked with as disciples had a much more difficult time of it because their minds had not been cleared of all their own thoughts, their own negativities. But that is what I worked on with them, in private, of course.

I did not do this work in public. This work would have been considered sorcery at that time. It would have been considered some kind of devil worship. It went against all of the laws of the Old Testament. It went against all of the Jewish teachings, and the priests and higher-ups in the Jewish tradition would have attacked me. As it turned out, that is what happened over time, but during my ministry, during these travels, I taught as many people as I possibly could and sent them out in small groups to pass this information along to other beings so that it could be shared. I could only teach so many; I could only instruct so many.

This was a time-consuming process, developing a meditation practice and developing an understanding of the energetics of the body-mind complex, so it was something I taught people, and I sent them off to teach more, but I did not have only twelve disciples. There were many beings whom I taught over the years. There were many women I taught over the years, and I taught women particularly to work with their children.

This was a society that was divided quite strongly between the domestic home life, which was the area that women controlled, and the outside financial, political, and religious realms that the men tended to gravitate toward. As healers and as transformers of lives, women held the key to the family home and to healing small children and birthing healthy babies, these kinds of things, so there was much communication between me and the women of the communities in which I found myself. This is something that, of course, is not covered in the Bible.

There were observations of some of my more public demonstrations, and these conformed more to the rules of the society. I did this for a reason, for I did not wish for the ordinary beings who came to talk to me to transgress the rules of their society. I did not wish for them to suffer for coming to listen to me speak, so I presented what was considered a more appropriate, a more traditional organization with men traveling with me. But in the privacy of the evening camps, in the privacy of some of the homes in which I stayed — and I stayed in many homes, as there were many families who put me up over the years that I traveled — there were many personal instructions given to women and to husbands and wives related to sexual energy, for I was also receiving information about this. There were many private teachings.

I will leave it at that. I do not wish to go into endless detail, but you get the drift: There was a public persona, and there were also teachings that went on in private. And these were kept private for good reason.

The oppressors of the people of that time were vicious, and they would stone those who misbehaved, particularly women. They would decry a person in public, and that person's life could be brought down in ruins when accused of something such as blasphemy. So I was very, very careful with the teachings that I gave. I did not wish for people to be persecuted. I was also protecting myself, of course, to the best of my ability, but this was far less of a concern. Although I knew that the body was not what it appeared to be, I was coming to a profound and deep understanding that it is our consciousness that is immortal, and this is what the higher realms that were in communication with me all the time were teaching me.

The Truth about Alleviating Suffering

When I received daily information, I would take myself aside from the people in my life. I would take myself aside to be by myself to receive downloads of information. I was guided all the time about the lack of solidity in the body when coming at it from a higher vision, and I was told about my own immortality. I was told about the immortality of consciousness. I was told about the dream that the physical world, in fact, was, and I was told that the reality that was the truth of our nature was not contained within the physical world, but it was contained within the mind. The mind held the key to the lock.

This is where my teachings that the kingdom of heaven is found within came from. I tried to word it in a way that would not be blasphemous and that would not be easily attacked. I could not go around telling humans that they should not listen to their authority figures and that they should do whatever was right for them. This would have caused even more suffering in the culture that they lived in. I had to find a way to word this information that allowed them to transform themselves from the inside out without causing a mass destruction of their current life. They were suffering enough under the auspices of these oppressive regimes (the Church and the Roman Empire's soldiers that were around at that time), so I had to provide them with a way to transform their experiences without destroying the very little that they had. So that was the way that I approached these teachings.

We do not have to do that with you in the modern world. We can talk to you openly about these processes. We can talk to you openly about the mind and the body and the dream that you are living, for you are much freer in some ways. You are free of the dogma of the Church. You are able to pick and choose what information you put into your mind without fear, although you still have a lot of conditioning that keeps you limited and fearful and afraid to connect with higher realms of the spirit world. I wish to explain to you why I did it the way I did in that time and place. It was for a very important purpose: to alleviate suffering. I did not wish to cause more suffering to those beings who were already bowed down under the weight of rules and regulations that brought them nothing at all in their lives but cost them money, cost them their freedom, and cost them their self-expression.

It was with mixed emotions that I traveled at that time. I saw the oppressive nature of the culture. I had been well aware of it all my life, of course. I had rebelled against it and had not conformed to it. I ended up having two children with my dear Mary, and we were very happy together. She was annoyed at times that I disappeared and went on these treks, but it was not something I did all of the time. There were many weeks when I was at home with her and my two sons.

We had a life that was unconventional because of my road trips, but we loved each other and lived a life that was restricted in many ways because of the oppressive nature of the culture, which is something that motivated me to continue my teachings. There were times when I wished that I could just live my life in my own town doing what it was that I did, but every time I ventured out onto the road, I saw how people lived. I saw how fearful they were, how sick they were, and how much suffering they endured. I felt I was obligated. I felt a desire in my heart to assist, so this is what I did.

Balancing Life and Purpose

I had to balance my personal desires as a human, as a man, as a husband, and as a father with my higher purpose, which was to assist beings, to heal their limited thoughts and beliefs, and to try to teach them some new ways of seeing the world, for this was my purpose. I was told on a regular basis that this was my life's work and that I was to continue in this form for as long as I was physically able and as long as it worked. However, I will talk here about the information that I was given.

I was told that I would be attacked by the powers that be. I was told that I would be put to death by the powers that be. And, of course, this was a very difficult thing to hear, but I understood from the communications I received from the nonphysical that this was part of the teaching — that I was going to have to show people that the human body was not lost in death and that the spirit, the human consciousness, carried on; this was part of my work.

I was informed of this quite early in my ministry — I would say two years before my crucifixion — and so I was very appreciative of time with my family. I was very appreciative of the freedom and self-expression that I had. I knew that I was being asked to do something that was very difficult. I knew that I was going to be asked to do something that would be very difficult for all of the beings who loved me. Because this information was given to me early in my ministry, it indeed motivated me to teach more, to travel more, and to be more present in my life, for I knew that it would not carry on forever.

This awareness does change you. You have some idea of this, that if you were told you were going to die in two years, you would live a completely different life than if you did not have this information. And so this is exactly what happened to me. I began to speak more passionately. I began to exert all of my energetic focus in communicating with people, and the crowds that came to see me became quite large and onerous to manage. Some of the stories in your Bible speak about this, of having to preach from a boat off the water's edge because of the crowds of beings, and this was indeed the case. There were many thousands of people, at times, who would congregate, and often I would have to escape by boat to another part of the land to remove myself from the crowds that were relentless at times in their following. They were desperate to experience the miracles I was able to work. They were desperate to experience the truth I was able to speak about.

There was an energetic shift within the crowds of people as I spoke that transformed their consciousness, and they felt it as peace, and they felt it as love. Whenever they were in my company, they had a sense of well-being that disappeared when they left. This was an energetic projection that I was able to afford to the beings in my presence because of the input of information and energies from the nonphysical that flowed through me. It was really not my human self that did this. It was the energies that were flowing through me from the higher realms because of the clarification process I had been through.

This is something that you all will be able to do, and I was clear about that in the Bible. I wish to reiterate that statement here: *There is nothing that I did that is not feasible for you all, given clarification, given study, given focus, and given understanding.* I will go into this further later, but for now I will say that despite the exceptional experiences, despite the exceptional stories that are told about me, I was indeed instructing my disciples in how to do this, how to affect healings, how to change their minds, and how to use the practices of forgiveness and compassion for clarification purposes. That is why that particular teaching was in the forefront of the Bible's accounts. I taught forgiveness, for judgment is indeed the biggest interference to connection to the nonphysical world. It is judgment that will keep you in the dream, separated from your Source, this being that you call God that is an overall, overriding energy that pushes you toward love, acceptance, and freedom.

These beings I worked with were not free and were not loving. They were judgmental and believed in sin, punishment, physical death, and sacrifice, so my teachings were radical and, indeed, against the grain of society. I moderated my teachings considerably for the crowds — there is no doubt about it — and I couched the teachings in words that they could understand. But in my one-on-one time with beings in my evening instruction and meditation groups, I spoke the truth and told them what had happened to me and what was ongoing and happening to me. I told them that they too could achieve these transformative, energetic experiences. I was not different; I had merely been on the path longer, and I had reached a point on my journey where I was receiving considerable assistance from the nonphysical realms.

This is exactly what we say to you now: You are immersed in a materialistic and ego-driven culture that focuses on the body, that focuses on judgment, that focuses on the belief in sin and retribution, and these kinds of lower vibration ideas. As long as you are involved in these kinds of concepts, you will not be able to achieve connection to the nonphysical. This is one of the things that these writings that we are involved with are helping you to see: There is a reason why you are not connected to the nonphysical. It is what you are taught. I wrote this book with this channel to show you where your culture is off track, off center, and out of alignment with truth.

So that is where I will leave it for now. Suffice to say that I worked miracles, but I was also in the process of teaching all the people who were close to me and had shown some interest and lack of fear in learning this new material how to do this too. That is not obvious in your Bible, although there are stories of my sending out disciples to heal. Of course they could not have done this without some instruction. This is an example of contradictory information within the text that beings have not thought about very logically. This is what I taught them, and this is why we worked together so closely. This is why I referred to the fact that you all can do this. This is not something that I alone was privy to; although, as I said, I was further up the ladder, further along the road. And I was trying to get as many people as I could to understand the processes and to teach as much as I could while I was allowed to while I was incarnated in the physical form.

The next chapter is the beginning of the end of my life, so to speak, as you are aware of it on this physical plane.

CHAPTER THIRTEEN

Biblical Tales

I WAS SPEAKING ABOUT MY MINISTRY IN THE LAST INSTALLMENT, AND THERE are, of course, some major events described within the Bible that come to mind. I begin with the idea of my walking on water.

In the physical world, you have rules that you must comply with: gravity, time, and these kinds of things. You must eat food, and you must breathe air. To get somewhere, you must walk from one point on the planet's surface to another; you cannot instantaneously move yourself there. However, in the vibrational elevation of the human consciousness, there are things that happen that allow you to break these rules. That is all that was happening in the story of my walking on water. It was an illusion. My friends were not actually seeing my physical body; they were seeing a representation of my body.

At the time when I was walking on water, I was in fact meditating in a cave not far from the edge of that particular body of water. The disciples saw a projected image of me and had a conversation with my consciousness. This ability to manifest a virtual body, if you will, for other beings to see is not unusual in Eastern yogic practices. This comes from the enlightenment process, the full awakening process. You are able to see that the body is a projection. You are able to see that your body is created, second by second, from your thoughts, and this is the same principle that applies to miraculous healing. The body you experience as a solid object, or the body that you experience in your current consciousness as something that is immovable, is very difficult to change. It is one of the great illusions that you are immersed in, so that was what happened in that circumstance. I was meditating, and I projected my consciousness to where my friends were. And of course, because the body they saw was not the solid kind that they were used to, they mistakenly believed that I was walking on water, when in fact I was just suspended; the image was suspended slightly above the water.

The calming of the seas was the same effect. The mind that is completely connected to Source is incredibly powerful. It is able to work miracles, and— you must remember this — all of your environment in every way, shape, and form is coming from your mind. So a mind that is in absolute connection to God, to Source, to All That Is, and that is completely aware of the laws of manifestation can change anything. Changing the weather is no more difficult than changing the television station. That is all that is happening. The effects of fear — which is what that storm was, a manifestation of the fears of the beings in that boat — could be changed by my calm and loving consciousness. That is what happened.

These miracles are not as miraculous as you think they are when you begin to comprehend that everything you see is playing out in your mind as a dream, for you know that in the dream state, in your normal sleeping experience, you can change things instantaneously as soon as you realize that you are dreaming.

You do not comprehend that this idea of lucid dreaming can also apply to your life as you live it now. That is all I was doing: I was expressing my ability to lucidly dream in what you consider reality. However, as you raise your consciousness out of the physical world and into the higher realms, it appears to be another level of dreaming that the world exists in. As you pass over into the afterlife experience, into the life-after-life experience, your life will be recalled as a dream, just as you do when you wake from sleeping. When you pass over into the nonphysical, when you return to the higher realms, you remember your life as if it were a dream. And for some of you, it has been a nightmare. That is what we wish to change. No one needs to live in a nightmare. You have the ability to change your dream, but you must understand how the system works.

The same, of course, applies to the feeding of the many. When the mind is in tune with that which is creation, with that which is connected to All That Is making all that is observable (for it is only a small part of the creative process that is observable, and there is much of it that is not observable in your world; you miss many things), there is no problem in multiplying objects and in transforming objects. So essentially, all that happened was objects that were small in number were magnified into objects that were large in number. And again, when you realize that this is a vibrational result of being in touch with truth, you understand that your world can be shifted in any way.

Again, the principle I was teaching in my ministry is that the kingdom of heaven is within. The kingdom of heaven is the idea that your world is exactly as you want it: full of love, wonderful relationships, abundance, and joy. That kingdom is contained within your mind, just as the resistance to that kingdom is contained within your mind.

That is what my ministry was all about. I was showing the potential that the human mind can create, the absolute end result of the connection to Source, connection to love, and connection to creativity. It was through miracles that I demonstrated my point of attraction, and it was also the contrast between that visual experience of healing, of abundance, and of transformation of physicality. These were all the things that I demonstrated to convince people to listen to what I was saying. Yet I bumped up against the conditioned mind of a very narrow and materialistic culture that was based on the spilling of blood.

Do the Work Where It Is Needed

There was a profound belief that death brought something and that it was a positive act, so I was working with a difficult crowd, so to speak. I had a lot of hecklers, and there were a lot of beings who believed the very opposite of what I taught, which was that love is the way. This is why I taught in that culture at that time. Earlier I described my trek to the Far East and into the peaceful and esoteric mind investigations that were taking place in Tibet and northern India, and really, my heart wanted to stay there. I loved the passivity of it, and I loved the calmness of it, and I loved the intelligent investigation of mind that was taking place there, but my work was in a different part of the world. It was with regrets that I returned to it, but my Mary was there, and I knew that it was where my work needed to be done.

You do not need to do this work where it is already being done! You need to do this work, teaching the relief of suffering, where people are suffering. You do not need to preach to the converted — this is the phrase, is it not? You do not need to preach to the converted; you need to preach to the people who are suffering. The other side of that coin is that beings who are suffering are far from where you are, and so you must find a language they can hear from where they are. That was why I taught in the way I did in my public encounters.

As this ministry continued, there was much dissent. The more the crowds gathered and the more influence I had over the local beings, the more concerned the priests and officials of those areas became. There arose a groundswell of desire to put an end to this disruptive force, for you must understand that I created events by my teaching and by my presence that would at times put a town out of business for a day. There would be so many people coming to listen to me speak, so many people with sick family members or needing their own bodies healed that entire towns would stop functioning for the duration of my visit. So I kept my visits short and sweet, as you say.

Still, there was much grumbling and dissent from the powers that be within those areas, so I kept moving. There were officials higher up in the realms of government who heard these stories, and there were higher-ups in the Church, the religious structure of that time, who were completely threatened by me and who saw that I was having more influence over the parishioners they had previously controlled. They were losing their power, and this was the beginning of the end of my teaching ministry.

I had talked to many, many thousands of people, and I had healed many, many hundreds of people. I had instructed many people in private on the principles of my teachings so that they could affect other beings with their own alignment with truth and their own vibrational congruency with love, which shifts the body into a state of healing, into a state of well-being. But there were whispers, and there were conspiracies arising to get me into a state of criminal activity.

This is where the story takes a turn that is difficult for you to comprehend. For in your love of life and your belief in life, there is not always love for your life; there is often just an attachment to it, which is not love. But in your attachment to life and the belief that it is who you are, you cannot comprehend that I could step into a catastrophic end, as I did, with equanimity. However, you must understand that throughout this period after my enlightenment, I could remove myself from my physical body at will. While in meditation, I could manifest myself in other places. I could have conversations with people, and they would see a physically manifested illusion of my body in front of them in what you would call full third-dimensional real time. Yet I was meditating quietly in a cave somewhere. I had come to a complete understanding of my reality, of the real reality that you can experience when the mind is awakened.

The hardest thing for me, of course, was my family. This is a part of the story that becomes difficult for me because Mary was not in the same spiritual vibration that I was, despite our love for each other and despite the family we had created together. This was something that was very difficult for her to bear, but she knew through our many discussions (I had discussed this with her for some time, and it caused her to shed many tears and to ask me not to participate, but I told her that a momentum was building) that I could not stop teaching and the powers that be would not allow me to continue teaching. It was a perfect storm that was bound to end in confrontation.

I did not want it. The human part of me did not want it, but the part of me that was connected to Source and had known these out-of-body experiences and my true nature was fearless in the face of death, for it knew that death was an illusion. I knew that death was not real, and I knew that I would be able to present myself in physical form and that I would be able to re-create a body as easily as these beings intended to destroy my body.

The most difficult aspect of my teaching, the most difficult aspect of my experience on Earth, was convincing my beloved Mary that this was the path of highest intention and of highest result.

Our sons were completely oblivious of my life, just as your children are oblivious of your careers. They do not know if you are a criminal lawyer or an actor of some other kind. They do not know what you are up to in your day, and they do not care. You are their parents, and that is all they care about — to sit on your laps and hug you, to play with you, and these kinds of things. My children were no different. We did not involve them in what was going on in the adult world.

Judas

As this conspiracy began to breed in number and grow in power, it became clear to me that this was the time for the reckoning. I went toward the eye of the storm rather than trying to avoid it. That is what happened when I went to Jerusalem, fully knowing what I would be subjected to. The betrayal by the one that you call Judas, this poor being who has become the symbol of hatred and unreliability and deception throughout your society, played a divine role in my transformation, and his part in that journey was a very painful one for him as a human. But on a spiritual level, there was no judgment.

This being has not been condemned in any way, and in fact, he passed into the nonphysical very shortly after I passed into the nonphysical, and there was a communion of our minds, a meeting of our minds after the departure from the physical, for he was brought into awareness of his full participation on a spiritual level in this, what would be considered a terrible betrayal. But that was his job in his life. He had volunteered to play that role in this drama, and after he passed over, he was given this information. He did have a difficult time for a little while, believing that he had killed me and that he was totally responsible. When he passed over, however, he was given the information that this was a cooperative effort and that I had gone willingly into the experience to prove what I was speaking about. This is exactly what happened. I demonstrated that I was not a body. I demonstrated that death was not real and that this was the most magnificent of opportunities, showing my disciples the truth of my existence.

The Body Is Nothing

You must understand that from the perspective of the crowds of beings who were of no particular consequence, I was just another badly behaved person killed for that bad behavior. That was all they took from it, nothing more. But for all the beings whom I had taught — all the disciples who I had instructed, all those close and loving friends I had been preaching to and teaching for many years — this was a powerful event. This was an event that demonstrated my ability to overcome the physical — but not because I was the son of God. I never claimed that. That is not what I said. I always proclaimed my equality with other beings. I always proclaimed my sameness to others, and I continue to proclaim that throughout this text. But I did have some skills because of my practice and because of my enlightenment that other beings did not have at that time. So I was in a place of instruction.

There was no sacrifice here. This is a very important part of this book. For your culture, having misinterpreted this act of crucifixion and death, believed that I sacrificed my life for other beings. That is not what I did. I did not die. I sacrificed my body, but my body was nothing. This was the message of the crucifixion: The body is nothing. It is already a corpse; it is already nothing in and of itself. It is the animating force, the spirit, the awakened mind that can animate the body on its own volition, and that is what I was teaching. For many, many, many generations, your culture and the Church have mistaken this act of raising awareness for an act of sacrifice, and this is not the case. It is not what this was for, and it is not required.

I did not sacrifice anything. I merely handed my body, which was of no consequence to me whatsoever, over to be destroyed and killed to offer up the example that this was not going to stop me; this was not going to be the end of me. This was not, in fact, going to hinder my teaching in any way, shape, or form. So this teaching that the Church has taken on itself to promote, which is that sacrifice is holy, is something I wish to put to bed now. This is something I wish to put to sleep now. There is no need to sacrifice anything. You do not need to sacrifice your happiness, and you do not need to sacrifice your body, and you do not need to sacrifice yourself in any way. Your obligation is to live your life to the fullest with the greatest awareness, love, and self-expression that you can.

That is what I did. I lived my life to its absolute fullest, and because I understood the lack of meaning of the physical body and because I had mastered the art of manufacturing a new body whenever I desired it, I truly comprehended how meaningless the body was. And I attempted to demonstrate this to my disciples; I attempted to demonstrate this to the beings I had taught.

Shifting Consciousness

There were forces at play here that were grander than the individuals contained in the story. My disciples did not wish me to leave. They wanted me to carry on in the way that I had been carrying on, but this was part of my destiny. This was part of the path that had been preordained for my experience.

I had a magnificent time on Earth. I had a magnificent time of teaching and healing and expressing these divine truths on the plane for all to see, but there was a limited time for this, and it was part of my journey, part of my teaching ministry, to have this experience of overcoming death so that beings could witness it. And of course, this is the message that has transformed me in your minds and in your culture from an ordinary being into a divine being, this thing you call the son of God, which of course I am not more than you are. You are all children of heaven, just as I am.

There are different levels of evolution, it is true, but one is not more valuable than the other. A child in kindergarten is not less valuable than a graduate from college; they are merely at different places in their experiences. You must start out in kindergarten before you can get to college. So there is no less value in the earlier stages of the awakening process. You are all equal, as I am equal to you.

However, this was part of my life's framework, my destiny, if you will. It was a difficult time, as the human aspect of me loved my wife and my children. I would have liked to go back to a simple life of carpentry and fishing a little bit and the occasional trek into the woods. This is something that I would have liked to do. But this teaching and this experience was not something I could go back on. I couldn't undo what I knew. I couldn't change all of the people who had come to know me as this teacher and as this healer. The momentum was massive, and the ultimate lesson that my life was going to demonstrate was not a sacrifice; it was a conscious decision, albeit a very difficult one.

I went to this experience with mixed emotions; there is no doubt about that. But I went voluntarily into the death experience because I was aware of this agreement I had made to do this work. It is hard for you to comprehend this, we understand from this side, because you are attached to the body and you are fearful of pain, but you must understand that I was able, in that time and place, to remove my consciousness from my body so that the suffering was in fact quite limited. The observers of the event from the outside did not experience what I experienced. I was able to lift my consciousness out of my body very early in the process and was gone far sooner than people think.

Because of many years of practice, I could at that time just shift my consciousness and remove it from the physical body. So the body that was hanging on the cross was not me. The consciousness that was me had already gone into the nonphysical and was communing and communicating with my higher guides, my higher self, and the beings who were in charge of my ministry from the nonphysical side (they were as directors and managers, if you will). I was informed of the purpose, and I was informed about the reasoning, about the structure of this event, and about all the associated beliefs and ideas that were challenged by this event. I was told that this death experience, undone through the idea of resurrection, would be the most powerful aspect of my teaching. That was the truth. I was not contained within my body, and I did not raise up a dead body. That is not what happened. The body was merely dematerialized, and I materialized a new one.

That is what my dear Mary saw when I first came back, and that is documented (although, obviously, not through an eyewitness account). These are stories that were recounted, so their accuracy is not very good. I returned to Mary after several days to spend some time with her and my sons. They were not aware of any difference in me whatsoever.

Returning to the Family

Mary was treated as a mourning wife, so nobody disturbed her. We spent several days together, and I was in my astral form, but it was solid in the sense that it was touchable. It was visible, and it was a speaking, breathing, talking, laughing, loving body. So there was no resurrection of the dead body. I merely created a new one. This is what happened.

I showed myself to my disciples, and of course, I did not need to walk in any particular way; I was able to dematerialize my physicality and rematerialize it. I was able to disguise it in a way that allowed only certain beings to see it. These are principles you are not familiar with because you do not understand the nonphysical. Once again, that is a reason this book was written: so that you understand more of the truth about the physical form in which you live.

I was given the opportunity to show these beings who had been so close to me, such good friends to me in my life, that the death experience was not what they thought. It was important for them to understand this as I moved into a new realm.

Now, you may wonder why, if I was able to manifest a physical body whenever I chose, I did not continue on with my life. Why did I not just live this way? You must understand that when you have ascended into a different realm, there is a driving force to keep you moving forward. There is a driving force toward evolution, consciousness evolution. There is a driving force to step into the new realm and to begin to investigate that, and it is an inexorable force. It is not a force that you can go against.

I was allowed to visit several beings I loved dearly in the months following my "death." I spent many days with some of these people, speaking about what had happened and speaking about why it had happened. But many of my disciples could not understand at all what was happening. It was so far out of the realm of their reality that they made up stories to explain these activities. They made up explanations that made sense in their world because what was happening did not really make sense in their world.

The concepts that came out of that experience were not as high as I had hoped. They were confused by the materialistic and earthbound minds of my fellow travelers. Mary did a much better job because she knew me so intimately and so well that she truly comprehended what was happening. However, there were consequences. She was by herself, but she was guided, with the assistance of my consciousness and with the assistance of some very good friends, into a new location. And indeed, we go into that in the next section.

Now I wish to go into what happened to my family after I passed and what happened to *me* after I passed, for this is only the midpoint of the story. There is much yet to cover. That is enough for you to contemplate; that is enough for you to think about.

CHAPTER FOURTEEN

After the Resurrection

BEFORE I TALK ABOUT MY CONSCIOUSNESS AND WHAT HAS HAPPENED TO IT since the incarnation as this one you call Jesus, I would like to wrap up the story of my life on the physical plane. There are many tales of what happened to my family after my death and after my apparent abandoning of them on the Earth plane.

You must understand that as I disappeared from the physical as you know it, I did not disappear from the Earth plane. At any given moment, I was able to manifest a body that was physical in all ways. I am not talking about a ghostly image. I am not talking about an image that had no texture or quality to it. I am speaking about a body that you would recognize as human in all ways, in all shapes, in all tastes, in sound, and in touch. That is what I was able to do, given the experience and instruction that I had been given.

There were many examples of my appearing over the years following my crucifixion to beings who loved me and whom I loved. It was not that I was restricted in any way, shape, or form. However, as years went by, I was called more and more into the nonphysical, and so it was an easing for my family. Initially, I spent a considerable amount of time with them to help them with their grief, because they knew on an intellectual level that I had died, and they were feeling it on an emotional level. But every time I showed up in this physical form that they recognized as their beloved Jesus, I eased their pain and convinced them of what was happening.

So this was their experience after my crucifixion. On the outside, it was a family bereaved because of the loss of a husband and father, but behind closed doors, I would often spend evenings with them. I would often spend time with them in the physical body that I was able to manufacture.

The same happened with my disciples. For several months I appeared to them to teach what I had experienced, but what I very quickly found was that their conditioning on death and their fears of persecution from the powers that had killed me shut down their willingness and openness to experience my consciousness in the way I intended. Very quickly after my death, their influence once again became their culture. Their influence became their fears. Their influence became their concerns about their physical safety. It was a testament to my understanding of the power of the belief in death, for even though I gave them evidence that death was not real, their conditioned minds still believed in it. So it slowly became difficult for me to manifest myself in front of them — not because I was incapable of doing it; that was not the case. It was because their minds did not wish to experience it, so they shut down that avenue of communication through fear.

This is, indeed, what we on the nonphysical side experience with most of you in human form. Your fears of death, your fears of possession, your fears of evil, your fears of spirit, and your fears of ghosts and haunting play into your part of putting up barriers to that which we consider love, that which we consider higher information, that which we consider wonderful opportunities for communication with the nonphysical. You limit yourself within your cage of fear to the physical world, and you become even more fearful, for it is a fearful world that you have created in your mind. It is a fearful world when you are limited in your vision and do not understand the nature of this reality in which you live, that it is not the only expression of what you consider experience and that there are many others out of your realm of interpretation. You must shift your mind into a place of focusing on the nonphysical to access these areas of nonphysical reality.

This channel, for example, has gone through a decade of prayer and practice and focus on the nonphysical, shifting her conscious thoughts in a way that allows fearlessness and defenselessness to express itself. And through this fearlessness and defenselessness, connections to the nonphysical have been made. That is why she is able to communicate in the way that she is and to receive these transmissions. But she is not unusual; she has merely gone through a mind-training process, using a book called *A Course in Miracles*, which was a book that was transmitted by me, through the mind of a being in your twentieth century, that was a training manual for transformation of mind. This is, indeed, the process that I was teaching my disciples, but they were seduced by my physical form and by my charismatic personality and ability to perform in the physical world to such a degree that they did not shift their consciousness enough after I had left to maintain their connection with the nonphysical, and their materialistic and attack-based society once again caused a problem for them.

The Church Is a Human Creation

When I was in physical form with my disciples, I provided them with a constant state of reassurance that allowed them to continue on the learning process. But after I had gone, they were unable to maintain that connection because my departure was such a traumatic and negative event for them. However, there were several beings I had taught who are not necessarily known to you but were working with my family afterward because they had the ability to connect with me. They were not so much in the public eye, so they were not as fearful. A teacher always has some students in class who are better than others, and these were the ones who were at the top of the class. I asked these beings to assist in moving Mary to a different location. I did not suggest this move through any controlling aspect of my personality; it was for the purpose of safety. That society was on full attack mode as the teachings I had promoted began integrating into the political and religious system of that time and place.

You must understand that my purpose was not to create a church. I was not setting the foundation for a church. I was setting the foundation for a change in paradigm. I was setting the foundation for a shift in consciousness. It was the human element. It was the power, control, and influence elements in the society at that time that decided to build a structure around my teachings and call it the Christian Church.

I intended for each being to have independence, to have freedom, to have self-expression, and to go through a personal transformation process to connect with the nonphysical and have a personal experience of enlightenment and awakening. That was my intention. It was not my intention to start a church, despite what people say about my actions. I never suggested that people build buildings in my name. I never suggested that people make sacrifices to me in any way. I never told anyone to worship me in any way. I always told them to go inside, to shift their thoughts, and to shift their way of perceiving the world. That was my ministry. It was not to build a church. It was not to create the structures that have resulted from my experience on the planet. You must understand that has been a human creation.

However, there has been a result of this church edification, this structural enforcement of what I taught, if you will. It was a manifestation of the ideas of men; but over time I have been influenced by the thoughts and prayers of millions of people. I will go into that later.

Escaping to France

There is a curiosity on your plane as to what happened to my family and how they lived out their lives. I return to that aspect of the story to tie up those loose ends before I go into the grander scheme of things, into the Catholic Church and the powers of manipulation and influence that have resulted from my life on the planet.

Two disciples were able to continue to connect with me and to work with my desires as they manifested through my astral body. I call it an astral body because it was not a body in the sense that you understand a body to be. However, you all manufacture your bodies every second — do not forget this — I was able to do it in such a controlled way that it appeared to be magical or miraculous. *But you all manufacture your bodies every second through your beliefs. You can transform them; you can change them by changing your beliefs.* I say that now emphatically just to remind you that you are not different from me. You merely do not understand the principles, and you do not understand the methodology of transformation. You can all heal yourselves. You can all transform yourselves, and you can all turn your nightmares into dreams of happiness, abundance, health, joy, and love.

My family was shipped to the Mediterranean coast of the country you now call France. It was not that long a journey. There were many trips over to [Italy]. Dear friends hired a boat to assist my family — my wife and my two sons — in traveling to the country you call France.

I was with them on that journey. They were not frightened, and they were not alone. We all traveled together, for the beings who were with us on that trip understood the principles of manifestation that I had mastered, and they were not surprised or shocked at all. They had been studying with me for many years, just as Mary had. And of course, my children — despite our not telling them about the political machinations of the end of my life because they had been quite protected — knew me, and they knew what I taught, for I taught it to them as well.

We arrived in southern France and ventured into the interior of that country. I will not go into specific locations, but with assistance from the beings who were my compatriots, my disciples, my dear and trusted friends, Mary had enough money to settle herself in a home in that area, and she began to live her life out.

Throughout her life, I came to visit her. We continued as husband and wife in the ordinary sense. We would sleep together; we would make love, for I was there in physical form frequently. As she became older, I began to focus my attention more in the nonphysical, but our relationship was always close. It was not until her physical death of natural causes at the age of seventy-four that she joined me in the nonphysical on a permanent basis.

I will not go into a discussion of my sons' lives and what happened to them; this is not the purpose of this story. The human mind wants to know who did what, where they did it, who they married, how many children they had and who were the offspring. It is irrelevant.

I am here now, speaking, and that is all you need to know. The nonphysical is real. The nonphysical is tangible in your lives if your minds are vibrating at the correct frequency. The physical lives that my family members lived are irrelevant in this story, and I wish to emphasize that by my refusal to go into more detail. The location is not important. We, on this side, do not wish to make a physical location sacred; it reminds you of the material world, keeps you locked in the material plane, and makes you believe that somebody else is more special than you. That is not the case, that is not the truth, and that is not what our purpose is.

Our purpose here is to convince you that you can connect with me every single day of your life in a real, tangible, and meaningful way and that you can transform your own mind from that of the lower physical realms into the higher realms so that you can live a miraculous life. You can live the kind of life that I lived: helping people, creating abundance, and living in a loving and fulfilling marriage, all these things. These are all your possible futures if you grasp this concept that the physically manifested world is the effect of your mind and not the cause of all your suffering.

That is the message behind this book: how to shift your consciousness so that you can manifest that which you wish into the physical world and live a life of abundance and peace until you are awakened completely, and then you no longer need to manifest a physical world to represent your limited thoughts, your limited beliefs, and your limited concept of self.

This world is a physical representation of your limited and untrue beliefs, and that is why this world is difficult for you. As you take on these concepts of the nonphysical being that you truly are and the physical world as a representation of that which you need to change within yourself, you will be able to climb the ladder to enlightenment, and you will begin to climb into the realms of the miraculous, the immortal, and the ever-living energies in which I and many of my dear friends reside.

PART THREE

The True Lessons

CHAPTER FIFTEEN

The Nonphysical Realms

WE ARE NOW AT THAT POINT WHERE WE HAVE SETTLED THE EARTHLY EXPERIENCE to some degree. Some beings will not like the brevity with which I describe some of these events, but I do not wish you to become burdened with history; it is pointless. Those bodies existed a long time ago. We are answering questions to try to put your thoughts about this part of the world's history to rest. To be obsessed with the past is pointless. Your point of creativity is here and now, and that is why I am here, using this channel in the form that I am.

No Room for Inequality in the Spiritual World

I am not using a male. I am using a woman. This is important. It is important for you to know my maleness was no more significant than her femaleness. It is all part and parcel of the same journey. Misogynistic, or woman-hating, theories in your culture based on the misinterpretation of my work and on the fact that I was often around men in a culture that was male dominated have caused much suffering in your world, much suffering on your planet in what you might consider Christian societies. Women have been subjugated, brutalized, and bought and sold with the idea that man is more valuable than woman. That is not the case, of course.

Woman and man are equal in the eyes of God. One is not better or worse than the other, but your society is tremendously out of balance with these essences of male and female, yin and yang, active and receptive, all of these things. This is a subject that I speak about quite considerably through this text, the whole idea that Mary was my equal partner. She did not have the enlightening experience, but my physical expression on the Earth plane in that time and place was as an ordinary human being who needed a partner, who needed a moral arbiter, and who needed somebody to support and love him. Mary absolutely did that job with flying colors, as you say.

I could not have lived the life I lived and would not have enjoyed living it if I could not go home the way I did, if I could not close the door on my home, be with my family, and forget about what I was. Those times of respite at home were wonderful for me. The inundation of bodies and the inundation of requests and requirements and questions were exhausting. And I want you to know, whatever your backgrounds, that there is no room for inequality in the spiritual world. You are all of equal value; you are all of equal import in understanding the universe and in experiencing your lives.

A small female child is no less valuable in our eyes than the male president of a country. We suggest you pay attention to that piece of information. Many are under the illusion that they are more valuable because they are white males who are powerful and rich. That is not the case. Their experiences in their next incarnation may not be as pleasant as they hope. Instead, they should use their power and influence to assist in educating and caring for the youngsters who do not fit into their description. Their use of their awareness and influence will determine their next experience in the physical world. If they are narrow-minded and convinced of their value over other beings, they will be given an experience to prove otherwise.

That is not a threat on our part; it is merely the way the system works. We all get to experience everything. We get to experience all of our delusions from both sides of the coin. You get to be the one who is in charge of the delusion, and you get to be the one who is the victim of the delusion so that you can understand both aspects and come to a place of letting the delusion go completely. That is the purpose of your incarnations: It is to wake up, to let the dream go, and to realize that your misbeliefs are not who you are.

You are all divine aspects of God manifesting to see where you are mistaken, and it is in waking up that you are relieved of your burden of suffering. It is in understanding that you are all the same, that you all deserve love and care and compassion, and that you are all on a difficult journey of awakening. It is not easy for anyone to wake up in the three-dimensional plane. It is a tricky place because it is laden with booby traps, which are your misunderstandings coming to life in the dream for you to see. Monsters lurk behind bushes; this is the idea of your life, and there is no doubt it is not an easy one.

I was very grateful for Mary and for her loving support. And when I look back on that particular incarnation, I am always grateful to her for her participation in the support and loving kindness that I needed to be able to do the work that I did.

Shifting Realms

We are at that point in the story where I was crucified and resurrected. (However, the word "resurrection" is not the correct one. That body was not healed; it was not made good and reused. It was deconstructed, and a new one was constructed.) My ministry continued on the earthbound aspect of my interaction on the plane with Mary and my children until Mary passed away. I did not continue to spend too much time with my children after that. They had their own lives to live, and they had their own personal growth to undertake. It is not that I did not love them. That is not what I am saying. What I am saying is that my focus shifted.

I was shifting into the nonphysical realm, and I was accessing layers and realms of intelligence, spiritual awakening, and improvement that were magnificent. I had done my work on Earth, and as a being of light, let us say (because I had become awakened), I did not have attachments to Earth as such. When Mary and my children were younger, they were the only things that really drew me back.

But what I had was a desire to teach the truth of life, which is what all nonphysical beings try to assist you with. They try to guide you into the realms of spirit so that you can wake up and get the correct information about what you are.

Removing the Blindfold

You must understand that from our point of view here in the nonphysical, in the awakened world, you are like blindfolded people walking around in a beautiful environment. You bump into each other, which would be considered conflict, and you trip over each other, hurting yourselves and sometimes others. There is a most magnificent garden around you and magnificent views and landscapes off in the distance into which you can venture and explore, but you are blindfolded, and you are bumbling around in a field together, trying to come to some sense of organization without really having the vision to understand where you are or to understand what is happening. We are able to lift the blindfolds from your eyes, little by little, in our efforts to assist you in seeing the truth of your world, which is that it is a minute part of reality. You have great adventures waiting for you in other lands when you take off the blindfolds. Yet you get used to the blindfolds. You get used to living in a restricted world, and the idea of removing these limitations can actually frighten you when you have been doing it for a long time.

Beings tend to do this for many, many lifetimes. You have a deep and profound history in your mind of all of the experiences that you have ever had as a physically incarnated being. And sometimes the longer you spend incarnating, the worse your attachments and fears and inaccuracies become. We have to make concerted efforts all the time from the nonphysical to assist physically incarnated aspects of the mind in shifting consciousness to begin to wake up, peak out from behind the blindfold, and realize that there is a most magnificent landscape to use and to explore.

Reaching across the Veil

After I passed over into the nonphysical with the awareness of complete awakening, there was no need for me to reincarnate. I began working with beings all around the planet in their sleep time and in their waking time. I could manifest with people in different locations and continue teaching, and this is what I did.

I came into the physical plane in various locations. It did not matter to me what country I was in; I was not concerned with political or national boundaries. This is of no concern whatsoever to the nonphysical. We do not see these boundaries. We see human suffering and minds in pain, and we attend to them in the physical world if we are required to do so. We can do that by manifesting a body, if that is required. Not all nonphysical beings can do this, however. I should explain.

Some nonphysical beings must work through the mind only, and they must work through the dream state and the communications that can be infiltrated through experience to help teach beings. I was able to manifest my physical body in various locations, and this I did.

I would often go to a village or town for a little while, and I would make myself known in the physical form. Of course, I was not restricted to my previous size and shape of body; that was not important. It is important in your world, but it is not important in our world. I have manifested myself in many forms, both male and female, to achieve certain goals, and I have continued to teach about self-awareness through forgiveness, compassion, and loving kindness, understanding that this is how you get in touch with the higher vibrations. When you are in touch with the higher vibrations, nonphysical beings find it much easier to communicate with you and teach you the truth about what you are.

There are many stories in your world of my appearing in certain places and at certain times. Sometimes it was me, and sometimes it was not. I did indeed spend more time in the realm that you call Tibet and northern India. My soul has a particular affinity with this area, and I have done many works there, living and working with people to heal and teach them how to live in accordance with their true nature, which is love and light, and healing those who are sick. Sickness is an expression of lack of alignment. It is an expression of fear. It is an expression of mistaken identity, and that has been my work.

The Power of Prayer and Spiritual Wealth

I would like to speak about the effect people's prayers have had on my consciousness and on my ability to help beings. I would like to speak about what has happened over the centuries of humans praying and praying and praying to me, making sacrifices to me — if not in the physical life form, then certainly in their life experiences. There are many people who have offered up their lives as sacrifices to me, and what I say is this: The focus of human consciousness on one being shifts that being's consciousness. Because I have had such adoration and love from so many — albeit misguided in some ways, for they have believed a story about me that is not true, a description of me that is not accurate — the prayers and focused consciousness of so many millions of people over such a long time have indeed shifted my consciousness far beyond that which I could have done by myself. So you can see that the inadvertent belief in my divinity has caused that very thing to arise in some ways.

I have become so enlivened by these wonderful prayers. I have become so connected to so many humans through their willingness to speak to me — not any other nonphysical beings, just a willingness to speak to me. I have been given a lot of responsibility in the nonphysical to offer truth out to beings who speak to me, commune with me on a consciousness level, and try to meld with me through prayer.

Of course, the most distressing thing from my point of view as this being you call Jesus, this being you refer to as the son of God, is the suffering that comes in my name. There are people who live very sad and restricted lives of penance and scarcity and poverty who do not need to live this way. They have mistaken what my life meant. I did not speak about being poor in the sense of suffering without enough food or enough clothing or enough housing. That was not my message.

My message focused on the nonphysical so that you could reap the rewards of heaven, which are abundance and health. The misinterpretation happened early on with this idea that when I was speaking about the nonphysical and about relinquishing attachment to the physical world, people thought that I was in fact speaking about poverty. I was not speaking about poverty. I was speaking about wealth of a different kind that will indeed bring wealth of a physical kind. It was a cart-and-horse issue, and people have, over the centuries, believed that they must be poor to be good. That was not the case at all. I was not poor in my life; I was well-off and had tremendous abundance flowing my way because of my connection to Spirit. I could always manufacture anything I wished to support me, and that is wealth in the truest sense of the word.

I did discuss with people the idea that if they were obsessed with the material to begin with, then they would become locked in it and wouldn't be able to enter the world of heaven. You cannot wake up when you are obsessed with the material world. But when you approach it the correct way — which is to focus all of your attention on the nonphysical, to bring your vibration up high, to focus on loving kindness, and to forgive so that your mind can become at peace — then you begin to attract to you the kind of abundance and wealth that all beings dream of, such as ease of life and lack of sickness. This is the kind of wealth that will come your way, and financial wealth might very well be part of it. It might not. You might not really care about it, so it might not come to you, but when you have woken up and when you are in the higher realms, you can focus your attention on anything that you wish.

There is no more or less divine aspect of this world than any other. This is not a divine place in the sense that you have been taught. This is the place that you learn to leave, and that is the truth. So that is one of the things that I would like to speak to people about, the idea that you have to be poor to be a good Christian. That is not the case. Your Christianity has been so distorted in your minds by 2,000 years of Church influence and editing and manipulation that you really do not have an idea of what I was.

So those of you who are sacrificing abundance for me, do not do it anymore. I want you to live in an abundant world, but in an abundant world that is full of love, full of connection, full of financial ease, full of physical health, and full of intellectual and emotional health. That is the abundance in which I wish you to live, and you will live in that if you follow these teachings. You will begin to understand why the Western world looks the way it does and why you are all confused and suffering in the ways that you are.

If you believe the declarations of poverty and refusing to own anything are arbitrary requirements, think again. They are not. They are my suggestions for focusing your attention on the nonphysical. Do your jobs, Do your work. Do the things that keep food and all those other things flowing into your lives, but pay attention to the nonphysical. Study spiritual material to shift your consciousness, to shift your focus from judgment, hatred, fear, and the body into the higher realms, and your life will take on an abundant nature that is beyond your wildest dreams. That is what my teaching is. It is not to suffer and to live in sackcloth and ashes. This is not the purpose of it; this is a mistaken interpretation of my words.

If you pursue spiritual matters, if you remove judgment from your mind, from your actions, and from your words, you will achieve a state of peace. You will achieve a connection to the higher mind that will inspire you in your life and will allow you to create the abundant, kind, and generous experiences in the physical that are possible in the awakened mind.

CHAPTER SIXTEEN

Church History

WE ARE NOW IN THE PHASE OF MY EXPERIENCE THAT IS NOT WHAT YOU CONSIDER the historical Jesus. I am speaking of the time since this story transpired. Your reality, your concept of time and space, now becomes a challenging concept, for you think of me as an individual body, and you think of me as a restricted mind. You see your own qualities in me, but they are not the qualities that a being such as I would possess.

Cracking the Mind Open

As you transition into the higher realms from a state of enlightenment, you are able to be in many places at one time; you are not even in time, as such. You may travel to the past. You may travel to the future. You may dip into the minds of any and all beings who are of a high enough vibration to communicate. You can dip into the minds and hearts of humans, who are, in fact, in a very dark place. For the ego mind or the conditioned mind cracks open in times of deep and dark despair when the beliefs that cause the pain are seen to be untrue.

Moments when a mind cracks open through deep and profound suffering — the loss of a loved one, the realization that a life is falling apart or not working, or the dissolution of a marriage — are the times when the conditioned mind, which believes that it is correct and its actions are right and true, has a loss of power over the mind of the being involved, and the true nature cries out for assistance, knowing that the path that has been taken has made it lose its way. It is in this profound and deep crying out that I can reach a human mind and connect with the true nature that resides inside it.

Some of you come to this in a dramatic moment of terror. Some of you come to this through a near-death experience. Some of you come to this through years of study of understanding the truth. But I now have the ability on this side, after my transformation from a human into a nonphysical being, to access many things that are beyond your comprehension.

You might ask, "How can one being be in so many places at one time?" You must understand that this world you live in is an illusory one. The time and distance and space that you believe in so truly are not real. This is what I mastered when I lived on Earth. I mastered the ability to create physical, material objects and to transform material objects. The possibility of a miracle shows you that something else is going on in your world that you are not aware of. It is the fact that your space-time reality is changeable. It is malleable, and it can be shifted by a consciousness that is aware of the truth of its nature and of its creation.

So I have, in my ministry, continued to work with beings throughout history, throughout this space-time reality that you consider to be so true, so real, so hard, and so tangible. You must understand that your consciousness comes into this space-time reality at your birth, and it is very limited in its focus. It does not truly understand the passage of time or the creation process, and it does not understand the experiential process.

It sees separation as reality, and that is not reality. That is an illusion. It sees attack as a form of positive action to get what it wants, and that is the biggest lie that you live with. It sees the other as less than or better than when in fact there is no other. There is only you represented in the outside world for you to see yourself and to come to understand yourself. And so we speak at cross purposes in a lot of ways when you think of me as an individual working from an individual state of mind, as you recognize yourself to be, even though it is not true.

Church Censorship

I am not an individual in the sense that you see it. I am an energy of thought, a level of creation and recognition and self-expression that can be shared, that can be imparted to many beings, and that can be "teleported" to many times and places. I will use that word, as you understand it in some way as defying the laws of physics that you believe in so strongly. You cannot envision a world that does not bow down to these physical laws that you believe you are dominated by.

My purpose in coming to Earth was to express myself as a spiritual being, as a teacher, and as a philosopher. I was not given this job by God as his son; that is not the way life was organized. I was as you: an ordinary human being with a life's purpose. Each of you has a life's purpose, and you feel it in the guidance system that you have been given.

The Christian Church has taught many beings over many centuries to ignore their feelings, to ignore their guidance systems, and to ignore energies that naturally work through their bodies at the behest of this force that you call God, this benevolent loving force. You separated yourself from oneness, which is what this world is. It is created by all of humanity; it is created by beings who see themselves as individuals. These are aspects of mind that have manifested a world to represent this belief in separation, and that is why this world looks as it does. This is why you feel alone. It is why you feel separate, and it is why you think others are your enemies. This is the state of mind that you have brought to this world; it is not the state of mind of the one you call God. This is why it does not make any sense when you hear that God is love, all is love. You look around and you see that this is blatantly untrue.

The structures of the Christian Church, as they have existed over the past centuries, have taken on the egoic structures of the human mind, and they have distorted my teachings. They have edited my teachings. They have edited other beings' teachings who worked with me in concert and supported my teachings on Earth through that time and place of the Middle East 2,000 years ago.

Many of these doctrines were edited out of this document you call the Bible. They were taken out because they encouraged self-expression, they encouraged self-awareness, and they encouraged self-empowerment and connection to the divine powers that all of you have the right to access. The beings in the early Church — the popes and political rulers — decided to take the passion, the fervor, and the delight that I had created in my ministry and the disbelief with which so many witnessed my preaching, my ministry. They took that energy and decided to use it for their own purposes. They decided to use it for their own power and aggrandizement, and they edited from the Bible anything that did not agree with and support the maintenance of their own power structures, their own Church infrastructure, and their own financial well-being.

These were all motivating factors in the transformation and the editing of these documents, the weeding out of any words that implied that any being had personal rights, the ability to create, or the ability to form a life that he or she chose, reflecting individual desires, wishes, and self-expression. And over the centuries there has been such abuse heaped on beings in my name.

There have been schools designed to teach children that they are sinful, they are wrong, and they are less in some way. There have been institutions that have punished people physically, mentally, and emotionally and have used my name as they perform these terrible, terrible attacks on the bodies, minds, and spirits of beings who have put themselves in those places, believing that they were following the word of God. At other times, they were put in these institutions by other beings who did not wish to deal with them.

Now Is the Time for Both Freedom and Fear

This time and place in your history is the first in which a wonderful combination of events is happening. There is a wonderful combination, a confluence of energies, that allows this transmission to be made and that allows it to be sent out to many, many millions of beings at one time. You will not be crucified, and you will not be hung, and you will not be burned at the stake, and you will not be thrown in a mental institution. The freedom to be yourselves has at last come to your planet, but you are lost in your ego mind. You are lost in the teachings of your modern society, and this is also one of the confluence points. There are many of you looking around at what you have made, and you are terrified. You are fearful of your governments, and you are fearful of your medical service providers. You are fearful of the army, and you are fearful of the education system. You see that a terrible monster has been let loose in your world, and that is the ego mind, which feeds on the images of the material and on the images of bodies and lusts and finances that are all self-centered and not based in spirit.

When I say "lust," I do not mean sexual energy. I do not mean that you should be celibate or that you should remove yourself from divine sexuality. That is not what I am saying here. That is a doctrine that has been adopted by the Christian Church. That is not what I taught. I will go into this subject later, but I do wish you to understand that when I say "lust," I mean the ego's use of the body — the use of the physical structure to take, the use of the physical structure to abuse, and the use of the physical structure for simple body gratification that is of a lower level, not of a higher divine essence.

Your world is in a time of distress, disillusionment, and fear. Yet, you also have tremendous freedom. You have the ability to read whatever you choose and to share whatever you wish with other beings, but it is time for you to understand that there are basic structures of your society that are built on lies, and I did not teach these things.

I did not come here to restrict you as the Christian Church teaches. I came here to help you understand how to reach awakening. I came to Earth to help you understand how you can commune with divine energies and become that which you are designed to become, which is a fully expressed part of the Divine Mind — expressing, experiencing, feeling, creating, growing, and learning. That is what you are designed to do on this plane, for it is only in the self-expression of your desires that you will come to a full understanding of what you are. And it is only in the full understanding of what you are and what this world is that you will be able to leave it behind and venture on to new and elevated landscapes and experiences that are the most wonderful things.

CHAPTER SEVENTEEN

The Guidance System

THIS WORLD IS A DIFFICULT PLACE; THERE IS NO DOUBT ABOUT THAT. I LIVED on it and struggled through my own humanity as I experienced it. I had many incarnations on the physical plane. The one that you saw as Jesus Christ was the last one, and I awoke in that lifetime. It was after that awakening process that I taught the things I taught on your world, but they have been taken and distorted. And it is time that you knew it. It is time that you understood that you are guided by a system that is infallible. You are guided by an internal guidance system that will not lead you astray but will, indeed, lead you to exactly that which you need to experience to understand yourself, to understand the world, and to understand how to wake up.

Your guidance system is your feeling body, your emotional body. This is the guidance system that you were given when you separated from All That Is — when, in your mistaken idea of self, you removed yourself from the mind of God and created a world in which you could play out your mistaken identity and your fearful thoughts. This is the world that you have created. This is the dream in which you find yourself, and that is the dream I have come to wake you from.

The dream has given you information that is erroneous about my teachings, and I come at this time, in this place, and through this channel to tell you the true story of what I was, what I still am, and what you are. We are all divine aspects of Mind, divine aspects of that which you call God, this loving benevolent force that wishes to pervade, to express itself, and to extend itself all the time, in all directions and in all ways. And your guidance system is designed to assist you in aligning with that energy. That is what it is.

You decided to take a journey by yourself, separate from God, from All That Is, and you were cut loose to experience this freedom and to experience the choice that you made. You always have free choice, but you were not cut loose alone; you were given a system that allowed you to find your way home. The love for you is so profound that you were given the freedom to become lost, but you were not given the freedom to become lost without a way home. This guidance system is the string that is tied to your home, and if you follow it, it will inexorably take you there. It will take you through all the twists and turns of your mind. It will take you through all the mistakes you have made. It will take you through all the delusions and illusions you have created to make yourself feel better, and it will inexorably take you home to that place where you can be at peace, where you can be connected once again with All That Is.

This guidance system is your feeling body. This guidance system is your minute-by-minute response to that which you feel and that which you experience. Here I will go into what this guidance system is and what it is telling you and how it works.

In speaking about the guidance system you were given, I refer to my statement in the Bible of giving you a "comforter," this Holy Spirit that you feel is a separate being from what you are. It is not. It is contained within your mind, and it is your guidance system. This is what I was referring to when I made this statement. Church people will not like this. They see the Holy Spirit as something else other than this, but they will not like anything in this book, so it is of no real consequence. We are not trying to shift those beings. We are trying to shift the flock. We are trying to shift the parishioners to spread their underdeveloped wings and begin to exercise their self-expression and come to an understanding that it is divine in nature. There is no rebelliousness about it; it is indeed what you are destined to do.

Pointing the Compass to Peace

This guidance system that is the comforter that I referred to in the Bible, this source of solace that I give you, is not something I indeed bestow on you; the *awareness* of it is what I bestow on people. It is the awareness that your guidance systems, your feeling selves, are your clues as to where you are on your paths. If you hold a compass and you want to maintain true north, you must follow the point and go in that direction. To maintain east, you must go in that direction. Your guidance system is your feeling body, and if you are not at peace, you know that you are not headed in the direction that Spirit — or God, or All That Is — wishes you to head in. It is telling you that in the alignment of peace, just as when the arrow points to the "N" on your compass, and you know that you are headed in that direction.

Your guidance system is just like a compass. It will tell you when you are aligned with All That Is, when you are aligned with God, by giving you a sense of peace. It is in peace that communion with the nonphysical can take place, allowing your intuition, your guidance, and the information coming from the higher realms to reach you. It is peace you seek when you tune out in your television-watching processes, for example, and this is a mistaken use of your guidance system. Your mind is agitated, tired, fearful, or some such thing, and you require relief. So you plop down on your couch and tune in to your television shows, and you find relief, for the mind is quieted. And you become immersed in a world that is not yours, problems that are not yours, and issues that are not up to you to solve. You go to a place that is out of mind and below consciousness.

Many of you also reach this state of peace through drugs and alcohol. Again, you come home from a day of stresses or work that you don't like, and you take some substance. We will not be specific here, for the substance does not matter; we do not prefer one over another. Some are more socially sanctioned, but that is irrelevant as well. Socially sanctioned drugs and alcohol are not necessarily better than those that are illegal. So do not take that as evidence that one is better than another. They are all shifting your consciousness from a state of agitation or stress in a desperate attempt to reach peace.

What is happening is that your guidance system is telling you something, and you are misinterpreting it. Your guidance system tells you to find a state of peace, but you do not go about it in the correct way. Now, this is not your fault, because your culture does not teach you how to interpret this information, and this is very important. So do not feel that because we are going into what could be considered "New Age-y, airy-fairy" business here that it is not of any consequence. This is the core of the matter and the heart of the matter. So pay attention to what is being said: We wish you to understand that it is important for you to reach this state of peace without the use of any substance, object, or other thing.

Seeking Peace Culturally

Your guidance system wants you to be at peace, and so you feel this, and you understand this innately in your consciousness. When you are not at peace, you are stressed out, you are worried, or you are fearful. You understand that you are not supposed to feel this way, so you seek, through your culture's teachings, a way to find peace. You are taught and trained to watch television very early on in your lives, which is detrimental to the spiritual awakening process. We say to parents who have been medicating their children with movies and television that it does bring the children or parents peace, but it is a numbing out. It is a lowering of vibration. This is very important for you to know.

You have been trained to seek your peace within your culture in many ways — through shopping, eating, drinking and drugging, watching television, and these kinds of things. We would like your attention to be drawn to the ideas of creativity, nature, self-expression, loving kindness, and communication. These are ways that you can find peace. They are drug-free and higher in vibration, and they will take you on your path.

Each of you will have a version that appeals to you. Some of you will enjoy technical drawing; some of you will enjoy pottery; some of you will enjoy cooking — it matters not what your creativity is. It is irrelevant. It is your own message from your own guidance system. You will have the urge to paint or draw or whatever it is that is coming up for you. This is going to be a bit of an exploration, for you have had many decades of training not to listen to this and to numb your consciousness with substances and behaviors that are condoned by and have become normal in your culture.

This is one reason for the creation of these texts by this channel with assistance from nonphysical beings such as me and the group of teachers known as Ananda. These documents show you what you are doing so you can understand that if you are suffering, if you believe in the world and if you are stuck in the material, then your vibration is low. You are doing many things that contribute to this system and to these negative vibrations that you experience in your lives and re-create through the manifestation that is your external experience of the world. You create your world from your internal belief systems, and you create your world from your vibrational state of mind, or your vibrational state of being. So it is very important that you understand that you lower your vibration in many ways throughout your society and you live the consequences of this vibrational lowering.

It is not a punishment from a God that is chastising you for watching too many television shows. This force does not care! It merely vibrates at a certain level, and when you are out of accord with that vibration, you feel bad. It is a guidance system designed to assist you in shifting yourself toward that which is truth, that which is your natural self, and that which is your home state.

You have come to this place, to this world, to this creation that you call the three-dimensional plane in a form of delusion that you have decided to explore. You are given free will. You are given the ability to do whatever you wish, but you have separated yourself from the very force that is your nurturing, that is your calmness, and that is your peaceful experience. It is important that you understand this and you understand how to interpret the guidance system that was given to you as an act of love from Divine Mind to assist you in your journey home.

Take Responsibility for the World You Make

We are speaking about the body-mind complex and its expression through thought and emotion. You must understand your beliefs about separation — and you *do* believe in separation or you would not be in this world experiencing what you are experiencing in a body at this time. Your body is a manifestation of your belief in individuality and your belief in separation, and this is why things such as sharing and communion and love are challenging for the human mind, for you have actually created this world to prove to yourself that these are not things you want. So you have much evidence coming at you all the time from the expression of yourself, which is your world, your life, and your experiences. You have much evidence coming to you to prove that you are right, that you are alone, that you are separated from God, that there is no God, and that you are bad in some way. This is the untruth of where you see yourself, and this is why some of the doctrines of enlightened beings, some of the beings who have come to your plane to wake you, seem so counter to what you are actually living. They make you feel as if you will live a dull and boring life if you follow these doctrines, such as removing drugs and alcohol from your life.

For those who constantly or repetitively turn to those things to find relief from their minds, the prospect of removing them can become terrifying. Many cannot imagine what life would look like without those drugs or alcohol, for they provide you with relief from the stress, boredom, and disillusionment that you have not been taught to cope with in any other way.

You must understand this: It is through reading these documents and beginning to shift your mind, even if you are not shifting your behaviors yet, that you will find peace. We wish you to begin to shift your mind, for when you begin to shift your mind and begin to understand the principles that are at play with the world, with your physical experience, and with your guidance system, you begin to change your behaviors a little bit. Your behaviors come from your beliefs, so we seek to implant new and truthful material in your mind so that your beliefs can change and you can affect your own behavior in an easy way. For if you actually start to study truth, if you actually start to come to a comprehension and understanding of what truth is, your behaviors will change. They arise from what you believe to be true .

So when you lie in front of your television drinking a bottle of wine every night, you act that way because of your belief systems, and it is not who you are. It is the conditioned mind. It is the delusional mind that causes these behaviors, so there is no judgment from our side. We wish you to understand that you are all magnificent beings who have the ability to create the world you wish. You can tap into abilities and talents that are beyond your comprehension at this time, but you have no chance of getting there if you continue medicating yourselves in the way you are in your society.

We bring this information to get you to truly understand what it is that you are doing to yourselves, why you are suffering, and why the world looks the way it does. It is created from all the minds that are here experiencing separation, fear, and a lack of love, if you will. We are not here to preach to you or to judge you. We are here to say to you that there is another way. There is a beautiful path that you can walk in consciousness and in love with your brothers and sisters. There are many beings reaching a state of disillusionment and fear on your planet who wish to change and to create a new world, and that is why these transmissions are coming at this time. There is a multitude of you who are asking for change, who look at what has been created and see that it is not in alignment with what you wish.

Change Your Mind to Transform the World

You must understand how the mind works, how creation works, and that you are all responsible for the world you see. You all contribute through your fear, your low vibration, and your judgments and hatred of each other. It is a transformation of mind, a raising of your internal vibration, and the consequent spontaneous shift in your behavior that will shift the consciousness of the world. Behavior, in fact, is the least significant, for it is in your change of mind that you will transform the world because that is what your world is made from. Your world is made from thought, and your action is inspired from thought. Your thought comes from your beliefs, and your beliefs come from your conditioning and understanding of what is going on here.

We are attempting to give you the truth so that you might begin to change your world from the inside out, because that is the only way that it can be changed. You must change your vibration, and you must understand what your guidance system is, how it works, and how you can shift it higher and higher and higher — a little bit each day.

You cannot go from low to high in one leap. It would jar your mental structures, your psychology, too much. The human mind must be shifted in small increments or it becomes imbalanced and frightened. This is what you see in psychotic breaks when people try to change things too much: They have a fracturing of the mind.

Manifesting Health

You are able to manifest anything you wish, and many of you are living in a nightmare that you do not need to live in. You can live in a wonderful dream, and eventually, you will wake from the dream — but that is a long way away for most of you, and so we do not speak about it too much. We just speak about raising your vibration so that your simplest experiences of day-to-day life will become better and better and better and your relationships and bodies will be healed.

This is a large one for all of you, of course — this idea of sickness. You do not realize that your sicknesses are your negative thoughts manifested in your physical body because your physical body is also an idea that is representative of separation and of your disconnection from Source. It is a place where you put your fears and your limitations so that you can see them and come to understand what they are.

This shift in consciousness that we ask you to undertake will heal your body, and we hope that those of you who are sick, disillusioned, or sad will indeed take this information to heart and study this material .

Do not worry if you do not understand some principle. Do not worry if this sounds too esoteric or difficult for you. We wish you to understand that your guidance system is how you feel in this very moment, and you have the ability to change it by what you focus on and what you believe to be true. So if you can come to some understanding of vibrational manifestation — that lower vibrations feel bad and higher vibrations feel good — then all you need to do is find a way to feel better by what you focus on without the use of drugs, alcohol, or television. We ask you to do this today in your life.

What can you do through your focus to shift your appreciation of where you are? Do you have a job that you hate? You can shift your consciousness and say, "Ah, but I have a job. There are people who are unemployed." Appreciating the fact that you have a job will raise your vibration a little bit. If you have a body that is working well, you can say, "Ah, I could be much worse off. I can focus on the fact that I am healthy and I have the ability to move. I can motivate myself to do certain things. I can go for a walk in this body in this moment. I will walk in the woods today, and I will focus on the appreciation I have for this physicality I am contained in."

These are simple behaviors that we wish you to employ to shift your vibration. It is very, very simple. This is not some grand spiritual plan that requires you to become a priest to understand. It is very simple, and that is why this guidance system was given to all beings: Every being can understand it. Seek that which you can do in the next minute that will make you feel better without the use of drugs, alcohol, shopping, or television (I am adding things in here, I understand that). We ask you to do this without the usual techniques that you use. This is important. It must come from your consciousness, this shift in vibration. It cannot come from something outside of you. A shift in vibration requires you to think about something differently. Entertain the idea that perhaps you feel bad because you have been looking at the world in the wrong way and that there is, in fact, nothing wrong with the world; the problem is the way you have been taught to look at it. We are retraining your mind to look at the world in a different way so that you will begin to feel relief from suffering.

These are simple teachings and simple techniques that you can use to wake from the suffering that you are in and to shift your consciousness so that your world will actually shift in front of your eyes. You will begin to have a different experience, and you will begin to consume different things — different foods and different entertainments — as you come to see that you are responsible for your state of being. You are responsible for how you feel in this moment, in this time and place, and you have arrived where you are because you have been listening to your guidance system and perhaps mistaking its direction.

Understand that you have gotten yourself where you are, and if you are suffering, let us say that it is through the misinterpretation of your guidance system. Your guidance system is telling you all the time when you are in alignment and when you are out of alignment. So at first it is about looking at where you are; knowing that you have created this situation you are in; and going into your mind to listen to your thoughts, judgments, and assessments of people, places, and things. See whether you can spot where negative ideas live in your mind and where negative sayings are repeated thousands of times a day. This is where you will shift not only your consciousness and your vibration but also the manifestations you see in your body and in the world in front of you represented by the people, the places, and the things around you and by the experiences you have.

CHAPTER EIGHTEEN

Leaving the Garden

IN THE PREVIOUS CHAPTER, I EXPLAINED HOW YOUR GUIDANCE SYSTEM ARRIVED: It was given to you as a road map out of the mire, out of the journey you insisted on taking into darkness, into separation, and into fear. The journey into fear is what you are being led out of. Your journey into fear is manufactured from the world of your mind, manufactured from all your fears and beliefs and mistaken ideas of what you wish to experience. You see, you are given the opportunity to experience all of the things that you believe in. The idols you worship of the body, of money, of sex, of individuality — these are things that lead you into suffering.

Demolishing Untruths to Rebuild the Foundation

You look at this world and wonder how God could make such a mess, but of course, this world is not God's creation. This world is your creation, and God merely waits for you to come Home. God merely waits calmly and in peace, offering love, offering love, offering love to those who are in alignment with that vibration. You are not punished, you are not chastised, and you are not cast into a sea of fire for your choices. This is where many of you are very mistaken on your journey through this world. There are sources of information that somewhere in their deep and dark past had this tidbit. For example, the Christian Church was supposedly founded on my teachings. I am going to be very tentative about this statement because they have used so few of my teachings that it is laughable, in a sense, considering the structure that they have built.

Many of my teachings were eliminated from the texts that form your Bible, so there are only snippets and small, encapsulated items that I spoke about in it. Most of my ministry was done in private for a reason. The thoughts, ideas, and practices I taught beings were revolutionary. They were designed to take down the structures that be. As you come into this understanding of what the Bible is, what the Christian Church is, you must keep this historical fact in mind. I brought information onto the Earth plane that was designed to free people from oppression, to free individuals from suffering, and to give them understanding of the creative process as it exists within the human mind.

The structures of power that were in force at that time and that observed these teachings — the public teachings anyway — were pivotal not only in my crucifixion, but also in the perpetuation of my teachings after I died. You must understand that there is a profound paradox here in that eventually some of my teachings became accepted by the powers that be, but many of them were not. Many of the teachings that were the most powerful were indeed taught in private and were subversive in their nature in the sense that they encouraged people not to listen to any authority but to their own connection to their divine Source.

So you can imagine that this information, as I disseminated it at that time, was considered dangerous and was considered likely to topple the house of cards that the human beings in power had created at that time. You must keep this history in your mind as you approach your own understanding of my teachings. You must understand that there has been a Church built on untruths, small snippets of truth elaborated and embroidered with untruths. There are these small gems of wisdom contained in there, but there are lies woven around them, and so some unraveling is required for you to truly understand what is going on in this history of my teachings as they relate to your guidance system.

Forgiveness and the Fall from Grace

What I will speak about here is forgiveness because this is one of the ideas that the Church has taken under its wing, has taken into its bosom so to speak, and kept as one of its own. My definition of forgiveness is very different. What I taught and what I am teaching now is this idea of forgiveness when you understand that all of the things you experience in your world are your own creations, so there is no point in attacking them judgmentally because you are literally attacking yourself in unawareness.

I go into this foundational principle a little bit, so bear with me. It is a little theoretical but not beyond your ability to comprehend. You have read this far, so you are an open-minded soul who wishes to learn new things, who wishes to transform your mind and your experience.

You have created this world from the idea of separation, this idea of wishing to be other than what you were, which was one with God, one with higher mind, one with Divine Nature, one with All That Is, whatever you wish to call it (there are many names; it matters not). At one point, you were at one with this consciousness, this loving is-ness, but an aspect of mind decided that that was not sufficient or acceptable, and there were other things that were to be experienced. Because of the power, the unbelievable power of the creative mind in alignment with divine Source energy, you immediately created an experience of that which you desired, which was separation from where you were. That is how your world, your mind, and your experience were created.

This plummeting, if you will, from Divine Mind through the idea of mistaken thought is what you refer to in your scriptures as the fall from grace, or being kicked out of the Garden of Eden. There is a collective memory of plummeting from a place of peace and total acceptance, total love, and total connection with All Being. There is a memory of this in the deep recesses of the mind. What happened when you did this was you ended up with a deep and intense sense of guilt and a fear of retribution. There was an understanding, in the second that this thought was created, that you made a terrible error and that there was some awful consequence about to be dumped on you for making this mistake. And the mind, in its creativity, began to shore up the "reality" that it now was experiencing. It is not reality; it is a dream of separation, and it is not a real separation. You are never separated from God. You only think you are and lose your awareness of your connection.

It is a place of deep fear when you first experience it, and that is the physical world that I speak about. This is a concept that is very difficult for the human mind to understand because it is limited in its ability to comprehend what it has done to itself. That is why beings of higher vibration repeatedly come down to this plane to try to explain to you what you have done to yourself, and this is what is happening in your experience. In your deep fear-fractured and guilty mind, you are unable to comprehend what you have done. You run around, putting your finger in the dikes of fear that you have created for yourself, making a more and more elaborate world full of more and more choices and more things to blame for your fear and suffering. This is what is happening in your experience.

Recognize Your Wonderful Creation

You do not realize that this is what you have created. It is disguised in a wonderful story, which is your life. It is disguised in a wonderful vehicle, which is your body, and it is disguised in a wonderful movie, which is a projection of these thoughts into the world that looks like your experience, your physical experience. You use your body to prove the reality of your experience, so you have a self-fulfilling prophecy that constantly seeks information to prove to itself that it is okay — to prove to itself that it is not going to die, not going to be punished, and not going to suffer.

What you do to make yourself okay with this situation is you project all the things that you hate, all the things that you do not align yourself with, all the things you accuse of this complete and utter mistake that you have made. You project it into your world in the form of enemies, in the form of behaviors that you hate, in the form of people who distress you, in the form of accidents, and in the form of all sorts of negativities. And you project it into the body because, you must remember, your body is a symbol of this separation; it is not divine in nature. It is not what you think it is. It is a projection of your fear and isolation manifested into an object. You project negative ideas into that, and they manifest as sickness.

So you have created this elaborate dream in which you are living, and you do not know it. This is why higher beings — such as myself, Ananda, and many of the great teachers throughout your history — have come with information from the nonphysical and from Divine Mind: We are trying to help you come Home.

This is a very basic description of what is at play, and it is your desire for individual representation, your desire for separation, that has created your world, and that is why your experience here is painful. That is why you will feel cut adrift much of the time until you become aware of what has happened and how to remove yourself from this intense and visceral dream you are immersed in.

Awaken and Exit Your Own Hell

Many of you these days are beginning to wake up, and it is time for you to hear the absolute truth. It is time for you to begin to deconstruct all the ideas in your own world, in your own creation. Remember that you are ready to shift. There is a groundswell of energies representing the desire of your mind to wake up, and it is coming into your world. It is coming into your mind through these streams of consciousness. You must remember that you have called out to us in higher mind, you have called out through prayers, and you have called out through your desire to wake up. You must remember that your entire world, your entire mind as it sits at this moment, is going to balk at what we are saying because you have created a world to prove that the opposite is true..

Some of these ideas are going to be very challenging, and some of these ideas are going to be thrown out, but we ask you to repeatedly read this material if you find it offensive or if you find it difficult to understand. Know that there is nothing wrong with the material. Know that there is nothing wrong with you. The ideas are merely so far away from the dream you have created that you know on some level you are going to have to relinquish the dream to believe these words. If you begin to believe these words and if you begin to integrate them into your mind, then things will shift in your physical world. For many of you, this is a frightening idea because you do not trust. You are still immersed in this idea of guilt and fear for what you have done, and so there is a part of your mind that thinks you will be punished. You will not be punished.

This is where the idea of hell has come from. There is a belief in the unconscious mind that is dreaming, living in this world of projection and in this world of separation, that there is an omnipresent God that will punish you for what you have done, and that is not the case.

Forgive Yourself

This idea of forgiveness is multileveled. You must forgive yourself for the error that you made in creating this world. When you look around the world and do not understand it, when you look around the world and hate it, when you look around the world and see injustice and suffering, then you do not understand the principle of projection. It is not until you understand the principle of projecting the unwanted into the world that you will begin to be able to come to some place of forgiveness and peace. As long as you believe that it is real (in the absolute sense of the word) and as long as you believe that enemies and evil exist out there, you are in the powerless place of the victim. You are in a powerless place of unconsciousness, which is an uneducated state. You do not understand truth — you do not understand that God is love, that All is love — other than what you witness through your mind, which is the projection of all your fears into the world so that you might hate them.

The reason you have projected them is you cannot contain that kind of conflict within the mind. The guilt and fear would overwhelm you, and you would go into a state of catatonia, let us say, or have a psychotic break. So what you have done is separate all your fears, all your hatreds, out into the world so that you might judge them. You have heard this phrase, "Judge not, that ye be not judged" [Matthew 7:1, KJV], and you will not accept this until you understand that this world is your own creation and that your enemies are your own frightening aspects of mind that you have separated out so that you do not have to live with them.

When you see an enemy or when you see something to judge, you must understand that it is a part of your fractured mind represented outside of yourself to give you some relief from your distorted ideas. When you judge that, then you judge a part of your mind, you feel it as pain even though you might not be aware of it. So this is where the concept of forgiveness comes in, and it is so very important for you to see it not as the way that it is represented in Church teachings and not in the idea that a good person forgives and therefore overcomes badness. What you must understand is that forgiveness is the act or the statement of your comprehension of truth, which is that any crimes committed by other beings are projections of your own mind's separation and your own mind's fearful concepts. To love and forgive those will allow you to integrate that aspect of self into mind, and you will become more whole.

It is this state of peace — through the practice of forgiveness via the understanding of the truth of your creative process — that you will be able to return Home and return to a state of peace and wholeness. In this state of peace and wholeness, the nightmare will be transformed into a wonderful dream.

Punishment Comes from Within

You do not need to worry about losing everything that you have; that is not what this is about. This idea that you will lose everything that you value is one of the fears that will keep you from what is called salvation. That is not the case. You will be gently woken from the nightmare into a nice dream, into a wonderful dream of love, abundance, and communion, and at that point, you will step easily into the world of your home state, which is connection to All That Is, the oneness of love and the oneness of what you call God. But there is no punishing God. The only thing that you have ever been punished by is your own mind, and the only hell that you will ever visit is the one in which you are living at the moment.

Do not fear this process. Do not fear this information. Your mind will think that there is some lurking punishment waiting, but that is not the case. The only punishments that you ever give yourself are the hateful thoughts in your mind, the unconscious fear of guilt and retribution that you expect to be bestowed on you by a God that does not exist. It is not that there is no God; the God that you believe in does not exist.

There is no punishment, there is no sin, and there is no hellfire and damnation. These are concepts from the ego mind that have been integrated into teachings that were originally sacred, and they have all become mixed up and entangled and very confusing for you. This is why religion is confusing; this is why secular life is disillusioning. You are trying to make sense of an insane situation, which is the manifestation of everything you fear, everything you think you have done, and every sin you think you have committed (but have not indeed committed).

Forgiveness is a subject that I speak about more. Next, I speak about how forgiveness looks in your life on a daily basis so that you have some idea of how to handle situations, how it will improve your psychology and your internal experience of self, and how it will transform the outside world for you to enjoy far more than you are at this time.

When we teach this material, we are excited for the potential relief it can bring humans. We have experienced our own physical incarnations, so we know what it is like to be deceived by the dream that you have created. But from our point of view now — in the nonphysical, in the higher realms of consciousness — there is great sadness in seeing how the human mind suffers. You become so deeply immersed in the dream that you cannot wake up and you cannot hear the voice of sanity and love calling to you to come its way.

So we offer these teachings with absolute conviction and love, and we know that if even one of you hears, it will be the dissolution of one person's hell and a new journey into heaven. That is a powerful thing to think about: Even one person's relief from suffering is worth the effort. We hope you will appreciate the energies and love that are behind this material. We are here to offer you a hand out of the quicksand in which you are floundering.

CHAPTER NINETEEN

Forgiving Yourself

THE WAY THAT FORGIVENESS IS USED BY THE EGO IS VERY DISTURBING TO HUMAN beings if they are deeply immersed in the ego mind and in the illusion of their lives. They believe they are alone, that they are separate from others, and they can be hurt by other beings profoundly and with tremendous result. If what I say is true (which it is) — that your life is a projection of all your beliefs in physical form so that you can see them — then everything that is contained within that experience is within you. This is the idea of treating your neighbor as you would like to be treated yourself. You can see how this message becomes so profoundly important when you see that, indeed, you are only treating yourself a certain way whenever you act in the world.

This is the idea of turning the other cheek when you are assaulted by the world in any way. To retaliate reinforces the belief in separation, the idea that you are not connected to this world. So if you retaliate, it is an act that keeps you in the belief of separation. These things that I taught when I was on the planet so long ago and that I am reteaching now are not taught to make you submissive. They are not taught to make you a doormat or a passive being with no passion in your life. They are taught so that you can understand that the way you act is the way that you reinforce beliefs.

Much of my teaching was eliminated from your book called the Bible. It was not a book I wrote. It was not divinely inspired in the way you believe it to be; that is not the case at all. That book was assembled in its current form by political and religious leaders who had a desire to keep their systems in order and in a position of power. And many of the teachings — the majority of my teachings — were eliminated.

Stories about women, stories about sexuality, and gospels about personal power and consciousness raising were eliminated because they undermined the ability of those in power to maintain their control over the populace of the time.

Prodigal Son

My purpose in being born, my purpose in incarnating so many years ago, was to teach freedom, to teach the truth, and to teach people how to raise up their minds out of the material world and out of the illusions they had created to keep themselves "safe" from a god they believed would punish them. Of course there is no such god. It is merely a figment of your deluded and separated minds projecting this fear that you will face retribution of some kind for separating yourselves. This is not the case.

This, of course, is the story of the prodigal son. This is what I meant in that particular text in the Bible, although I was not creating the Bible at the time. You must remember, these stories were recounted by witnesses who might or might not have accurately reported them, so there is a lot of room for error, and there indeed have been errors — profound errors — reported in what I said and what I taught at certain times.

The prodigal son is the story of a son who leaves his father — which is the very journey that you have undertaken in this detour into fear, this separation experiment of wanting to have your own adventures, to find out things, and to experience things, believing that they would make you happy. Then you realize that it is not so much fun being away from home and that the terror of returning has kept you in poverty, in the illusion, and separated from your Home — your Father and your Mother, if you wish to use those words. Yet you will be welcomed as a returning son or daughter when you decide to come back.

What I am teaching now, this idea that your journey into fear, this detour into a separate experience, is of no consequence to the Divine Mind. There is no punishment waiting for you. There is no retribution waiting for you. These are merely illusions in your mind that you have projected out and created in your world: a punishing god, a cruel god, stories of hellfire and damnation. None of these things exist. They only exist in the separated, fearful mind, and because they are so horrible, they cannot remain in there, so they are projected into stories and mythologies that are not true.

Forgiving Projections of Your Separation

So it is through these teachings that I attempted to convey this understanding. You must understand that many of these teachings that went along with these statements and even remained in the Bible have been eliminated from the teachings. So these stories stand alone and do not really help you understand because the foundational information they were based on has been removed. That is why this information, in its completeness, is being given to you now: so you can understand why I taught beings to turn the other cheek. Turn your cheek, for to retaliate is to perpetuate fear and separation. If you do not retaliate, you are, indeed, loving an aspect of yourself that has heretofore been unloved. This reintegrates it into the mind, and you become more integrated, more whole, and closer to your return Home.

When you forgive beings, you see that these are the unlovable aspects of yourself projected outward. Forgive that being in the sense of not judging him or her in the first place. You do not witness the sin and forgive the sin. You merely say, "That behavior is unacceptable because it is an aspect of myself." And as you witness that behavior, knowing that it is not another separate being but an aspect of your own mind presented to you for healing and raising awareness, you immediately go into your mind and say, "Do I have that aspect in myself, and have I not been aware of it?" Indeed, you will find that aspect in your mind beyond your conscious awareness. It has been brought into your conscious awareness by the activity of the apparently separate outside being that you are observing, and it is a gift indeed to be able to love and forgive that aspect of yourself!

This is not about other beings. It is about the forgiveness of self, the reintegration of self, and this is why the practice of forgiveness is so important. This is why it is so important to not be violent or vicious in your actions, because you attack yourself. As you attack yourself, you feel terrible in this place of judgment because you are reinforcing the separation, and the further into separation you travel, the more pain you feel.

This is what you feel when you judge somebody, when you attack someone. You feel this awful sickness, this horror inside, and because you do not understand the principle of creation, you think you feel terrible because others were mean; you think you feel terrible because they attacked you. In fact, you feel terrible because you engage in viciousness — malicious talk, violent behavior, or judgment — and when you do that, you move further into the idea of separation, further away from that which you call God or Oneness, and you suffer.

The Truth behind the Confusion

That is why these stories were told in my ministry on Earth, and that is why it is very confusing for the ego mind to read this information: You are asked to act in a way that makes no sense, given the incomplete information you have been given. There were many, many texts that were removed from my teachings because they did not suit the powers that be at the time. If you do not have those other texts to support the behavior, it seems insane behavior to the ego mind, and indeed — given the belief system that most of you practice, which is that you are a separate being, that you can be hurt, that there is no God — these kinds of remedies that I presented so many years ago do not make any sense to your mind.

This is why so many people have left the Church: They see the suffering that this partial knowledge causes. When you live in the ego mind, believing in your separation and believing in the material without any connection to Source, these acts seem to go against your well-being; these acts seem to reinforce the danger in your life.

Who cannot retaliate when a being is attacking you? This seems to be something that is impossible. You are not spiritually evolved enough to do this. But when you understand all of the teachings, when you understand your true power, when you understand the constructs you have made from fear, and when you understand how the mind works, then indeed these activities begin to make sense. You are not doing them in the dark without any understanding. You understand the purpose for them, and you are able to integrate other aspects of the teachings into your life, which will shift your life. You cannot act as an elevated, awakened being in a mind that is fearful, materialistic, and uneducated. It is impossible.

So it is very important for you to understand the principles of creation, as we lay them down here and as Ananda teaches in their books. This grouping of materials is important to read as a whole because it teaches you about all of the different aspects that the ego mind has taken and all of the different layers of behavior that you participate in that reinforce the separation concept. It is not until you truly understand how profoundly lost you are in illusion that you can begin to climb the ladder. It is not until you approach it in a multi-faceted way — through practicing thought training and mind discipline, shifting your focus, transforming your body, understanding energies, and focusing your mind on particular teachings — that you will be able to practice these teachings with understanding and empowerment. If you do them from a place of fear, out of a feeling that God will punish you if you do not, then you are very disempowered in this action and there is no force of love behind it, so it does not work.

You must act in accordance with your beliefs and thoughts, and then you become aligned with creative power and are able to affect the world by your behavior. So this is why you have these misunderstandings that come from the fractured nature of my teachings. They were edited and eliminated, and only the smallest pieces were allowed through the filter system of the patriarchy, oligarchy, and all of the facets of power and influence that were at play at the time.

Your Internal World versus Your Social Face

If you wish to find peace, if you wish to find happiness, and if you wish to wake up, these teachings will allow you to do so. Forgiveness, as I teach it now, is a reinforcement of your belief in oneness and your connection to Source. As you act in accordance with the new beliefs, they will become more firmly planted in your mind. As you exist now, you have many misbeliefs and untrue teachings planted in the mind, and the teachings here are going to seem strange because you have had many, many thousands of occurrences of reinforcing untruth.

Now you must begin to systematically teach yourself truth, and it will seem like a foreign language when you begin. It will not necessarily feel like truth. It might ring true to you, but you are going to be taught things that might seem insane because they are the opposite of what you believe, which is separation, fear, death, aloneness, and defensiveness. This is how many of you function in your world, even though it is disguised in a happy and smiling social face. These beliefs seethe underneath the surface.

As you learn these new lessons, you will be able to shift your internal world. You have an internal world and a social face. The social face is what you are conditioned to present, and all of your fears and terrors are hidden. That is why life can seem such a struggle; you feel you cannot share who you truly are. You feel that you cannot share the terrors and feelings of isolation and loneliness within you. You desperately grasp at other bodies to relieve you of this pain, and you get into relationships that are unhealthy. You cannot have a healthy relationship until you know what is going on, until you understand the principles that are at play, and until you understand that your partner's behavior is there to show you something about yourself that needs to be changed.

As long as you attack your partner in judgment for behavior that you think is incorrect, then the relationship cannot live. And that is what you are witnessing in your modern society. You are witnessing beings who are so deeply involved in the illusion that they are attacking and destroying each other out of ignorance and who have the belief that this will bring them what they want. They don't understand that it is going to bring them the exact opposite of what they want. Peace, love, joy, harmony, and abundance are the things you will receive as you study this material.

Do not feel that you are going to lose anything. You are not. You are going to have to readjust your priorities and your way of looking at the world, but most of you do not come to this place of seeking salvation unless you are truly disillusioned with what you have and are ready to do something different because you witness the insanity of what you are making yourself and you know this cannot be right because it is no fun whatsoever.

Physical Manifestation of the Divine Mind

This is why forgiveness is taught. It is a physical manifestation of the belief in oneness. It is a physical reinforcement of the ideas of Divine Mind being your connective, parental energy, if you will. There is no loss at all in the practice of forgiveness. You gain connection to Source; you gain peace. You gain relief from the relentless attacks in the mind of the ego on the being, place, or thing that has apparently committed the sin. The voice of the ego is relentless in its harsh condemnations of those it perceives as having committed a sin. So you will receive more peace, and as you receive more peace, you will be able to receive more knowledge from the nonphysical. You will receive energy by not expending it on a relentless attack on the outside world, and so you will receive the ability to focus more on what you wish to create.

As your mind is removed from these magnetic attachments to sin and judgment and as your thoughts become more easily controlled because you exert a force of discipline on the mind, you will be able to focus on a world that you wish to make. As you take away the disempowering idea of separation, as you cease this reinforcement in this idea of separation, you start to see yourself as the being that you are. You start to see yourself as a magnificent, creative expression of Divine Mind temporarily lost in a dream, and you become excited about your life. You become excited about the journey Home. You are taken out of the endless rounds of death, decrepitude, and sickness, and your body becomes healthier. Your vibration will rise, and your sicknesses will pass. Your ability to live a long and healthy life will increase. There are thousands and thousands of benefits to be accrued from this basic practice of forgiveness, and you will never regret it. You will transform your mind into a most wonderful, fertile, and peaceful environment, and your life will reflect it because your life reflects your mind.

Forgiveness is the most important practice based on this understanding. I am not asking you to forgive for no reason; I am telling you to forgive because it is the key that unlocks the door to knowledge. Through the practice of forgiveness, you achieve peace, harmony, and love, and when you are in that state, you are in alignment with the nonphysical and Divine Mind, and you will receive information from that higher vibratory source. Your life will begin to change in a way that is beyond your comprehension at this moment.

— CHAPTER TWENTY —

Sexual Energy

THE HISTORY OF THE RECOUNTING OF MY TEACHINGS IS VERY INACCURATE. There is no mention of celibacy in my teachings whatsoever. I was, indeed, a practitioner of what is now known as the tantric arts, as I learned them on the journeys I took to the Far East to the areas where yogic practices were mastered and taught willingly to those who were interested, which I was.

This sexual energy that has caused so much pain and suffering through the misteachings of the Church needs to be brought into the light and understood. It is divine energy. Sexual energy is the physical manifestation of divine creativity within your physical body; this is what it is. It is nothing else. There is no sin attached to it. Only the sexual energy used by the lower vibrational mind is dark and difficult in its manifestation.

The mind that is awake, the mind that is connected to the Divine, the mind that is aware of itself and that practices loving kindness, compassion, and caring for others and self will use this energy in the most delicious and loving and kind way. It is a connection to the Divine; there is no doubt about it. I state unequivocally that it is a connection to the Divine Mind. That is why it has been given to you, as a path to awakening, as a path to divinity. The tales and lies about it have caused much distress in your history, much stress in your individual lives, and it is now time to bring this out into the open and have a discussion about it.

The grips of the Church have lessened, and this allows us to have these discussions, but the grips of pornography and promiscuity and lower-vibrational

171

expressions of sexual energy are now causing as many problems as the Church caused, just at a different end of the spectrum. So we are going to attempt to bring this into balance by expressing the truth and by speaking of reality, which is that in your physical creation, you have been given many gifts, but you have taken yourself away from truth.

You have separated yourself from truth, but you were given two gifts from the Divine to take with you on your journey. One of them was your guidance system, your emotional guidance system, which helps you to find your way Home, and the other is sexual energy. This is an energy that is a direct opportunity to return Home in the sense that it can take you to oneness. It can take you to a state of bliss and ecstasy that is divine in nature and that is offered to you as a reminder of what you truly are. You must remember that you have stepped away from oneness because you have the ability to do whatever you choose, but you are offered this reminder of oneness, and that is why it is such a powerful force; it draws you incessantly Home.

I tell you now about my experiences in the physical, sexual energy in my life because there have been so many lies perpetrated about this.

I was married to Mary. I was her husband, and we had the normal physical relations of a man and a wife. There was no celibacy involved in my life; I was a passionate and healthy young man and loved making love to my partner very much. I was skilled in the tantric arts, and this became part of our spiritual practice. We were involved in tantric practices together as a way to access Divine Mind. And of course, I was directed from the nonphysical in these techniques. Mary and I enjoyed a sexual relationship that was full of bliss and connection to the Divine. We loved each other very much physically, spiritually, mentally, and emotionally. It is a wonderful gift indeed to give yourself and to allow this energy to flow in clarity and love with divine inspiration as your guide. You will find that all will be well, and the pain and suffering that you have experienced will disappear.

Align with the Divine

You have a deep and profound misunderstanding of what it is and what it is for. You have a deep and profound confusion because you have been taught so many untruths by the Church. The Church has used this energy for its own devices, and the secrecy and veil of lies that it has placed over this act within its confines is abhorrent indeed. This will come into the light in the future, and it will not be too far in the future. This teaching will begin the discussion. It is a very powerful energy, and this is of course why it is used in negative and oppressive regimes.

You must align yourself with the Divine. You must align yourself with the higher realms as you venture into the use of this energy. To use this energy in a negative way will distort your mind and your body. So this is a warning of sorts — not a threat of any kind but a kind and generous warning, asking you to pay attention to the lessons offered up in the book that was written by Ananda, that was written by our co-creators on this journey, through this channel. It is important for you to understand that clarity, love, and divine focus bring up the most powerful connection to this energy. It has no sinful aspects to it at all unless used by the ego mind to manipulate or hurt, and that has nothing to do with the energy itself; that has to do with the mind that uses it.

I truly wish you to understand that the mind can use energy for whatever it chooses; it does not reflect on the energy. Nuclear energy can be used to kill or it can be used for benefit; food energy can be used to kill in gluttony or it can be used to heal and help. Every energy on this plane is dual in nature in this expression in your three-dimensional world, and sexual energy is no different. It is not sinful in and of itself, and I was a practitioner of divine sexual practice. I state that firmly and unequivocally. I have, indeed, been involved in teaching humans that truth throughout the past 2,000 years.

I come now to speak the truth that sexual energy is divine energy. Understand that you are a multifaceted being and that there is no isolation of this energy from what you are. You cannot put it in one section of your life and expect it to flourish and bloom, when in other areas of your life, you are being lower in vibration, judgmental, and these kinds of things. These are all connected aspects of you. You are a holistic being, and you have to understand that. Every act, every thought, every word, and every deed that you participate in creates something, is very powerful, and will take you either toward heaven or away from it.

There is no such thing as hell; there is only that which is separated from the light, from oneness, from this energy that you call God, All That Is, or the Divine Mind. It is hell when you get far away from it, when you are immersed in cruelty, separation, and judgment. But it is always your choice. You have many beings around you who wish to assist you out of your darkness and who wish to assist you into the higher realms so you can begin to have a happy dream rather than the nightmares that many of you exist in.

Embrace in Wisdom

So sexual energy is to be embraced, but it must not be embraced in ignorance. It must be embraced in wisdom. It must be embraced when you are informed in the right use of that energy. It must be embraced when you are informed in the correct power of that energy. When you are informed in the connection that it has to the Divine, you are able to shift your focus and your consciousness and your thoughts into those that are in alignment with truth, and that energy will flourish and grow within you in a way that is most delightful and empowering and enlivening.

The way many use this energy now, it is considered a dark and dirty secret. It is kept behind closed doors in fear of judgment and exposure because they have been taught that it is dirty or wrong in some way. It is not; it never is. It is misused or misunderstood, and there is always forgiveness on this side for beings who get confused through bad teachings or inaccurate instruction from those in authority.

If you have misunderstood sexual energy up to this point in your life, do not think that you are going to have any kind of punishment heaped upon you when you pass over. That is not the case. But if you have the opportunity now to reeducate yourself, to relearn the truth, and to understand that you are divine beings and that sexuality is a divine energy that will assist you in your awakening process, then take that opportunity. You will be able to shift your mind in this lifetime, and you will not need to return to learn the lesson again.

You are not returned to learn lessons as a punishment. You are returned to learn lessons so that you can have a full and complete understanding of what you have misunderstood. You are incarnated into this physical plane and you have these difficulties because you believe in things that are not true and because you worship things that are not deserving of your worship. Sexual energy is a divine gift from heaven, and it will arise in your body.

What I would like you to understand is that when these energies begin to arise in your body, offer them up to God. Offer them up to Divine Mind, and ask your perceptions to be healed of any misunderstanding of them. Ask for healing, ask for clarification, and ask for love to be focused on you in this area if it causes you distress. There are many of you who are distressed in this area and need assistance, and we are here to help you in this understanding.

You do not need to shut down this energy in your life. It is part of your vitality, and it is part of your holiness. I ask you to begin to relearn the truth about sexuality and the truth about your connection to the Divine through this most wonderful energy that is available to you at any time during the day, any day of the week, any month. You have the ability to tap into this divine connection, and it is a blissful and ecstatic one. It is given to you as a gift, as a guide, as a way Home.

I offer you my blessing and my love, and I ask you to forgive yourself for any sins that you think you have committed and to now reeducate yourself in the truth of love and sexual energy. Understand that it is of God and for love. And that is that!

CHAPTER TWENTY-ONE

A New Paradigm

I LIVED LONG AGO ON YOUR PLANE AND ROSE OUT OF THAT CONSCIOUSNESS and into the consciousness in which I am now immersed, the otherworldly consciousness, the out-of-body consciousness — if you would call it that — the nonphysical. But this does not mean that we are not complete beings in this realm. This is not some ghostly replica of your world. In fact, the opposite is true. You live in very limited, proscribed, tortuously closed-off psyches that do not allow you to tap into that which you are.

You are tremendously creative beings. You are spiritual beings whether you realize it or not. You are temporarily and at times mistakenly ensconced in a physical form, but that is where you must wake up; that is the choice that you have made — to follow your ideas, as distorted as they have been, and to follow your idols, as undeserving of your worship as they are. And it is that experience that causes suffering. It is that experience that gives you your feelings of separation.

Those of us who have risen out of that mindset, who have risen out of that limited concept of self, now turn back and see the pain and suffering. Having been there, we know what it is like to be limited within judgment or fear. There are many on this side, of course, who have not been ensconced in the prison of the body of an Earth being, the unaware Earth being, so they are somewhat confused at what happens on this plane. However, those of us who have been on the plane can explain it and ask for their assistance in waking you up. That is what is transpiring at this time.

Free the Mind

It is time to free the human mind of its constraints. It is time to free the human mind of the bondage of religion. It is time to free the human mind of the misperceptions that limit it, the misperceptions that keep it contained within a vehicle that is far too small for its magnificence and for its creative abilities. This information is designed to wake you up so you can begin to experience your own Christhood, your own arising into the Christ Mind.

I taught that you can do all that I did on the physical plane, and I repeat that here. I am no different from you; I am merely further up a ladder that you are on the bottom rungs of and in the darkness. Perhaps you see a little light ahead, and you climb, hoping to find some relief from the fears and the grasping energies that you have chosen to experience. There is always your own choice. It is in your minute-by-minute choices of what you focus on, what you say, what you think, and what you do that you create your experience. There is nobody doing it to you; there is no punishment from the past, and there is no god destroying the hopes and dreams that you have. Even though you may experience that, these are your own beliefs being manifested in the physical world.

But if you do not know this, if you do not have proper instruction — as you have not had in your society for many, many generations — you become lost in the mire of mind and in your own misdirected thinking, so you keep creating things that you do not wish. You have the ability to create whatever you wish. You have the ability to live a life free of disease. You have the ability to live a life in a body that does not age and that does not die; you have the ability to do this. It is only through awareness, it is only through awakening, and it is only through practicing all the principles that we speak of that you can, indeed, awaken to the natural and true self that you are.

However, you must come to understand what has been done to you. You must come to understand the lies and the misperceptions that you have taken as truth in your mind, and you must take over as teacher from those beings or those experiences in the past that have shown you something that was not true.

Reflection on You

You have not been taught the principles of meditation. You have not been taught the principles of focused thought. You have not been taught the principles that underlie the consequences of judgment, that show you what happens when you are judging and separating yourself from your brothers and sisters on this journey. You have not been taught the liquid and malleable nature of your world. You have been taught that it is a reality that is hard and objective and fast, but it is not. It is absolutely and in all respects a reflection of you. Yes, everything on this plane is an aspect of you.

Sickness is a reflection of the aspect of self that is not healthy, that is not making healthy decisions, perhaps intentionally. Wars on your plane are the reflections of the battles going on in your mind. Perhaps those battles are with relatives or ex-lovers, or perhaps they are future battles that you fantasize about having with your enemies. All are creators of war on your plane. Your separation from your brothers and sisters, these judgments that you make about your value over theirs or their value over yours, creates the disparity between wealth in your plane: the poor and the rich, the valuable and the valueless, the ugly and the beautiful.

All of these relative experiences exist within your mind, and as you heal them within your mind, you will change your experiences in the world. This is the simple science of it. This is not spiritual in the sense that something is being done to you or for you by a god that is more powerful than you, a god that is outside of you. That is not the case. You are being shown what your mind believes in. That is what your world is, and that is what you are seeing.

Live Your Life Now

It is a simple reflection, but you have not been told this. You have been told that this suffering you experience is the fault of other people. You have been taught through misteachings related to my life that sacrifice brings you something. All it does is bring you pain and suffering and a life unlived. It does not make you holier. It does not make you [better] in the eyes of God after you pass over. There is no reward for sacrificing yourself; in fact, the opposite is true. You come to see that you wasted an opportunity that was given to you by the Divine Mind, an opportunity to heal that which is within yourself, and you did not take it because you did not live your desires or make your own experience. You sacrificed yourself as valueless in comparison to somebody else. You might have learned this from a teacher, a priest, or a family member who wanted you to sacrifice yourself for his or her benefit, and in your youth, you misunderstood and believed him or her. You did not know that you had the right to live your life free and clear, choosing whatever you choose and creating whatever you wish to create.

There is also no punishment, as such, at the end of a life of sacrifice; there is only the opportunity to learn again. You are given the opportunity to experience another lifetime and to choose again. But what we are asking all of you to do is to choose again now. Do not wait until you have passed over and come into awareness of what your life was for. We are here now, telling you what your life is for.

Your life is for you to live it. Your life is for you to express the unique being that you are, the unique aspect of Divine Mind that you are that nobody else can fulfill. The experiences that you choose to have because of your innate desires are the path to your awakening. You cannot live somebody else's life and wake up. You can only live your life and experience what you choose to experience, which is guided by your desires, by your passions, by the things you are curious about, and by the things you wish to better understand.

This is your map to your awakening, and it is only through your honest self-expression and living an authentic life that you will come to understand who you are and where your mistakes, misperceptions, and truths lie. You will only know this by following your inner guidance system, which is clearly marked out in wonderful descriptions of passion, joy, and happiness.

There is no need to be unhappy. There is no need to suffer. I did not teach this on the plane when I lived in physical form. This is a distortion of my teachings, taught by the structures and powers that wished to maintain control over beings, that wished to hurt them, and that wished to manipulate them in any way they saw fit. They changed my words, turning them around and deleting parts that did not suit them, and they began to teach untruths in my name.

You Must Rescue and Reeducate Yourself

You must begin to look away from the material world as your salvation. You must begin to look away from others as your rescuers. Nobody will rescue you except you. This world is your creation. It is a reflection of your mind, and only you can change it. Only you can shift it. Only you can make it into what you want it to be, and you do that by listening to your desires, your passions, your wishes, and your heartfelt callings.

You will have to be strong to do this. There is much teaching in your culture that says to not do what you wish because it is self-indulgent or cruel — to family members, to children, or to grandparents or whomever it is. But you can follow your heart kindly. You can understand that you can make decisions for yourself, but do not do it from the place of ego.

You must clarify your perception. Your perception has been distorted, and the decisions you make are not going to be clear. They are going to be tainted by conditionings that you are not aware of, and that is the purpose of *A Course in Miracles*. That is the purpose of that steadfast and determined way through the mind. Clarify the mind so that you can begin to see clearly and you can begin to interpret your thoughts and ideas clearly — with a clarified, healing sense of self.

So do not hear these words and make rash decisions based on distorted ideas. Come to understand yourself in the situation in which you find yourself, even though you might feel that you want to run away and hide. You have misunderstood your thoughts and your guidance system. If you react to these few sentences that you are reading here, you will make poor decisions based on egoic fears, egoic limitations, and conditionings that are not yours.

Make New Decisions

You must clarify the mind before you begin to make different decisions and before you begin to change your life's direction, if that is what you feel is necessary. But your life as it exists now is based on your state of mind as it exists now, so you cannot run from yourself as you exist now. You must begin to make different decisions. You must begin to reeducate yourself. You must begin to put new information into the decision-making device, which is your conscious mind.

If you have made a thousand bad decisions that have resulted the life that you are in right now, begin to make new decisions, but do not make new decisions rashly about ending a marriage or selling a home or adopting children or these kinds of things. To begin to make new decisions, pray for guidance. Be kinder to yourself. These are the beginning steps to transform a life. It will go much faster than you think.

The ego mind will immediately tell you to do what it wants you to do, which is to attack or to run and hide. That will not help because you will take the mind with you that created the world that you are running from. There is no point in running. There is only a point in changing the thought processes that are contained within the creative device that makes your world.

Of course, this is logical when you understand it, but many do not understand what they are doing and why they are doing it. Every decision that you have made, which creates the life you are experiencing, was made from a mind that believed that decision. You are still that mind, that belief, that decision.

You must make new beliefs from self-understanding. You must make new thoughts from new beliefs, and then you will have new feelings from those new thoughts and new beliefs.

Quiet the Ego's Static to Hear Our Voices

Do not panic. Do not feel that you must run away from your life, but begin to make new decisions. Do not burn any bridges or make any large financial shifts, but begin to make new decisions, and your life will begin to reflect that. Nonphysical beings will be able to assist you; we are able to help you when you ask for our assistance. We are present, and we are real, and we hear you. We are connected to you, but you must quiet the mind. You must come to an understanding of self to be able to hear our answers.

When you are in fear, when you are in judgment, or when you are deeply immersed in ego thoughts, you have static around you that you cannot hear through. It is only the voice of ego that you hear. Spirit cannot be heard; our voice is much gentler. We do not force anything. We do not insist on anything. We merely wait until there is a break in the thoughts, in the judgments, in the fears — in the static — and then we can infiltrate ideas. So your job at this stage of the game is to begin to quiet the mind, to quiet the static so that you can hear us. We are here and we wish to help you. We are making a concerted effort from the nonphysical to shift many, many minds into peace.

Wake Up

This is the time for it. You are all sick of war. You are sick of all the money you spend on war. You are sick of all the money you spend to fix up your bodies so that you feel less self-hatred. You are sick of spending money on fancy cars and homes to impress people who you do not even like. It is time to stop this madness. You are destroying your beautiful planet; you are destroying this beautiful world that needs care and loving attention. And you are destroying yourselves by keeping yourselves locked in the material and locked in the physical when there are worlds and realms above the physical that you do not have any idea about.

You call these realms heaven and believe you will get there when you die, but that is not the truth. You will pass on to realms that are of a like vibration to your internal world, not the face you present to the world but your internal world. This vibration of mind in which you are immersed, which you have to listen to twenty-four hours a day and seven days a week, is the vibration that you will slip into.

You will have a temporary respite. You will be shown your errors. You will be shown the opportunities that you missed or the wonderful opportunities that you took, and there will be a reckoning of sorts. But there is no judgment in it in terms of sin or punishment. You will merely be shown where you could have made better choices. You will be shown where omissions were made that needed to be taken in. You will once again be offered a physical existence in which you can make different choices and in which you will be given opportunities to choose again.

But do not wait until your death, dear ones. This is the purpose of your life — to wake up. Do not keep repeating the endless cycle of physical incarnation — remaining asleep, suffering, and believing that the material world is all there is. It is this material world that you are given to show you where you are off track, and if you can interpret it correctly, you will indeed create a new mind. From that, you will create a new world.

CHAPTER TWENTY-TWO

You Are Divine

Interpreting the Guidance System

When you begin to clarify the mind, you will begin to experience Divine Mind manifesting in your world. When you are ensconced in your ego mind, you are ensconced in the mind that believes in the physical body and the material world completely. That mind believes that you are responsible for all of the things that come to you, so you must work hard for them and make everything happen that is going to happen — this is the ego's way. It does not believe in a god as such. If it does believe in a god, it believes in a punishing and hateful god that will be cruel to you when you pass over and will rub all of your errors in your face, so to speak.

This is the ego mind's way of looking at God and spirituality, and it is a terrifying view indeed. It is terrifying to think of yourself alone on this planet with no assistance or help from any other realms. This is not the truth. You know it is not the truth by your guidance system's response to these ideas. Your guidance system will feel fear at the idea of a judgmental god. This means that you are experiencing your guidance system's feedback. It is telling you that this is not true. Whenever you hear a truth, your guidance system will be at peace, and it will be happy, and it will be content.

So this is basic training for what is going on in your body-mind complex. Your emotional guidance system has been given to you as a way to find your way Home from the lost place in which you find yourself now. But if you do not understand how to interpret this guidance system, you could go astray, and that is what is happening for many. They believe it is okay to feel negative; they believe it is natural to feel fear. They believe it is good to sacrifice themselves on the altar of whatever causes they have chosen, but this is not the case. These are all untruths that will manifest as negative feelings in their guidance systems.

At this stage of your learning, we would like you to understand that if you feel happy, if you feel at peace, if you feel calm, if you feel content, if you feel joy, if you feel passion, if you feel creativity, or if you feel eager anticipation, these are all signs that you are on the right track — that you are indeed aligning with your guidance system.

If you feel fear, if you feel anger, if you feel rage, if you feel sick, if you feel paranoid, if you feel depressed, or if you feel disempowered, these are clues from your guidance system that you are out of alignment with truth and that something in your mind needs to shift and change. This wonderful, wonderful guidance system, this thing that you have been taught to override, this thing that you have been taught to medicate, and this thing that you have been taught to ignore is the thing that is your custom-designed guidebook Home.

Your guidance system is deeply affected by your beliefs and your misunderstandings, and so we suggest that you undertake the clarification prescribed in *A Course in Miracles* before you begin to listen fully to your guidance system for major decisions. Of course, you must listen for small things from your guidance system immediately upon embarking upon this course, such as what to eat, where to go for exercise, who to be friends with. But even as you are listening to this guidance system, it will be distorted by your conditioned mind, and it is *A Course in Miracles* reconditioning process that will bring further clarification, and will bring you a truer ability to interpret your guidance system.

This guidance system that you have is liable to lead you astray unless you have undergone a clarification. However, you can listen to it today. You can listen to it in the simple responses to the choices in your day. Do you want to go for a walk? Do you want to have communion with other beings? Do you want to eat something? Do you want to read something? Listen to your guidance system.

If you are in a life that has been manufactured from a deeply conditioned mind that is out of alignment with truth, you are immediately going to come up against conflicts. You are going to have people in your life who disagree with you and perhaps want you to do something that you do not wish to do. You are perhaps going to have to go to a job that is not in alignment with what you truly believe you should be doing. Yet, you have a life structure that is based on these poor decisions that you have made, based on a poor interpretation of your guidance system, perhaps for many years.

What we would like you to do is to take this information and begin to make small decisions based on your guidance system, decisions based on what you would like to do now.

For example, imagine you live with a partner who overrides your wishes and what you would like to do, and you have put up with this for many years. This is a habitual dance that the two of you do. Our first suggestion is that you forgive your partner for treating you this way because you allowed him or her to treat you this way for so long. You stood in the fire of this person's judgment, and you allowed him or her to develop a habit of negativity or attacking behavior that you do not like. However, you did not stand up or remove yourself from it. So we would like you to do two things: We would like you to forgive this person for the offending activities because the behavior comes from ignorance. We would also like you to forgive yourself for allowing this pattern to develop. This would be the beginning stage of healing and changing this relationship that is not what you want. This will be challenging enough for you for a few weeks — to forgive, knowing that this person is acting in ignorance, and to forgive yourself because you have allowed someone to treat you badly.

We would like you to exert your freedom of choice within your mind. This is a place that nobody can affect. This is a place where you are in charge. So you may be forced to continue in a pattern that you do not like because of fear or confusion or not knowing what you should do instead. We suggest you begin to change your mind. This is where creation begins and where your life is manufactured: in the thoughts that arise from what you believe to be true.

We do not require you to do this work as a statement in front of anyone else; this is a private journey for you to undertake to change your life.

Forgive Your Body

Perhaps your body is in a state that you do not enjoy. Perhaps it is overweight. Perhaps it is sick, or perhaps it is too thin or weak, or perhaps it is distorted in some way. The same process can be used. First, forgive the body for manifesting these negativities. The body does only what you tell it to do. It does not do anything of its own volition. You must come to understand this. The body is speaking in a language that you cannot ignore, so you must forgive it for manifesting things that you do not like, because you misunderstood the creative process.

The creative process of the body's manufacture comes from your thoughts and beliefs and emotions. The first step in healing the body is to forgive it and stop attacking it and stop judging it. Thank it for manifesting the negativities in your mind in physical form so that you can understand them, see them, and begin to change your internal workings, allowing the external workings to also change. Then you must forgive yourself, once again, for believing things that are untrue, for acting on information that is incorrect, and for sending hateful and judgmental messages to the body and to the self, which caused these negativities. These are the two forgiveness practices that you must start with to heal the physical body.

You must always start with forgiveness, for forgiveness brings about peace in the mind. When peace arises in the mind, then you can receive information from the nonphysical, and you can calm the energies in the physical body and in the mind allowing the natural healing processes of the system to take place.

You see, your body-mind complex is designed to function in the vibration of love, and it is your responsibility to get yourself to that vibration. Whenever you are angry, whenever you are fearful, or whenever you are upset, you indeed inflict wounds on your body-mind complex, and you choose to do it through your judgments and your misunderstandings. So forgiveness is always the place to begin. Forgiveness brings peace to the mind. Resentments against other beings, resentments against yourself, and resentments against the body only induce a state of agitation and judgment that is further fueled by fear and anxiety and these kinds of things.

So we would like you to always start with forgiveness of self and other, of self and body. It is in practicing these acts of forgiveness that you will provide an environment in which healing can take place. Continue to take the medications, the prescriptions from doctors that you have been taking if you feel you still need them, but include the practices of forgiveness for yourself and for your body. You will find that the conditions you experience in the physical body will subside, and you will be able to decrease your medications.

This is something that you must do cautiously and with awareness. You cannot suddenly stop your medications if you have a mind and a belief system that inherently believes in them. You will become sick again if you do not change the structure of your mind along with changing the structure of your behaviors.

Consequences of Your Creative Power

Your behaviors are a consequence of your thoughts, and your thoughts are a consequence of your beliefs. So we are retooling your beliefs. We are going to the foundation of the creative aspects of your mind, and we are gently and with love and forgiveness dismantling the beliefs that are untrue. We are replacing them with true thoughts of your divine nature, your incredible power to create your body and your world, and your natural state of being as a creative, loving being. These are the beliefs that we are going to instill in the mind that has forgotten them.

This is the purpose of studying new material. You must understand that you are putting material into your mind twenty-four hours a day when you take in information through the senses — talking to people, watching television, watching movies, and reading books. This is all information going into the mind, and so it is very important for you to understand that if you are unhappy, if you are living a life that is not bringing you the experiences you wish to have, or if you are in relationships that are detrimental or painful or abusive, you are the creator of these. These are outward representations of your inward beliefs about yourself. These are the idols you worship, these beliefs that you have in the mind, and it is important now that you come to understand and take responsibility for your own creative power.

This is what all these stories are about. I told you my life story in the beginning of this book so that you would understand what I was, what my life represented, and what I taught. It was so that you can eliminate the untruths from your mind that churches and religious dogmatic structures have perpetrated on ordinary beings seeking salvation — these untruths about martyrdom, suffering, sacrifice, and the evil nature of sexual energy. These kinds of belief structures contained within the churches and religious structures have been the foundational elements of your society.

These untruths must be undone in your mind. I started this book with my autobiography so that you could hear my voice as an ordinary human being. You could hear the story of my life and how it unfolded, and you could begin to discern the truth of my life story in that time 2,000 years ago.

I am returned, and I have returned many, many times. I return now to begin a healthy and healing dialogue about my teachings. It is time. The world has reached a point in which you must understand your divine nature; you must understand that you create all of the problems that you experience not only in your physical body but also in your relationships and in your physical world. You are the creator of your world in all ways.

Every experience coming to you reflects a vibration of your self, of your mind, of your belief structure. It is only in shifting the belief structure and the consequent thoughts and emotions that you will be able to create a different experience. You will be able to create a different life. You have the ability to transform every aspect of your life if you so choose, but you must understand the creative process. You must understand where ideas are formed, and you must understand that the clarification of the mind and the installation of peace and love in the mind are necessary for you to begin to accept ideas from nonphysical.

Getting into Alignment with Truth

We are all here, many great teachers, many enlightened beings, and many divine beings. We are here in the nonphysical, disseminating information in this conscious contact way. We do this with all of you in your dream states. We do this with all of you through intuition and connection of mind, but many of us find we cannot communicate with you because you are so out of alignment with truth that the communication channels are fractured and out of sync with each other. It must be done by transforming the mind, inputting true information into the intellect and changing behavior, such as turning off your television sets (which disseminate so much hatred and violence into your world) and video games (which disseminate hypnotic information into young minds that will cause them great troubles later on).

We wish you to begin feeding yourself not only the nutrition of sound knowledge and information, but also the sound nutrition of organic foods grown locally and with love. These are the changes that must be made in your life to begin to facilitate these shifts in consciousness. It is worth your while.

Your experience on this plane is long and painful if you are out of alignment with truth. Your experience on this plane is long and painful if you are out of alignment with your guidance system, your God-given guidance system that wants you to be happy and wants you to express this unique nature that you have, this wonderful, divine self that is unique unto you. It is heartbreaking for us to witness your denial of your natural passions and of your natural self, thinking that God wants you to be unhappy and suffer in silence and that God wants you to be a martyr and to sacrifice yourself on the altar of marriage or religion or some such thing. That is not the case.

Divine Mind, God, All That Is — whatever you wish to call it — wants you to vibrate at the vibration of love, wants you to be happy, and wants you to be creative. This is the natural state of being an aspect of Divine Mind. That is what you are. When you do not express your true self, when you are not creative, and when you are not in alignment with love, you feel bad, and that is because that is not what you are.

Accept Responsibility and Stand Your Ground

You are happy, you are joyful, you are creative, you are kind, you are loving and compassionate, and you are divinely creative beings. And when you believe anything that is out of accord with that most magnificent definition, you feel it as a negative response in your guidance system.

So when someone tells you to do something that you do not wish to do, but you do it, and you then feel resentful and hateful toward that person, understand that this is your guidance system telling you that you need to follow your heart and your directive. When you do, you will have feelings of peace, love, and joy. Do not mistake the feelings of negativity you have in judgment for the other being, who forces you, apparently, to do something out of your realm of choice. You choose to do this, and you must stand your ground and begin to make your own decisions.

Some of you have put yourselves in quite a pickle, and you have set yourselves up in relationships of home and work and family that are not conducive to your happiness. Perhaps you have a complicated system that has been built around you based on your own misunderstandings and poor choices. What we would like you to do, instead of slamming the door, walking away, and leaving those beings — such as partners or children or employers — high and dry, is to make a concerted effort to begin to change your mind. In the smallest increments, begin to do what you wish to do. For example, you might wish to read a book instead of watching a television program with your partner. Lovingly and kindly tell him or her to enjoy the show but that you would like to read a book.

These are the kinds of statements you can make that do not attack or hurt someone else or leave him or her feeling abandoned. You can begin to make such changes. They may seem inconsequential, but you will begin to feel a connection to something greater than yourself, and it will be us, whispering in your ear. We will be connecting with you and offering you inspiration, and you will begin to find opportunities arising in your life that you could not have anticipated. These are manifestations of Divine Mind responding to your shift in consciousness and your shift in vibration. They will be powerful, they will be frequent, and they will come quite quickly.

Reject Societal Teachings

Your creative abilities are magnificent! If you keep the mindset and the vibration the same as it is now, you will continue to receive the same feedback, and it will look as if things are not changing. But when you begin to change your input to the mind and you begin to change your output through kinder words and less judgmental thoughts, you will see changes very, very quickly manifesting in the physical world. Minute by minute, you re-create your world every day, but because you keep your mind the same, you do not see the changes that are possible because you are not changing.

You are designed to be an ever-evolving consciousness. You are designed to be an ever-creative, ever-learning consciousness that challenges itself, but your society insists on sameness. Your society insists on security and on things like thirty-year mortgages, which do not suit the creative, divine, spiritual mind that enjoys exploration, growth, transformation, and evolution.

The same can be said about your relationships. Over and over again you repeat patterns that are excruciating for the creative, divine mind that is your natural state, so you become miserable because you are taught that suffering and sacrifice are required in relationships. This is not the case. A relationship needs passion, and a relationship needs growth, and a relationship needs to provide each participant with self-expression and freedom so that each person can indeed be in alignment with his or her natural state of being.

So you see that your society has many prescriptions that are counter to what we say. We say that you are creative, so create. We say that you are loving, so love. We say that you are freedom seekers, so give yourselves and others you care for freedom. We say that you are most creative and divine beings, so treat yourselves and your fellows accordingly. Treat them as if they are divine beings too. How would you speak to God? How would you speak to me if I were standing right in front of you? Would you attack me? Would you denigrate me or use harsh sarcasm? This is what I wish you to think about, because you are, indeed, facing divine beings. Every being you meet on your journey is Divine Mind manifested.

You must treat yourself with respect and forgiveness, and you must treat your fellows with respect and forgiveness. And your life will begin to change. Your life will begin to reflect those shifts in your consciousness, and your body will begin to reflect those shifts in your consciousness. You will feel energy, enthusiasm, and health returning. However, you must recondition the mind because there are so many untruths in your society.

You suffer so unnecessarily from sicknesses, believing in the body's fallibility and that the body is wrong. The body is not. The body does nothing. It simply reflects your quality of mind and your state of vibration. It is your internal condition reflected outside, just as every aspect of your life is the outside reflection of your internal condition.

This is the basic principle we wish you to learn, this idea that you are the creative force in your life — not as an ego mind, manipulating and forcing things to happen but as a divine aspect of the creative mind of God. Also, if you are in a state of peace, you receive information all the time on how to act and how to respond to the environment around you.

As you read this book — this sentence — know that you have been placed in this situation by your higher self. Pay attention to these lessons. Pay attention to this prescription, and you will find that your life will go much, much better than it has been going. If you are happy and you are experiencing everything that you wish, then you still might add these prescriptions to your life. They will never, ever, cause you to lose anything that is in alignment with high vibration and loving thoughts. But if you are living a life that appears to be successful on the outside with a lot of material attachments to it, and on the inside you feel as if you are dying or you feel as if you are not able to keep up this social face, this façade that you pretend is who you are, then we suggest you take these prescriptions to reeducate and clarify your mind. You will find that your life will shift in a way that will allow you to be more honest and to live more in alignment with who you are, more in alignment with your true self.

I am the one you know as Jesus; I am the one who has returned to teach once again on your plane, using this female form to make a point that my energy as a male on Earth was no more valuable than the energy of [the channel's] body as a female. Equality of the sexes is paramount in healing your planet, and this is something that we speak about next.

CHAPTER TWENTY-THREE

Equality

I AM RETURNED TO CONTINUE THE DICTATION OF THIS MOST MAGNIFICENT BOOK. I am not arrogant when I say it is magnificent. Magnificence is of God and is in alignment with truth. Magnificence is what you are. Most of you, of course, do not see your own magnificence, and this is a dark area of your consciousness.

This is a consequence of many, many centuries of belittlement and of requiring people to shut down their natural passions, their natural tendencies, and their natural curiosities. When you look back on your history, you see that there is a long and painful record of this kind of persecution. I am going to speak about this a little bit as it relates to men and women, because this is a legacy that you are reaping the rewards of in your society now, and you do not truly comprehend the disparity energetically as we see it on this side.

Archetype Themes

Your society is very male and female oriented. Your images are very particular. You have your hero images of a muscular man, sword or perhaps a cell phone in hand, riding his stallion or his Lamborghini to rescue the female. These are archetypal images that you are familiar with. The female is asked to develop her physicality to flaunt her body, as if she is a piece of bait to catch a nice, big, juicy fish. This is an underlying theme in your society. Now, there are many permutations and convolutions of this. There are, of course, people who develop their intellect; there are, of course, people who develop their creativity. We are generalizing, so do not get upset about that. We are generalizing and offering a theoretical analysis of the kind of vibration that your society emanates.

So you have a woman who perhaps is developed mentally and emotionally in many ways, but she still feels an overriding urge to develop herself as a beauty or as a piece of bait. This is very demeaning energetically, and she misses a great deal of creative force and a great deal of loving energy by pursuing these artificially created structures.

Now, these seem normal to you, and they are normal, but they are not natural. Your natural state is one of partnership; your natural state is one of equality. You each have different qualities, but remember these are manifestations of separation. Your "coming together" is the remedy for the separation, and so this is how we would like to approach this problem. We would like you to begin to see the disparity between the two sexes as the solution to the problem. It is also the problem, but the problem always contains the solution; this is the gift of Spirit! Spirit brings you problems so that you can see where you are out of alignment with truth. Now, think about this as it relates to the separation of the male and female body.

You have created these physical structures to represent separation. They are designed for that purpose, so they emphasize difference. They emphasize the differences between male and female. They embody, literally and figuratively, all of the qualities that you are separated from. This is the experience here, and this is the battle between the sexes. You, in fact, experience the battle between the sexes, the differences between male and female energies that are supposed to be contained, balanced, and equal within each of you.

Female qualities are creativity, receptivity, intuition, gentleness, cooperation, and the ability to be multifaceted. Male qualities are action, judgment, war, mechanization, and the intellect. And of course, because your society has been patriarchal for a very long time, these values are profoundly ensconced in it. It worships the male values. The female values are derided; the female values are looked down on and considered weaker. It is manifested in all of your aspects of work and the world.

Experience the Realities of the Opposite Sex

You are seeing the destruction of Earth's environment. This is a masculine energy. The feminine energy loves nature. The feminine energy will lie gently down in a sunny glade of dappled light and dream about her lover. That is feminine energy. Now, those of you who are men will find that little snippet about feminine energy quite enticing. You think this would be lovely for you too, to lie down in a sunny glade with dappled light and wait for your lover to come to caress you and be kind to you.

You must take it on your own shoulders to correct your compass. You are all heavily conditioned in this society as it relates to sexual energy, to your maleness and femaleness. You must begin to develop those qualities in you that the opposite sex represents to you. Your experience of this is going to be completely individual. You will each have an individual experience of what maleness means to you if you are a female, and what femaleness means to you if you are a male. Those are the qualities that you lack. Those are the qualities you need, even if you look on them with derision or from a place of condescension.

This is a humbling experience, particularly for men because they have dominated. They have been in charge, so to speak, and their qualities are valued in this society. Your society is destroying itself because it is out of balance. It does not have the feminine adequately represented in its governments, in its medical industry, in its financial institutions, or in its social programs.

Balancing the Energies in Society

If women were in charge of these things, you would see a very, very different world indeed, but it too could become out of balance if there were no male energy. You must initially balance it on the outside. You must begin to see how you can be stronger where you are weak, how you can be gentler where you are tough, and these kinds of things. You must go inside. As we say, these behaviors arise from your conditioning. They arise from the mind that is trained in this system, and this system has been patriarchal. It has aggressively dominated women. It has been hateful to women, imprisoning them and taking away their rights. It still does this in many parts of the world; we speak here to the Western world.

There are many women in your civilized Western society who are violently attacked every day by the men in their lives, and it is deemed acceptable. There are many women who are paid less for the work they do that is of equal quality to that of men doing the same job. It does not matter, this history of the story around work, male and female work. You are all equal to each other. The playing field needs to be leveled, but this must come from an understanding within the mind. It must come from the understanding that these physical structures, these male and female bodies in which you find yourselves, are representations of separation.

Sacred Sexuality and the Asexual Divine Mind

This discussion leads into the subject of sacred sexuality in the mating process. When you bring disparate bodies together with the eye to oneness, with the eye to merging in the Divine Mind, then you are on the right track, and that is when you will feel the great energies of Spirit connecting with you. As long as you come to your sexual union with disparity in place — with inferiority if you feel weak or dominated or with your superiority if you feel strong and powerful — then you will, indeed, reinforce the separation because that is what you are focused on; that is the energy of separation. It is not the energy of love and Divine Mind.

Divine Mind has no care for bodies whatsoever. From our point of view, male and female do not exist. Spirit may have a particular experience in a female form, and a particular experience in a male form, but that experience is brought into spirit without any attachment to body shape or size or sexual orientation. So this information is asexual. We are asexual on this side. I represent myself as the male Jesus; that is the story that we are retelling here, so it suits the purpose of reeducation. But I am coming through a female form so that you are not caught up in my maleness. That would not serve my purpose because it is of the body. My life's teaching as it is revealed in this autobiography is that the body is of no consequence. It is not real but an aspect of separation, and it is to be overcome.

It is not to be denied in the religious sense. You are not to whip yourself or wear hair shirts or deny yourself your sexual expression or creative self-expression. This is not what I am saying. What I'm saying is that you must understand what the body is and how it functions and how to heal the separation. The separation is healed through the mind because it is the mind that is split, and it is the split mind that manifests the separated bodies, the male and female bodies. You do not need to be ashamed of this, but you need to understand what is going on so that you can heal the split.

The split is not physical, but you live in a world that is created by your split mind, and until you completely heal the mind, you will have to deal with these physical differences. You will have to deal with these physical manifestations of separation, and your physical male and female bodies represent split. We want to heal the split. We want to bring that split mind back into oneness. That is what the atonement is: the reorganizing and the reintegration of the split ego-mind.

Battle of the Sexes

You must change your mind first. You can begin to change your behaviors if this material resonates with you. If you feel the truth and the love and the unconditional offering of wisdom that is contained within these pages, then you know that you can look at yourself objectively in this moment and ask yourself where your male energy is, where your female energy is, where you are out of balance, and how you treat members of the opposite sex in your society. If you are female, are you afraid of males? If so, you need to begin to make friends with some of them. Choose your partners and your friends wisely; there is no reason to do it rashly. But there is no reason to reinforce the fear.

If you have been hurt in the past by a member of the opposite sex, practice forgiveness to heal that rift between you and the other half of the population with which you reside on this planet. You must remember that you cannot have half of the population of the planet as enemies. You must forgive the opposite sex. You must forgive them for whatever it is you perceive they have done, and look inside yourself honestly to understand what male and female energies are. The male and the female, the yin and the yang, the strong and the gentle, the nurturing and the active: These separations are well-known in your society now. We do not need to go into them ad nauseam, but you must look at yourself.

For example, if you are a woman and you are aggressively pursuing a materialistic life and an active, dominating career, you might want to look at certain aspects of yourself and ask, "Why am I doing this?" What is the feminine side of you doing? Are you being creative? Are you being receptive? Are you being gentle? Are you being kind? Or have you taken on the male traits of the society? We do not blame you for this: It is what makes you successful in this society's paradigm. We are not here to judge you. We are here to suggest balance, reintegration, and reunification.

But it begins with you. That is where the male and female war, the battle of the sexes, if you will, and the disparity in power begin. Reintegration and reunification cannot come to a mind that does not know itself. They cannot come to a mind that will not investigate what it is doing, what it is thinking, or what it is feeling, these aspects of self-knowledge. You must come to know yourself, and you must come to know your culture. You must come to know what your culture is based on. You must understand what your culture's history is — not to dwell on it or to blame it, but to understand it.

A Love Revolution

To work from that point of knowledge, it is like any other subject. You do not go into your car's engine without studying the manual or hiring a mechanic. You do not need to hire a spiritual mechanic. You must do this work yourself. This is entirely a self-created world, so you must do the work. This is why having intermediaries, such as priests, who teach you all the time and take the power from you does not really work.

I want to create a love revolution on this planet. That is what I have always wanted to create. That has been my purpose, forever and ever, amen. I want to create a love revolution in which you investigate yourself and look at your behavior, your thoughts, and your feelings, and you learn how to come to a state of peace. You learn how to come to a place of complete acceptance and joy. In that state, we can communicate with you and bring you information. But of course, many of you are frightened of us, and that is another subject that we will tackle here.

We are going to have to limit the subjects. We can go on and on about your society. There are many, many problems that you face, and that is why we are here. We love you. We want to heal the split mind, and we want to heal your dying world. We want to heal the wars and the punishment and the frustration that many of you feel in your lives and that many of you witness around this planet at this time.

As far as equality goes, from Spirit's point of view, you are all of equal value. I demonstrated that in my life with my partnership with Mary. I demonstrated that in my teachings, but it was hidden from view because it was not safe for women to be taught in public. Ridiculous restrictions were placed on them, and that is not acceptable. Those of you who restrict women in your lives because you feel it is your right are wrong, and we want you to stop that.

We want you to begin to see the women in your lives, your partners or your daughters or your friends, as equals, for they are absolute equals in the eyes of God. God does not create separation; you have created separation. You have brought this disrupted energy into the world through your belief in individuality, separation, and selfish interests.

So it is through the practice of forgiveness initially, through self-understanding, and through studying and reading material that is based in truth that you will begin to heal this. But if you are lonely, if you have been unable to find that wonderful, wonderful, sacred partner, then you have some work to do. This being is not coming to you because of something in your mind. That being is not coming to you because of beliefs that you hold in your mind that are untrue. Unification, or oneness, is the truth of your state. When you are not happy, when you are not united, when you are not in communion with your brothers and sisters, something is wrong. Something is out of accord in your mind, and it is manifesting as separation, loneliness, or isolation. These experiences can be healed. They can be healed by following these practices. They can be healed by forgiveness.

This is always the first step in the transformation of mind. Why? Because judgment reinforces the separation, and as long as you are judging, you are reinforcing the world as it is in its suffering, separated, isolated, and judgmental state. It is causing all of your problems; that is what is causing your sicknesses, that is what is causing your divorces, that is what is causing your wars. So always, always start with forgiveness.

Men and women are equal in the eyes of God. There are no differences whatsoever. Your hierarchical structures and your patriarchal, male-dominated history have thrown an illusory veil over the truth, and it is time now for this veil to be lifted. Any church that refuses equality for women is out of alignment with truth. Any teaching that teaches inequality between men and women is out of alignment with truth. God is unity consciousness. There is no separation, and that is what you will know is the truth, that demonstration. By their fruits ye shall know them. Examine the fruits of any teaching. If its fruits are war, separation, subjugation, or the usury of some being, then you know that teaching is out of alignment with truth. There is not an ounce of God energy in that. God is loving, God is equal, God is kind, and God is abundant to all beings. God is love. That is our comment on that particular subject. We feel that we have made ourselves clear.

CHAPTER TWENTY-FOUR

Passion and Purpose

AS I HAVE SAID THROUGH MANY, MANY OF THESE DISCUSSIONS, YOUR GUIDANCE system tells you exactly where you should be and exactly what you should focus on. As your guidance system or your passion arises, it gives you clues as to the path you should take. Now, this path is very, very clouded and dark if your mind is confused with conditioning and teachings of untruths. It is the clarification of mind that gives you the understanding of your guidance system.

The Little Things

Your guidance system will tell you where your purpose is and where your passion is. But as you have been told many times throughout this text, you have been conditioned out of that passion and out of that purpose. Early on in many of your lives, you were taught not to listen to your guidance system. You were taught not to listen to this wonderful, wonderful gift that has been given to you as a string that you can hold onto as you return Home.

Now, you have been taught that these small desires of yours — the way you like your food, the time you like to get up, and these sorts of things — are inconsequential, but your passion and your purpose are hidden in these minutiae, if you want to call them that. Your desires, your inklings of turning left or turning right, these are your guides; they are your teachers speaking to you. This is the language that we speak to you in, but we cannot speak to you in this language if you are filled with fear. We cannot speak to you in this language if you are filled with worry and concerns about the material world.

Throughout your history, you have been told that your body is not sacred, that your feelings are of the devil, and that you must not listen to your passions. These are the counsel of teachers in the Church. In your modern society, you are taught to do whatever you wish, but there are many, many things that you are taught throughout your conditioning process, particularly in your education process, that get you to override this system that is so important in finding yourself and so important to us as your guides and teachers.

Tuning Out the Static to Return to Oneness

We are always there, waiting for a crack in the armor of your mind. Your mind, this untrained powerful creator, is full of worry and full of static. It is, indeed, as a radio station tuned incorrectly and loudly, the volume up, the station not receiving well. And it is a painful thing for us to experience. When you are in fear, doubt, worry, or judgment, these negative, lower vibrations create static between you and us. And it is your job to turn the static down. Just as you own a radio and other beings in the room would not touch your station, we would not touch your radio. You must do it yourself. This is where you are given free will. You are given the opportunity to focus on whatever it is you wish to focus on in the experience that you are having.

You are loved so much that you are given the opportunity to step into individuality and to step into separation, but you have not been abandoned, even though you feel you have been. It is, in fact, you who has abandoned oneness. You have abandoned us, if you will. You do not know it. You do not have a conscious memory of it, but you have these feelings of guilt and fear. You have hidden the truth beneath these things, and you must face these fears. It is in clarifying the mind that the quietness will return to your guidance system, and this is something that we wish to emphasize: *You must quiet your mind; we cannot do it for you.*

We are waiting for those quiet spaces, waiting for those meditation practices, and waiting for those forgiveness practices. Forgiveness quiets the mind and stops the ego's rancor. It stops the ego's ceaseless attack on other beings, places, and things, and it is in that quietness that we are able to communicate with you.

Now, when your mind has quieted, your passions and your guidance will become louder. When you are focused on the ego's horror stories and judgments, you cannot hear the quiet suggestions we make. We are not brutes. We are not forceful on this side. We come to this experience with love, with compassion, and with gentleness, as love does. Love is always kind and gentle, and it does not scream orders as the ego mind does. When the ego mind is screaming orders, you cannot hear us or feel those gentle, subtle urgings of love toward that which you enjoy, toward that which you treasure, and toward that which you participate in with passion. These are the essences of the way we speak.

We speak to you with kind thoughts; we speak to you with loving ideas. We speak to you with inspiration, with song, with dance. These are the ways we speak to you, in image and at times, sound. You may hear choirs or at times, ringing in the ears. This is something that many of you do not realize is a vibrational tuning, if you will, from the nonphysical. You think it is something wrong with your body; it is not necessarily. We can bring you experiences of light, sound, or image in many, many different ways. We do not always speak to you in words like this.

This is an exceptional demonstration of clarity. This channel has cleared the way for this direct communication through her practice of forgiveness and through following the prescriptions from *A Course in Miracles*, which I transmitted many, many years ago now, on your plane. It is only now coming into the group consciousness, if you will. So of course, that is the book we say you should read if you want the quickest clarification of mind. But if it is too difficult, know some minds cannot tolerate the language, some minds cannot tolerate the discipline of that book.

If you are tired of not feeling your passion, if you are looking at your job and know that it is not who you are, then you must take steps. You must begin to clarify your mind. If you take a few minutes to honestly assess the quality of your thoughts, the quality of ideas in your mind, you can see that there is much fear there. You can see that there is anger there or judgment of other beings or self. It matters not whether you are judging others or yourself. It is still static, as far as we are concerned.

Making the Connection

It is in quieting the mind that you will begin to receive information about your purpose and about your passion. But you must honor yourself first. For those of you who have been conditioned to not listen to yourselves, to not do what you want to do, to not follow your own hearts' desires, you have some retooling of the mind that must take place first before you feel that connection to your passion, to your purpose.

There are many of you who, when asked what you would do if you were free, do not have an answer. That does not mean your purpose has gone. You are all born with a higher purpose. You have your idols that you worship; you have your lusts and distractions that you have pursued in your journey down into separation, but you have a higher purpose too. Each one of you has a talent; each one of you has something that brings you great joy. You might be disconnected from it, but you can reconnect. You can tap back into that connection, but it comes from Divine Mind. You must get yourself in a vibrational state that is in accord with Divine Mind before you can receive this passionate directive from that which you call God, that which you call All That Is.

I am connected to that energy. I am here to assist you in clarifying your mind. I am here to inspire you, once again. I am here to teach you. I am here to reclaim my name for the good. I am here to reclaim my name for the loving. I am here to reclaim my name for the teaching role that I have always had. I have continued to teach ever since my incarnation ended so many hundreds of years ago. But you do not know that. Because of the Church's teachings, you think that a silence has been in effect for the past 2,000 years except for very special, prescribed leaders. But that is not the case. I have spoken to many beings throughout these centuries. Some of them in cloistered situations, such as nunneries or monasteries. Many beings have been too terrified to listen to my voice. They have seen images of me, and they have prayed to me. Many, many beings, of course, have prayed to me every day, and I appreciate that connection, but to hear my voice or to listen to a reply? For them, it would be terrifying.

So this is one of the barriers we face on this side: your horror at communication from the nonphysical, your terror of possession, and your fear of losing control of your consciousness. This is an evil seed planted by beings who do not wish you to venture into this realm. They decided that they can maintain power over you if you are powerless. And of course I am preaching to increase your power. I am not teaching these words to decrease your power.

Tapping Into Your Power

We on this side want you to know your divine nature. We on this side want you to know the power that you possess. But your power must be used with discretion. Your power must be used with love. Your power must be used without the ego wielding its cruel and vicious attacks on beings. These are the first things that must come into your mind to see where you judge yourself or others and to see where you are fearful. These are your creations; these are your manufactured terrors that keep you small, that keep you from this consciousness expansion that we seek to provide.

If you wish to tap into your passion, this gift from God (if you wish to call it that), it is this unfolding story in your life that must begin with you. It must begin with you listening to how you feel. It must begin with you listening to the ideas that come into the quieted mind. That will be your first step. If you have not found your passion, if you have not been gifted with creativity and an understanding of self that gives you a clear directive, if you feel lost in your world, if you feel as if you are not being who you should be, then you know there is something terribly missing from your life. Begin to follow these prescriptions of forgiveness and excavate the fears in your mind. Face your fears with courage, and understand why they are there, why you make them in your mind.

We cannot deal with your fears for you. We must take a back seat until you have become peaceful, until you have raised your vibration enough for us to reach you. That is the quieting of the mind. These voices in the head — these attacking voices, these judgmental voices, these fearful voices — are not your true self. Your true self is at one with God still, even though you feel you are separated. You have, in fact, allowed a stranger, if you will, into your mind, and that stranger has been telling you tales filled with untruth, lies, fears, and paranoia, and you have mistaken that voice for your own. It is not your voice. It is the untruth you have learned from other beings who did not know what they were doing. It is the lower-vibration concepts that have traveled around your planet.

Thoughts do not disappear. They coalesce in groups and are tapped into by your guidance system. If your guidance system is disconnected and you are fearful and scared because of untrue teachings, you will tap into these lower thoughts. As you begin to input new information by studying these truthful texts, you will indeed raise your vibration, and you will be able to tune into our higher-vibration ideas, our higher-vibration inspirations. Then you will begin to tap into your true purpose, to your true passion.

Your true purpose is to wake up. Your true purpose is to leave this third-dimensional Earth. Indeed, in stories from the Church, you are told that heaven is the ultimate goal. It is not through death that you reach heaven; it is through awakening that you reach heaven. It is by waking that you raise your vibration enough to join us in the nonphysical realms, which are delightful, full of love, and completely different from the world in which you find yourself.

Your world is illusory in that sense. There are many, many magnificent realms that you will encounter once you wake up. But you must understand what you are doing to yourselves; you must understand that the stories you tell yourselves are untrue. So this is the material I bring you in this book. I tell you the story of my life so that you might begin to see your own divinity, so that you begin to see the fictions that have been fed to you for many, many centuries on this plane in the name of Jesus.

I am feeding you my story now. I am feeding you my energy now. You will feel the love; you will feel the joy of it. You will feel the freedom of it; you will feel the passion of it. Teaching is my passion and purpose. It has always been my passion and purpose, and so I want you to find your passion and purpose, because you have a gift for this world. You have a most magnificent talent that perhaps has not been tapped into, and it can be accessed by clarifying your mind, clearing and forgiving the past, and staying in the present with all of your consciousness focused on that which you choose to do in the moment, that which brings you joy in the moment. This is how you will find your way; this is how you will find this beautiful, beautiful experience that is your passionate life.

That is enough on that subject; you get the gist of it. You must become peaceful. You must become willing to first unlearn and then learn. You must erase from your mind beliefs of hatred, narrowness, and limitation, and you must implant in your mind the ideas of divinity, love, and creativity. This is your job, this is the way to happiness, and this is the way to peace.

There are many steps up this ladder, and you do not need to worry about how to get to the top. All you need to know is that this is the perfect place for you in this moment. You have arrived at the perfect point of awareness combined with information, and this is your moment. This is your moment to change your life. Begin to forgive those beings, places, and things that you have hated, disliked, or regretted. Begin to look after your body-mind complex by feeding it healthy foods, healthy entertainment, and healthy ideas based in truth.

Keep your mind out of the future. You do not know what the future holds for you. As you change your consciousness in this present moment, your future is ever changing, so there is no point in looking to the future to try to figure it out, because in this moment — as you forgive, as you love, as you nurture, as you care for yourself and your brothers and sisters — you are literally changing your future, moment by moment by moment. So stay present and follow the prescriptions that we have offered in these texts, and you will find that your purpose becomes clearer and clearer every day and in every way.

CHAPTER TWENTY-FIVE

Possession and Evil

THIS CHAPTER IS THE ONE YOU HAVE BEEN ANTICIPATING ABOUT POSSESSION and evil. This is a very important chapter because the topic is a very big block to your spiritual, mental, and emotional development.

Your society has been the victim of propaganda that has been systematically and repeatedly pummeled into your minds through very vicious means. I am speaking about the Christian Church, of course. It might seem as if I have a bone to pick with this particular institution, and you are right. I have a bone to pick with this particular institution because there are many, many things that have been conducted by this institution over the centuries that are abhorrent to me, that are completely the opposite of what I taught when I was on this plane and continue to teach throughout these interactions with various humans who are open to the vibration of the Christ Mind.

The Nefarious Vibration of the Church

This is all that is happening here. This being [the channel] has freed herself from the untruths in her mind by studying truthful material. It is science. It is not a dispensation from God, and it is not a reward for being good. It is merely vibrational science in which a person can raise his or her vibration and align the self with love and truth through the practice of forgiveness, compassion, and creativity. This is something that is in alignment with truth and creativity because God is creative. When you practice these principles, you bring yourself to a frequency that we can reach you at.

Throughout your history, the Church has punished — capitally and with great cruelty — anybody who dabbled in anything that was deemed the Church's territory. In the early phases of the Church, there was a great understanding of the power that I wielded in my incarnation. There were beings who witnessed me heal others. There were beings who witnessed miracles that I performed, and this brought home to them the incredible power that was contained within my teachings. Many of these beings would listen to me preach, but they were not listening to the preaching that you see in your Bible, the edited and "dumbed down" teachings — ones that have eliminated all the truthful lessons of divine power, your sacred nature, your divine nature, and your amazing ability to create your own experience. These teachings were present when I was on the Earth plane, so beings were able to hear what I was saying, and at times this was very frightening to the powers of the time.

They saw how people reacted to what I was doing. They saw the bodies being healed, they saw the resurrections that I accomplished, and they saw the transformation of the material world through this discipline, through this enlightened connection to truth and oneness. That is what I taught. I encouraged people to do the same thing that I was doing.

Now, you must go back in time and imagine people who wielded power over ignorant and uneducated beings, who were making a lot of money from this, and who were reaping rewards of land, influence, and political power. They did not want this to change. So when they saw what I was teaching, it was imperative for them to stop me, which of course they did. This did not victimize me; I knew it was coming, as I told you in the story of my life. I knew that I was going to be taken out of the discussion in the way that I was, and I was prepared for it through many, many hours of teaching through the nonphysical.

The powers that be could not allow ordinary beings that were under their influence to access this energy, so prohibitions were made, but not immediately. These prohibitions were calculated over many, many decades — even centuries — and over time these practices of meditation and of connecting with Divine Mind through the elevation of consciousness were forbidden. They were forbidden because they were powerful. They were forbidden because they undermined the absolute control that the leaders of that institution wanted to wield over ordinary beings.

Of course, that is one of the things that have upset me so much over these centuries. But this teaching could not be brought forth in this time through this particular format, spoken word, because of the danger to beings. It is only in the past few decades that this kind of activity has been permitted in your society. The Church has wielded great influence for a very, very long time, and you must remember that your institutions, your schools, your universities, and your social interactions are based on the Church's prohibitions. You do not realize it anymore, but they are still profoundly in effect in your mind and in your collective consciousness.

The terrors and the murders that were perpetrated by the Church on anybody who dabbled in the nonphysical, who entertained speaking in this kind of manner to beings who were out of time, out of the physical world, were so devastating that anybody who entertained this idea became terrified. This is what you are witnessing. Even as you read this material, even as you entertain this book's contents, you will have these fears arise because these fears have been so fed, and these fears have been so perpetuated. These fears have been inoculated, if you will, into your society. So the second you feel the slightest fear around this communication, many other thoughts of that vibration could tumble into your mind because you have tuned into that frequency, and it is a very powerful frequency.

The Church beings who orchestrated this prohibition understood vibrational medicine — vibrational tuning, if you will — exactly because that is what I was teaching. Many of these beings studied the material I taught as they edited it. They had access to this material, and they used the knowledge that was contained within my teachings for nefarious purposes, for the ego's purposes, which were to control, limit, hurt, and make fear in the minds of the masses.

So this is the history that you are faced with here in terms of these fears of possession. They have been taught to you relentlessly and with capital punishment as the consequence of not conforming. When you look at 2,000 years of this kind of teaching, you can understand that there is a profound and visceral reaction to anything that goes against what has been indoctrinated. You do not realize that you are still being indoctrinated.

Now, the indoctrination has been taken over by movies, facilitated by the powers that be — and yes, there are powers that be — who do not want you empowered, do not want you strong, do not want you focused, and do not want you wielding your Divine Mind for the purposes of loving communion with your brothers and sisters. Look around your world and see the separation. Look around your world and see the war. Look around your world and see the profits that are reaped from your hating each other, from the fear, the guns, the wars, the poverty, and these kinds of things. These are the consequences of ignorance. We do not want to offend you in any way, but you have been kept ignorant. You have been kept away from your true nature, from your divine nature.

The Death of the Ego

Of course, that is why I was killed, because I was preaching sedition; I was preaching revolution, as I am now. I am preaching revolution now! I am preaching a revolution of love. All I ever tell you to do is to be nice to each other. All I ever tell you to do is to love each other and forgive each other. But in the ego's world, this is poison; this is tantamount to predicting the ego's death, and it is, indeed, the death of the ego. And when you have beings who reap the rewards of the egoic culture in which you find yourselves, they will not support systems that bring that culture down. The fox is guarding the hen house, and you must understand that as you read this material.

You will fear possession, and it is natural, given this history. But we want you to understand that it is in changing your vibration that you guarantee there will be no negative consequences. In practicing these principles we teach, you guarantee that the only beings you will contact will be of higher vibration. When you are free of judgment, when you are loving, and when you are kind, you access the vibrations of the higher consciousness.

Now we will speak a little bit about the lower-vibration world because some of you have experienced it. Some of you have encountered what you would consider lower-vibration energies, and we say to you that there are many, many realms that you do not see. There are many, many levels of consciousness in other realities, in other dimensions, that you are not privy to, because you are tuned into a particular vibration. Just as when you raise your vibration and begin to tune into our realm, there are beings that you can connect with if you continue to tune your vibration down. These are beings of a lower vibration, and they are not your friends. They are not loving, and they are not seeking light. They seek darkness and have sought darkness over and over again. They are not put in hell by a god that judges them; they are merely reaping the rewards of the seeds they have sown. So those beings who are continually hateful and abusive, those beings who are repetitively cruel and malicious to their fellows (even though they know that it is not the right thing to do) are setting a tone.

Ask for Help to Create a Positive Life

There are stories, of course, between lifetimes, and we will go into this here. When your life ends, you will be given an opportunity to look back on it and make a different choice. However, your teachers, your guides in that intermediary life, also reflect your vibration. They may very well be higher than you are in an incarnation. Let us say you are a pedophile, and you have hurt many, many children in your incarnation. Your teachers will be of a higher vibration than you, but they will not be as high as those for somebody who practiced loving forgiveness. You will be offered another life that is in accord with the one that you have led. You will not make sudden jumps from one experience to another; you will do it incrementally as you glean experience in that incarnation.

So as you step into the next incarnation, it may not be much higher than the last one that you experienced. And if you continue to make lower-vibration choices, you will then experience a lower vibration in your next life. This is an experience that brings momentum — just as when you focus on the good you then get more goodness, when you focus on the bad, you get more badness. It becomes the tuning fork that you are aligned with, and it becomes more and more difficult to break out of that alignment. This is very important for you to know.

If you feel you are a negative person, then it is very important that you discipline the mind while you are in your incarnation because your seeds for the next experience are being sown in this one. You do not need to wait until you pass over to change your mind.

We ask you to choose again now. We ask you to look at what you have been doing, and if you are unsatisfied with it, if you see that you are making poor choices, then we want you to exert your decision-making abilities and begin to make different choices. Ask us for help! We cannot help you unless you ask us, and we cannot help you at times when your vibration is too low. We are there, and we are willing, but you must make the first step. You must begin to practice forgiveness; you must begin to practice kindness. You must begin to be the change that you want to see happening in your mind. Action brings new experience; new experience changes your belief.

The Western Pathway

If you would like to change your mind quickly, study *A Course in Miracles*. Now, there have been beings who ask if this is the only path. Well, this book is designed to change the Western Judeo-Christian mind quickly. There are other philosophies — Eastern philosophies and many, many kinds of tribal philosophies and shamanic pathways — that are all pathways designed for different beings. But if you find yourself in the Western mind, if you find yourself in the Judeo-Christian culture, or if you find yourself reading this book, then it has come to you for a reason. Because it is your language, it is the book that speaks to you. If you were on these other pathways, this book would not appeal to you, and you would not pick it up. It would not be in your vibrational resonance. It would not appeal, and you would not even see it. For those of you who are reading this, this tells you that you are on this frequency; this tells you that these words speak to you. These words resonate with you.

That is why I channeled *A Course in Miracles* through a being who was caught in the Western mind, in the Judeo-Christian teachings that caused her profound suffering. That was a demonstration, also, that you do not have to be perfect to connect with us. You need to want to understand truth, and you need to want to understand the mind, and you need to want to clarify yourself. We do not come to teach those of you who are already accomplished. Why would we do that? We need to teach those of you who are lost; we need to teach those of you who are frightened. We need to teach those of you who do not understand, and we are bringing truth to you because you need our help.

Open Yourself to Our Energy

You must reach your hands up to us and show that you are willing. This is where your fear of possession and evil causes you great detriment because the sensations in the body as we begin to connect with you can feel as if they are other than you. This is because you have not delved into your own energetic systems. The energy of the human mind that is awakened is powerful indeed. These energies are of you. These energies will appear when you are drifting off to sleep. They represent the conscious mind falling away, and you will often feel energies, but because stories and the punishments have been perpetrated in your culture, you immediately assume that they are evil, that they are bad because they feel different from your normal consciousness. But they are not always so.

If you continue to have these fears, we want you to ask us to assist you in becoming clearer. Ask us to gently wake you up, to gently communicate with you in ways that do not frighten you. We can do this. We can communicate with you through writing, or we can communicate with you through music, or we can communicate with you through conversations in public places. We can communicate with you through synchronicities; we can do many, many things that will not frighten you.

Our purpose is not to frighten you, and we are working with a difficult audience in this particular time and place because of the heavy indoctrination of the Church and because of the heavy indoctrination of the horror movies and these kinds of things that you have watched far too many times. It is important — if you want to wake up or if you want to connect with us, but you are afraid — for you to stop reading or watching any material that has these kinds of subjects in it. It is important for you to look back on what you have watched and to ask to have those memories or those ideas cleansed from the mind so that you can become open, so that you can become brave, and so that you can become defenseless.

If you are well defended, we cannot get in there. If you are terrified that you are going to be possessed and we make any attempt to connect with you in a nonphysical way — through a voice in the mind or a sensation in the body — you are going to shut down and run from the room in terror, and our purpose will not be served, so we will not do that. You are keeping us at bay.

We want you to understand this vibrational medicine, we want you to understand that if you are depressed, sad, lonely, or intensely self-loathing, then you should not try to communicate with Spirit directly in that state. You need to bring your vibration up before you do that, because if you have been in that state for some time, you will have a tendency to attract lower-vibration experiences, and we do not want you to scare yourself. We do not want you to be afraid.

What we want you to do is to begin to practice all of these techniques We want you to treat yourself better. We want you to think more clearly, and of course, this is the path of *A Course in Miracles*. It is my voice teaching you how to raise yourself up out of the ego's world, and it is the ego's world that you need to fear. That is why you are depressed, are lonely, and feel abandoned: you are in the ego's world.

Join Us Up the Ladder

It is not like that in my world. In my world there is communion, love, joy, and creativity, and we want you to join us in that world. We want you to join us in that realm of light and kindness, love, and compassion for each other. We are all here, teachers of great light, teachers of great love and integrity, and we are calling you up the ladder. But we will not come down the ladder. Occasionally we can communicate with you when you fall on your knees in surrender, but we prefer not to resort to that desperate measure. But often that is the only place where you will call out to us.

You can begin to call out to us now. Call out my name. Call out any name of higher beings that you respect, whose teachings you love, and begin to lift your own thoughts out of self-hatred, judgment, and narrow-mindedness into expansiveness, creativity, love, and joy. As you raise your inner world, you will tune into our radio station, and you will be able to pick up the wonderful, wonderful messages that are coming from our level of consciousness.

So that is our story on possession and evil. It is your own creation; it is not out to get you. Your creative abilities are godlike; you can create whatever you wish. You can miscreate through fear, judgment, narrow-mindedness, and hatred, or you can create through love, compassion, communion, and higher-minded ideals. It is your choice. You have free will. You are loved so much by this one you call God — All That Is, this oneness consciousness that is always calling you toward love — that you are given free will. Exert it wisely, and learn these lessons. There is nothing in this book that will hurt you. There is nothing in this book that will lead you astray. Your guidance system is divine in nature, but it is confused and often clouded by misteachings and conditioning. So clarify your mind, be patient with yourself, and direct your thoughts — focus your thoughts — on that which is good, that which is loving, and that which is kind, and your life will begin to change.

Conclusion

IT IS THE BEGINNING, NOT THE END. DO NOT FEEL THAT I AM NOT GOING TO carry on with this discussion. These discussions are going to take place in public with many, many beings. We are going to share this information with many, many beings over the next few years. This is the beginning. It is the turning of the handle on the door. The door is open now, and we are able to bring through information for you that you are curious about — information about how to change your world. How do you change your world? You change your mind.

The Beginning of the Dissolution of Untruths

There have been communications throughout your history from the nonphysical. They have been inhibited by your culture's fear of this particular kind of connection through the demonizing that has taken place in your religious structures. There has been a profound deception played out in your society, and it has been reinforced through fearful techniques of murder and punishment and chastisement in various forms through various different modalities. But it is time now in your world to stop this ignorance. It is time now in your world to take back your power — not to hurt others, not to control others, but to bring into your awareness the power that you possess as a divine creative being. You are, in fact, a divine creative being. You have been bestowed with the creative mind of a god. You have not been told this information in your training, so we are bringing it to you now.

Your world has changed over the past few decades. The fears and controls that the Church wielded for so many centuries on your plane have faded, and beings are beginning to see that some profound lies have been told. And now you are looking at the consequences of many of these lies in your world in the physical manifestation of wars, judgments, and attacks on other beings through very, very painful means. Yes, we are speaking about those who take advantage of beings financially and use people's ignorance to manipulate them, and use people's ignorance and fears to keep them small. You see wars based on lack of understanding of your divine nature. You see pain and suffering that is completely unnecessary, in a large degree, based on these untruths.

You do not see the connection. You do not understand that in keeping yourself small, you become fearful and you want to attack. When you teach yourself untruths and you believe in your fallibility, you believe in death, you believe in isolation, and you become dangerous. You feed the ego mind with untruths. You continue to expand the ego mind, bringing to it things to protect itself: guns, big houses to keep others away from you, and these kinds of things. These are consequences of the untruths that have been planted in your mind, but you do not realize it.

You do not realize that your fearful natures, your sicknesses in your bodies, and your combative relationships are based on these untruths that have been perpetuated planted as seeds in the mind throughout your culture in schools, religious groups, and these kinds of things. You have become unconscious to them. They have become normal, but they are not natural; they are not your natural self. They do not reflect your natural state of being, which is love.

The Mind of God

You are an idea in the mind of God, and so you must be like that force, which is loving, ever giving, ever expanding, creative, and kind. When you do not act in accord with that nature, with that natural self that you are, you feel bad. You have been taught to remedy that bad feeling by attacking others, by purchasing goods, and by doing many, many things, but I am telling you to stop these things. I am telling you to connect with that divine source of energy, to go inside quietly, and ask for connection, knowing that this connection has nothing to do with the god of your religion, knowing that this connection has nothing to do with the fearful propaganda that you have been subjected to on possession and evil. None of these things will manifest in your connection to higher mind if you come to it from a place of peaceful, loving curiosity or when you come to it in a prayerful, focused, and self-respecting way. Do not make a game of it, a party game performed in dark rooms where connecting with Spirit is attempted with alcohol and drugs around. That is not the way to do it; that way will take you into the lower-vibration realms.

What we want you to do is to connect with higher-vibration beings through the communication device that is the mind. You will find that you will reach those beings of higher vibration. We are all here, ready to help you, ready to communicate with you, and ready to help you understand your true nature. I am here to dispel the lies that have been told about me and to finally bring the truth out about your divine nature and about the deceptions that have been perpetrated upon you.

It is time now for you to begin to act in accord with that which you are, which is a divine aspect of God Mind. You are an idea in the mind of God. You have a guidance system that is infallible, that can take you wherever you wish to go, but you must understand how it works. You must understand that when you feel bad, you have had a thought that is out of alignment with truth. You must understand that your guidance system leads you to your path through passion, through feeling good, through feeling happy. God wants you to be happy.

This force, this benevolent force, is not a being. It is a vibration. When you are in accord with that vibration — loving what you do, loving the beings around you, and loving yourself — you feel good. When you are out of accord with this vibration — judging others, hiding from life, and hating yourself — you feel bad. And this is what you must understand: When you feel good, you are in the right place, and you are doing the right thing. When you feel bad, you have stepped off the path, and your guidance system — this divine, reflective device that is telling you how well you are doing on your journey — will let you know that you have stepped off the path, and it will do it through negative emotion. It is a very, very simple principle that you can begin to follow this very day as you read this material. You can begin to listen to your guidance system more, but you must understand what has been done to you. You must understand the erroneous ideas that have been planted in the mind that will confuse the guidance system.

Through practicing *A Course in Miracles*, this wonderful psychological exploration of self and Divine Mind, and through studying this material, you will clarify the mind and come to an understanding of who you really are. You will then be able to tap into these divine powers, and you will then be able to tap into this loving force that is always flowing to you and that wants to give you abundance and health. Because you are powerful and because you too are created as a creator, you have the ability to stop this energy from flowing to you. It is in lower ideas, hateful thoughts, attacking behaviors, spiteful words, and these lower-vibration expressions of mind that you will stop this energy from flowing to you. It will cause sicknesses in your body. It will cause a limited amount of abundance to flow to you. These are consequences, not punishments from a god above who is saying you are not good; it is vibrational only. You must align yourself with the vibration of love, and all will come to you. All will thrive — not only your body but also your relationships, your finances, your environment, and everything. And everything will come from you.

You are the creator. The being next to you is an expression of yourself being shown to you, and it is through your love for that self that you see in front of you that you will, in fact, become aligned with who you really are. When you judge that person next to you, when you hate that person next to you, or when you are spiteful to that person next to you, you are doing it to yourself. Judge not, that ye be not judged. That is what I meant.

Grow into Your Divine Being

You are all connected. You live in your own dreams, and if you attack the dream, you become more and more lost in the dream because you believe it; you believe that it is real. As you become wiser — as these new teachings enter into the mind and you begin to align yourself with love, knowing that that is your purpose, that that is what you are supposed to do — then more shall be revealed to you. As you become wiser, as your channel for this information begins to expand and offer you more and more and more knowledge, you will be able to grow into that divine being that you are.

You are merely separated from this awareness of what you are. You have been told many, many lies that keep the channels closed and that keep you small and defensive and fearful. It is in understanding what you are and acting in accord with that new understanding that you will begin to have new experiences. As you begin to open to new experiences, expanding the mind and your understanding of yourself, then you will begin to connect with us, and you will begin to have spiritual experiences that will bring knowledge to you that you do not have access to in your defensive, small, ego-driven self.

We do not judge you from this side. We love you; that is why we are here. We are here to bring this information to you so that you can become that which you seek to be, which is a divine creator of a world of love, self-expression, kindness, and assistance for each other. You have the ability to do this. This is what I taught when I was on the physical plane so many years ago. It is what I have always taught, and it is what I will continue to teach.

We would like you to share this information with those you love, those beings in your world. You do it through demonstration. You share these ideas through acting in accord with their vibration — which is love, forgiveness, and kindness — and if you do this, your world will change. It will change in ways that are beyond your understanding at this point. Miracles will happen. Things, relationships, and even global events will shift when you all begin to shift toward that vibration of love — love not just for those beings who act in accord with your wishes but for all of your fellow travelers on this plane.

We are all here together. We are all walking along the road to heaven, all walking along the road to hell. Every day you choose which direction you walk. Join us in this direction toward light, toward love, toward self-acceptance, and toward self-appreciation through the practice of forgiveness and the practice of letting go of the untruths in your mind. That is all forgiveness is: You only remember the loving, you only remember the kind from the past, and you choose only to bring that with you and to offer it to your fellow brothers and sisters.

This simple practice of letting go of the negative, the fearful, and the untrue will transform your body, will transform your mind, will transform your experience, and will transform your ability to tap into the creative powers that are given to you by this benevolent force that wants you to vibrate in accord with it in its loving, loving vibration.

— Jesus, 2014

Ananda's Final Words

Join the Love Revolution

Other beings are responsible for the dissemination, distribution, and success in the material world of this work. They have the strategies, the companies, and the abilities to bring this work to the forefront.

The love revolution is inevitable because you are all tired of the wars, tired of the poverty, and tired of the destruction of your beautiful, glorious planet. This material is incredibly important because the untruths that hide in the mind keep you small; the untruths that hide in the mind keep you limited and attacking, fearful and judgmental. These are not pleasant experiences. They cause profound suffering in the individual, and they cause cultural degradation and poverty in the greater meeting of your physical structures, your populations.

This is going to be a community process. It is going to be a collaborative process. It is going to be a process of unity consciousness. It is *not* going to be a process of individual exploitation or flamboyance. It is going to be a group project, and the group will form as the vibration of this work seeps into the minds of those beings who are ready.

If you are ready, if you have had this feeling that you are fortunate and have skills and talents and abundance that can be employed in the transformation of the world, but you do not know how to do it, step up to the plate and come into this group. Come into this amazing opportunity for assistance. This is how the world is going to function once the love revolution has happened. There is a separation mentality that must be overridden.

You have all been taught to do what is the best for you, to fear sharing with others, and to fear offering your assistance to others because they might take advantage of you. Do not worry about this. If you have abundance and desire in combination or if you have skill and desire in combination, then nothing will ever be taken away from you because you are coming to the creative process with love and an extension of that which you are. That is the purpose of your life: to extend that which you are with love to those fellow beings on your plane at this time. They are not separate from you.

That is our closing comment. We are bringing in much information, and there are going to be many, many opportunities for communal expression of love. You look around in your world, and you see hoarding, battles, judgment, and scarcity. Why? Because you are all ensconced in separation mentality, afraid of being taken advantage of or used. You must use yourself to bring about the world that you want to experience, to bring about that which is good, to bring about that which is abundant, and to bring about that which you all desire.

You must understand your conditioned mind. As we bring more and more information through, these blocks to your wonderful magnificence, your power, your influence, and your creative dominance — for you are the greatest creators — will all become clearer, and you will all be given the information that you need on your journey as you clarify yourselves. You must clarify the mind of its untruths, and you must focus on love, even when you do not have it in front of you. You may love many, many things; you may love many, many ideas; and you may love many, many creations in the mind that do not yet exist, and that is what you must focus on. Focus on that which you seek, that which you desire, and that which you wish to experience, and this will then manifest in front of you because you are the creative force behind this universe. You are the mind that makes your experience, and you are the mind that can change your experience.

Afterword

WOW, WHAT A RIDE THIS HAS BEEN! IT HAS BEEN OVER A YEAR IN THE MAKING, and I have been on a journey I never expected to take. I didn't even know it was possible to produce Jesus's autobiography, a book I never thought to write and, in the beginning, didn't even want to write. But now? I am so glad I was offered the opportunity and somehow found the courage to take the plunge into that deep sea of unknown experience and uncharted ideas.

When Ananda first came to me during an automatic writing workshop I took more than two years ago, they gave me a piece of knowledge that now makes sense, but at the time, it seemed quite outrageous and had nothing to do with my experience then. They told me that I had been Jesus's student in the desert all those centuries ago. They told me I had been a teenaged goatherd, a young man who followed Jesus on his teaching ministry, and that we had become friends. I had fallen in love with his ideas and his wisdom in that long-ago life. Ananda said I had many incarnations of teaching and learning his divinely inspired communications and that I had followed him relentlessly, sitting with him at night and talking in the firelight about all kinds of things.

I recall a vivid dream I had in my twenties in which I was a man walking in the desert, looking down at my sandaled feet. As my gaze shifted toward the flat and featureless Middle Eastern horizon, I understood it all; I understood the entire world.

Now that dream seems to make sense, yet I have more to learn, teach, and understand. This book has made me enter the most fearful of places in my mind, but there were no real demons there — just ideas, vague and forbidden. Forbidden by whom, I did not know, but as I entered into this dialogue, a wisdom and tangible love made itself obvious, both on the page and in my mind and heart. When I read his words — so full of passion, truth, and love — I am astounded, and I can feel his energy in these phrases.

I still hesitate a little when I tell people what my latest book is about, but each time it gets easier and easier. And every time I read these wonderful teachings about love and forgiveness, I know deep down inside that I could not have a better life's purpose. How could it get any better than sharing this most wonderful and healing information? What bigger book can be written than Jesus's autobiography? None that I know of. Is that arrogant of me to say? No, it is not. I have come to this job humbly, without any expectation or design and ignorant of the path I was to embark on. As Ananda said, this is not my work. I am only the messenger, but it is a joy and a great honor to have had this information come through this fallible body and mind that is Tina.

I hope you have enjoyed this book. I know I have enjoyed channeling it and, of course, reading it. Yet this is, as Jesus has told me, only the beginning. I don't know what Jesus has in mind for the next book — no idea at all. I wait in eager anticipation.

If you would like to connect on Facebook, like or join the Teachings of Ananda and Ananda Jesus pages where I post updates and newly channeled information. I look forward to my next adventure with JC. I can't wait to see what teachings come through next, and I hope you are as excited as I am. I know this work is challenging to our deeply conditioned minds, but I hope it has opened up some doors for you, whether to forgiveness of self or others, or even just to new possibilities. After all, if our past has been inaccurate and we have mistakenly believed untruths and errors and thereby caused some of our most painful problems, then a new past will offer up the possibility of a new future for all of us.

Peace,
Tina Louise Spalding

To send a personal message to the author, email her at blissistheanswer@gmail.com, or visit JesusAnAutobiography.com

Questions and Answers

DURING THE PRODUCTION OF THIS BOOK I WAS ASKED TO come up with some questions for Jesus to answer, so I canvassed some friends, looking for some challenging questions that seemed suitable, the kinds of questions you might ask. These people certainly asked some things that would not have occurred to me. The questions and Jesus's wonderful answers follow.

Marriage

What does the ideal marriage look like?

I am amazed at the work that you are doing at this time. You are becoming fearless in the pursuit of the same goal as we have. We are all here, seeking to bring enlightenment to this planet, seeking to relieve the suffering of the minds of many, many beings who are laboring under misconceptions and under untrue statements in their minds that they believe. This is how suffering occurs.

You have a guidance system that tells you when you are happy. You have a guidance system that tells you when you are sad. And yes, this relates to your question on marriage. We are building the cup in which to hold our story. This phrase has been approved of before, so we will use it again. You have this guidance system, and you are taught from a very small age to override that guidance system. A babe in arms is taught to override that guidance system.

A baby will cry when it is unhappy, and the parents will do whatever they can to soothe that child. They will distract the baby by giving it a soother, for

227

example, covered in some sweetness or some distracting sensory information. And then the child will give up its plea for what it really wants. It does not want a soother. It wants to be held; it wants to be caressed; it wants to be kissed; it wants to be fed; it wants many, many things. It may want to be bathed, or it may want to be exercised, or it may want to be taken outside. These are all things that the little child may be asking for, yet you just get it to shut up.

This is where the process begins. So this is a deep question. You are, in fact, marrying beings who have had their guidance systems essentially destroyed. It is not destroyed in the true sense — it carries on giving information — but the nurturing of that guidance system, the coming to understand its nuances, has been destroyed in youth. And so you have beings who have lost their ways coming together in marriage. They have lost their ways because they have no compass.

It is exactly the same as asking directions from somebody who has wandered out into the wilderness without any sense of direction whatsoever. There is no point in asking that person for advice because they do not know where they are, and this is the truth for many of you in this society. You do not know where you are. You do not know who you are, and you do not know what you are.

So to answer your question, this is the foundational information that must be brought to bear on this query. If you do not know who you are, if you do not know what you are, and if you do not know where you are, then you should not be marrying anybody! This is the first answer to that question.

If you have taken it on yourself to know yourself, to learn about your history, and to learn about the truth of your nature, you will be better prepared for marriage.

As we venture further into the question of what the ideal marriage is, you see that it is very difficult to answer in this time and place. If you want to have a good marriage, you must feel good. You must feel good about what you are, and you must feel good about where you are, and you must feel good about who you are. You must understand your divine nature. You must understand your physical body and what it represents and what it does not offer you. You must understand the nature of projection and the illusion of reality as you see it. These are basic guidelines of self-understanding, for it is the self reflected back to you. These are the basic understandings that must be in place for a marriage to thrive.

Many beings are married in your society, but they are superficial relationships because the beings are not in contact with their true selves. They are not in contact with their true natures. So an illusory self is married to an illusory self, and this is where the ego comes in. When you are in a relationship with someone and you are not in alignment with truth, then the ego is in charge.

The ego is every untrue thought you have ever had, every misbelief you believe, and every lie you have been told that you have swallowed as a truth. That is what the ego is. The ego is concepts in your mind, belief in separation, ideas that are separate from that which you call God, that which you call All That Is, that which you call the Divine Mind. So when egos marry, there is a battle zone, a war. You have people who believe in attacking one another. You have people who believe in verbal abuse, and you have people who believe in separation. You have beings who defend themselves from all kinds of perceived and imagined wrongs.

This is why the marriage situation looks the way it does, with infidelity and divorce and unhappiness. It is only in the awakening of the mind that you will have a marriage that is based on truth. Understand that the person standing in front of you is not different from you, is not anything other than you, and is, in fact, an aspect of you reflected back to yourself. Until you understand that, you cannot have the ideal marriage.

Now, this is not to be negative or cynical. I am not either of those things, for I have achieved that state that brings the ideal marriage, and that is what I experienced in my physical incarnation at the end of my life with my beloved, Mary. We had that ability to commune with each other absolutely in unconditional love, but that was because my ego had been completely dissolved. I understood truth. I understood how the world functioned, and I understood what relationships were for. Mary, in that particular time and place, was not enlightened, but she became enlightened later on in that physical incarnation, with help from me and the nonphysical. But, as it was within our marriage, one being who is awakened does not fall into the traps of the ego mind. The awakened mind does not fall into the battles and arguments, the retaliations, the hatefulness, and the restriction of energy. So when one being is completely open, the other being must follow suit.

It is that tuning fork philosophy, if you will. When one being holds a high vibration, the other must hold that high vibration or leave. Mary would not leave, so she had only one choice: to raise her vibration. That is what facilitated her enlightenment in her physical incarnation.

To make a long story short, the way to a perfect marriage is to remove the ego's control of your mind. You will have an ego as long as you are manifested on the physical plane until you reach that state of enlightenment, but by understanding the ego mind — understanding the desire to attack, the tendency toward defensiveness, and the concept of separation — you will make yourself into a person who is capable of the ideal marriage.

The ideal marriage does not exist in and of itself. It is made. It is created by beings who are awake. It is created by beings who are aware of the principles that are being taught in this material. So this question does not really have an answer. The ideal marriage exists only as you create it from your healed mind. That is the way to have an ideal marriage.

If you have a marriage that is not ideal, that does not mean you need to walk away from it. That marriage can be healed, but it must be healed by you. It must be healed by one partner changing the way he or she looks at the relationship. It must be changed by one partner's refusal to attack because he or she knows it will not bring anything of value. It must be changed by one partner becoming unconditionally loving of the other partner, regardless of the ego behavior the other being exhibits. The beings who exhibit poor behavior are not showing their partners their true selves. They are showing the parts that are out of alignment with truth, and the only way to return to oneness, the only way to return to truth, is by offering love. So that is the solution to marital problems. It is in coming to understand your own ego mind and the ego-mind behavior of your partner. Recondition the self so that you begin to forgive, and recondition the self so that you begin to refuse to attack, no matter what is happening. Yes, turn the other cheek; yes, that is what I taught.

So you learn how to have the ideal marriage by becoming the ideal marriage partner. To become the ideal marriage partner, you must wake up. You must understand that the illusion is not real. You must understand your true, divine nature, and you must understand that love is always the solution. If somebody offers you love, you return love; if somebody offers you hatred, you solve the problem of hatred — which is lack of love — by offering love. And that is what you do.

That is not a satisfactory answer for the ego mind, but it is a satisfactory answer from our mind. That is a mind that is united; it is a mind that is in touch with unity consciousness. So that is the answer that will bring you the result that you are looking for.

Death and Mourning

Why do we have to suffer the profoundly painful experience of the death of a child?

These questions, of course, are the questions of life; this is what humans struggle with so, so profoundly. So we will begin at the beginning.

Death is not real. It is an illusion that you have bought into because you are body worshippers. You believe in the body's reality. Now, you must understand that you use the body itself to prove its reality. You use your sense of touch to touch it, you use your sense of sight to see it, and you use your sense of smell to smell it. So in fact, you are always using the body to prove that the body is real; this is something that is paradoxical in nature. In a scientifically sound experiment, you cannot really use the thing you are trying to determine to try to determine itself, but that is what you do. You are using the body to prove the body's reality. You cannot prove the body's reality without using the body. It's a circular argument.

But in this society, you do not really question this; you do not really question that that is what you are doing. You do not really understand how the mind works. You do not really understand how creation works. You do not really understand what this life is.

The suffering that comes from death is based on your beliefs about what death is. If your beliefs about death are accurate, you do not suffer. You may cry a little bit because you miss the physical presence of a being, but if you were raised in a society that facilitated communication between physical and nonphysical, you would not lose contact with that being. You would have constant contact. That being would be in another realm, it is true, so you would not have the same sensory input from being in association with the person's body, but you would not feel that the being was gone. You would have constant communications and conversations if you both so chose.

This "veil" between life and death is an illusion based on belief. This channel, for example, has bridged that gap through diligent practice of scientifically proven principles. When I traveled to the Far East in my lifetime and studied with the masters there, I learned scientifically proven techniques for transformation of mind and body. That is what I brought back with me and taught in that time so long ago. But these powerful and empowering teachings were not allowed to continue, and that, of course, is what we are doing here. We are now able, through the freedom of information in your society, to teach these things, to allow these things to come out. But your society is indoctrinated in untruth, it is indoctrinated into the body, and it is indoctrinated into death, and this causes suffering and grief. So we will go to your guidance system.

Your guidance system, this emotional system that you have in your body has not been explained to you accurately [by others]. When you are in intense pain, your guidance system is telling you that you are wrong in what you are thinking. This intense feeling of isolation or grief — suffering, if you want to call it that — is a sign that you are not thinking clearly and you are not in alignment with truth.

So if your child dies and you are mistaken about death — you believe that this is the only world and that there is nothing after, or perhaps there is some terrible place after death — you are going to suffer terribly because you are out of alignment with truth and your guidance system is telling you so. If, however, your child dies, and you understand that this life is not real, that it is an illusory dream existence that is, in fact, a separation from real life and a descent into isolation and individuation, then you will suffer much less. It is very difficult for you to experience because as spiritual beings at one with God, this idea of separation is painful, and it is difficult for you to cope with, especially because you have not been taught about the truth of its nature, the truth of its experience as it exists.

Suffering is based on your beliefs. It is not a fact. Death is not a fact. This is what I worked to prove to my disciples in my life by allowing myself to be crucified. I could have walked away from that experience; there is no doubt about that. But I allowed it to happen to prove to them that death was unreal, that I could manufacture a new body at will. I showed that I could become fearless; I could become defenseless. I could stand in the fire of any attack, even an attack such as crucifixion, and not be afraid. This was a teaching opportunity.

But because of the profoundly programmed minds that these beings were working with, even though I had taught them for several years, they relied on me. These programs run deep and fast in the mind, and if you do not do the work, you cannot change them. And that was part of the problem in my ministry. They saw me as special, so they weren't taking it on themselves, as they needed to, to make themselves as disciplined as I was. So in that time and place, I was demonstrating the unreality of death, but because of the profound programming and belief in death that you all have, this teaching seems insane. It seems unattainable.

There are many beings on your plane who study the mind, who are disciplined practitioners of several different philosophies, and who have the ability to manufacture a body. You are manufacturing your own body as we speak. You are doing it unconsciously. The body that you are in at this moment is being made from all of your beliefs, and that is why you get sick and why you die.

So these concepts and even the questions are out of accord with truth. Why do we have to suffer the death of children? You do not have to suffer; nobody is doing it to you, and your children do not die. They merely believe in death, and they believe in the separation that they experience in this detour into fear, so it is real for them. Anything that you believe to be so is so. This is your free will, and this is your choice. This is what you have been given by this benevolent force that you call God, a creator that has made you a creator. You are a creator too. I am a creator. So I am creating my experience consciously. I am lucid dreaming, if you will. You are creating your experience unconsciously. You are in a nightmare, and it is the same process.

When you go to bed at night, you can have nice dreams, or you can have horrible dreams. You can have dreams that bring you great joy and pleasure, or you can have dreams that bring mortal fear into your mind. These are all made from the mind. As it is in your sleep, so it is in your waking time. You make your life from your beliefs.

If you are making a nightmare, your beliefs are out of accord with truth. If you are living a joyful and happy existence and you are creative and feel free and expressive, then you are more in alignment with truth. But if you are on this Earth plane believing that you are an individual existing in a separated body, you have great untruths in the mind, and you will experience death. You will only be able to walk away from death by truly understanding the dreamlike nature of this experience that you are having and by understanding the techniques that lead you away from separation to unity consciousness. That is what I did at the end of my life and what I continued to teach after my crucifixion.

It is time for you to take back your power. It is time for you to take back this knowledge that was brought to Earth long ago and continues to be brought to Earth. I am not the only messenger of this tale; there are many, but many of them are not in your society. However, your society is coming to the end of this particular section, this particular chapter in the book of life, so this is a perfect time for this information to come to you.

You are not forced to experience these things. God does not punish you by taking your children away. You believe in untruth, and you see the demonstration of it that is not love but death; it is not life but separation. But as you change your mind, as you heal your mind, as you begin to tell yourself the true story of what you are, and as you begin to act in accord with that true story, your experience will change. Your death experience will begin to change, and it will be less painful.

Beings will be able to leave their bodies at will without any suffering what-soever, and you will know that they are merely stepping into another reality and that you can join them whenever you choose. Then you will not suffer, you will not grieve, and you will not waste your lives wishing that something that has to happen did not happen.

The biggest regret we have when we observe this kind of grief is the calling back that it causes for the spirit concerned. There is a terrible calling, a yearn-ing, that the departed being feels from the Earth plane when its loved ones are in deep despair, and it prevents the being from carrying on its growth, carrying on its freedom-seeking, creative nature. So if you have lost somebody and they have been gone a while, put your grief aside and study the material that we bring through this particular channel. You will find your despair will fade, and you will be able to offer your dearly departed one freedom from your clinging ideas and thoughts.

As these teachings become more accepted in this society and as these truths become integrated into your culture, your death experience will change drastically, and eventually you will not need to experience it at all in the way that you do. But you are far from that. Look around. There is much death and destruction, and there is much belief in and promotion of death. Death is used as entertainment, and you must look at this part of your society. If you do not wish to reinforce the ideas of death and suffering, stop watching them for entertainment, stop watching movies that promote them, and stop voting for people who bring them about. Invest in what you want to grow. Stop looking at what you don't want, and start looking at what you do want. Start looking at life, start looking at love, and start looking at compassion and companionship. These are all things that bring you wonderful, wonderful rewards. Your obses-sion with and fear of death brings you nothing except more death.

It is time now for you to put that aside. If you are reading this particular book, it is because you have had enough of that. So now is the time to set aside your grief. All those who have gone before you are fine. They are in their new experiences — some in the nonphysical, some returned to the physical — and you do not need to grieve for them. They have moved on. It is only you who have not moved on.

So we send you our love, we send you our wisdom, and we ask you to reeducate yourselves about this particular subject. Reeducate yourselves about what causes suffering, what causes death, and what causes these misperceptions to be maintained in the mind, and you will find that your experiences will change and this belief in a punishing God, this belief in the need for difficult lessons such as this, will pass. You do not need difficult lessons such as this. There are joyful, wonderful lessons that are relatively easy to learn, but they do require discipline, focus, and a willingness to change.

Authenticity

How do we know this is real? How do I know this is Jesus's voice?

We are Ananda. Your question is one that so many beings ask about this form of conversation — channeling, this intangible, unconventional way of speaking — so we will add our little bit here because we are the gatekeepers. We are the channel providers, if you will. You cleared the way for our energies, and we cleared the way for Jesus's energies, so we are part of this question, and we are part of this answer.

Your body is your vehicle, let us say; it is what you drive around in. But in your society, you have made it a god. You have made it what you *are*. Now, this is not your fault. It is what you have been told. You have been told you are a body, and you have been told this body controls you. You have not been told the truth, which is that you control your body. You are the maker of your body. You brought it into manifestation so that you could experience and have power over separation and individuality. This is what you wanted when you made this experience, when you created this dream.

But in your world, you have been told that anything you can see is real, and so you use your vision, as you perceive it to be in your experience, as the determiner of reality. This is because your reality is created by you, and you are unknowingly using that which you have created to experience separation and to experience material things. You are using the very device that you made to prove that the material is real. So you seek evidence through that thing that is unreal to prove that the experience you are having is real. You only seek evidence that supports your case, evidence that proves you are alone and that underlies your belief in separation, which created your experience.

There are many other pieces of evidence available to you that are not material. We will go straight to your experience of love as an example. There is no solid evidence of what love is. You see consequences of love; for example, you see kindness between beings and say that they love each other, but you cannot prove it. There is no material effect of love. There is not a body. There is not an object. There is not something that you can measure. You cannot take love into the lab; you cannot take love into your scientific method and prove its existence even though you all know that it is a real thing. You know that it exists as a nonphysical experience. You feel it, you know it, you trust it; it is not physical, however. So here your laws of reality begin to crumble, but you do not really look at those because your evidence-based society is material.

When you begin to seek nonphysical evidence, you will have experiences that support the nonphysical. Now, your society is very determined in this way, and it does not want you to seek the nonphysical. There has been much training in your society not to seek the nonphysical. You have been taught that you will be possessed; you have been taught that it is evil; you have been taught that God and Jesus will be angry with you. These are not small ideas in the minds of ordinary humans who believe they are material beings. Even those who believe they are spiritual beings are indoctrinated into this idea of judgment from God or Jesus that are completely out of accord with their teachings, with their vibration, if you will. Their vibration is of love; they will not judge you.

But your world has become distorted. Your world has become fixated on the material and physical through this separation of religion and science. This is one of the areas that you must look at as a society. Your scientific method has swung too far away from Spirit. Now, in the beginning stages of your scientific method, this was important because the Church wielded too much power. It wielded too much influence, and it had to be separated out, but now as you enter into the quantum world, the nonphysical, your new science shows you that the world is not as hard and fast as you thought it was. It is, in fact, immaterial; it is, on a nuclear level, very, very "unsolid," if you will. (That is not a word, but we will use it.) It is very transparent; it is very ethereal in its nature. But the teaching in your ordinary school systems and in your ordinary minds is very much that the solid is solid, and this is not true. Your greatest minds know that this is not true, but it has not trickled down into your ordinary teachings, and that is what we are here to do. We are here to begin to reeducate you in the truth of the matter, which is that your obsession with the material was a reaction to religion and the pain that religion, in its oppressive and torturous ways, taught society.

Your world is a relative world, so it teaches through relative experience. You have had the religiosity of the Church, and now you have had the materialism of science, the traditional scientific method as you understand it to be. We want you to begin to blend those two. We want you to begin to blend not the narrowness of religion or the untruth of religion but the truth of the teachings that the religion was founded on with science to see how very powerful and influential you are as spiritual beings, to begin to redesign the way you look at your world, and to begin to see the physical as a consequence of the nonphysical. It is not objective in and of itself. It arises from what you believe in. It arises from what you emphasize and what you value.

Now we will pass you over, as we always do, to our dear Jesus, and we will allow him to continue answering this question.

✳   ✳   ✳

I am returned to continue on the teaching. This question, of course, cannot be answered to a satisfying degree for the Western mind. The Western mind — immersed in materialism, immersed in judgment, immersed in singularity, if you will — will not accept this material as truthful. It will cause too much conflict in the mind as it exists in this time and place. Unless you have been trained in spiritual principles, unless you have been trained in understanding how creation works — that the solid material world you see arises from your thoughts, and therefore your actions arise from your thoughts, and your actions affect the world — until you see this, you are unable to accept these teachings as real.

Now, there are beings who will say that this is manipulative, that this is brainwashing, that this is dangerous. All of these concepts and ideas are going to arise as we venture into this discussion because you have been deeply indoctrinated in the scientific method in which only the physical/material is real. Those minds that are deeply indoctrinated in that belief cannot accept this material because it is not provable. It is not measurable, but neither is love, joy, or hatred, yet you experience all of these things. We want to bring these ideas into the mind so that you are not out of accord with what you are experiencing.

You must accept that there are certain realities you experience that are immeasurable — for example, you might love your child, and yet you cannot prove it. Therefore, if that is true in your experience of love, the door opens to the possibility that other things can be experienced that are real but are not physical or measurable. This is logic, and you must use logic in this argument. Logic has not been used in spiritual practice as it has existed in your society. Terror has been used. Fear has been used. Arbitrary walls that you are not allowed to look around have been used to stop you from investigating these subjects. This was done by the Church because if you had investigated them logically and ventured into them with curiosity, intelligence, and open-mindedness, you would have discovered these truths long ago. But you were told not to go there. You have been told that you would be possessed. You have been told that you would be killed. Of course you are not going to go to those subjects because they are terrifying when presented in that way. But we are approaching this subject logically. We want you to investigate your own mind and your own experience because your experience gives you information that is in accord with your belief structure.

If you believe in love, you will experience love. If you do not believe in love, you will not completely experience love. You are a loving being, you are created in the vibrational essence of that which you call God, so you are love in nature. But when you step away from love, you begin to feel bad, you begin to feel the separation to such a degree that you suffer incredibly.

This is what suicide victims feel when they refuse to live in their bodies anymore. Through their thought processes, they have created a vibration that is too far from love for them to live with. This is the evidence of lack of love. If you think about it, it is logical. Those beings have had such hateful thoughts, such untrue thoughts, that they are unable to live with themselves, and so they kill the body because they believe the body is the cause of the problem. They do not understand that the consciousness is contained within the body and can be separated from the body. You are not the body!

That is what I was teaching when I allowed myself to be crucified. I was teaching my disciples that my body was of no consequence. The Church took that teaching and turned it to their own ends, but my purpose in being crucified was to show my disciples the lack of value in my body and to show them that I could create a new one because I had mastered these physical/material creation rules.

So is this experience real? For those who are too far into the material world and too far into science, it will not be tenable. There will be too many beliefs in their minds for them to accept it; it will cause too much conflict. For it to come into the mind as a new belief, it would cause all the conflicting beliefs held in their minds to come to the surface, and it would cause fear. That is what happens in the mind that is presented with conflicting beliefs — one of the beliefs or the imbalance of the beliefs will have to be sorted out by the mind. And if you have a mind that is ensconced in the physical world and believes too much in the physical/material world, then this belief will be the one that has to be kicked out, because the mind will not be able to tolerate it. But if you have already ventured into the nonphysical, if you have already ventured into the energetic expression of your spirit through your experience, then this belief and this experience will not cause too much conflict. It will always cause some conflict in the Western mind because of the teachings about possession, these teachings about evil, and particularly these teachings about my existence, my presence, and my name.

I am reclaiming my name, but you must be brave enough to step into a new experience around my name. And because my name has been used by the Church as the whip that you have been punished with, because my name has underscored all of the terrors that were perpetrated on ordinary human beings by the Church, my name will frighten you. That is why I am bringing this information through. It is so that you can begin to excavate those fears and those beliefs, because until you do, you will not see the truth of your nature; you will not see the truth of what has been done to you by this edifice and by this behemoth, the Church. All of you are suffering from it, and I want the suffering to stop. That is why I am teaching in this method at this time.

"Why do you not come in a body?" beings will ask because they want to reinforce this belief in the material. That is not my purpose. You believe in the material enough. You believe in the body too much. Those who insist on seeing me or touching me or feeling me do not understand what we are teaching here: We are teaching the unreality of the body. That is what I taught in my crucifixion, although that message was lost. It was not taught correctly by the beings who witnessed it. It was taught incorrectly by the beings who wanted to use it for their own ends. So to bring my body, something that does not exist and something that is irrelevant, into the physical world would only emphasize untruth, which is that you are your body. I am not my body. You are not your body. We do not wish to teach this lesson, so we will not demonstrate this lesson. That is the lesson of the physical. That is the lesson of the ego. That is the lesson of the material.

You are troubled in your world because the physical and the spiritual are not balanced. The material and the nonmaterial are not balanced. You can live in your physical bodies in ease if you understand what they are for. You can live in the material world in ease if you understand how it works and how you are making it from your beliefs. When you look at the world as an existing solid object that you have nothing to do with, you are completely powerless.

That is what the ruling classes have wanted from you: They have wanted you to be powerless. That is what I taught in my life! I was a rebel. I was a preacher of revolution, as I am now. You are no freer now than people were 2,000 years ago. You are hooked into televisions, you are hooked into consuming, and you are hooked into powerlessness. Why? Because that is what served the structures of power that existed then, and that is what serves the structures of power that exist now.

You will not be taught this information from the hierarchies that rule you; they do not want you to be powerful. They do not want you to reach down into your heart and soul and connect to the nonphysical and express your most wonderful divine self. It does not serve them! They will not be able to make you do what serves them if you receive this message.

So how do you know this is real? You do not know this is real. You must read this material with an open mind, you must feel this material with an open heart, and you must step into acting as if it is real for a short while. You must act on faith. Yes, Western scientific minds hate that word, but you act on faith every minute of every day. You believe in money; you have faith in money. You believe in the body; you have faith in the body. Do not think that you do not act as if you are a faithful worshipper. You are a faithful worshipper. You worship things that will not bring you satisfaction, and that is why you are unhappy in your society. That is why you are destroying your environment: You worship things that take, take, take.

These principles are different principles. They are the principles of love; they are the principles of compassion, of forgiveness, of caring, and of sharing. But you have been worshipping the opposite of these. You must be willing to entertain the idea that the fruits of your worship are war, disease, death, and the destruction of your environment. Those are the fruits of the gods you worship!

We, on this side, want you to entertain the idea that these gods are not worthy of your worship and that love is worthy of your worship and, therefore, action! When you can entertain the idea that these ideas are the right ones and act in accord with them, you will begin to see fruits coming from those actions, and those fruits will be sweet. Those fruits will be relationships that blossom. Those fruits will be health. Those fruits will be communities that care for each other. Those fruits will be pacifism — not in the weak sense but in the sense that you are putting your energies into love and peace rather than war and hatred.

So can we prove these experiences are real? No, we cannot prove them. But we can say this: Keep walking along this path and practicing these ideas, and you will begin to get evidence of your belief. This world is a mirror showing you what you believe, and if you have worshipped the gods of hatred, war, and separation, that is what you will witness. As you step more into love, as you step more into acceptance and kindness and sharing, you will see the fruits blossom on that tree, and you will begin to understand what truth is. Truth is alignment with love. Truth is alignment with oneness. That is the origin of your mind.

You experience yourself as a separated being that has no connection. It is not so. You have drawn veil after veil across the truth of what you are, and we are attempting to unmask the truth for you. But you first must take one step in that direction, and that is to entertain the idea that perhaps this is true. You cannot explain it to anyone else. You must go by your feeling, and you must go by your guidance system. You must go by your emotional guidance system, which will tell you. By their fruits ye shall know them. Look at the fruits of your society. Look at the fruits of your government. Look at the fruits. If they are poisonous fruits, if they are depressing fruits, if they are scared fruits, then they are not the truth.

Try this path, and begin to experience the fruits. You will have a new experience because your beliefs will change. We are not trying to manipulate you here. We are merely trying to alleviate your suffering. We are trying to show you that truth is true and untruth is not true, and you will know by the experience and products of that belief system.

Offering Assistance

What can we do for you, Jesus?

There is no "me." I am not the individual that you think I am. I am the consciousness of many, many beings together. The voice is one; the name is one, as you know it in your experience. You experience yourselves as individuals, and so we present ourselves as an individual, but you must understand that the being incarnated as Jesus on your plane so many, many years ago was a pointed focus of consciousness, just as you are a pointed focus of consciousness. You have separated into your physical reality. You have experienced yourself as separate from what you call God, what you call Oneness. But in my incarnation, that awareness of Oneness was returned to me. That is the state of enlightenment in which I found myself in that incarnation.

So now, as a being you are listening to, this apparently individual consciousness has separated itself from Oneness once again to have this conversation.

Why? Because your society needs to have this conversation with the "old me," if you will. This old me can be retrieved from Oneness — this consciousness experience that you call the life of Christ, the life of Jesus, the birth through maturity through the crucifixion and resurrection, as you know it in this biblical story that your society is founded on. This consciousness can be retrieved from Oneness, and that is what is happening. We are retrieving that experience so that you might understand it more clearly, so that you might understand it in a way that allows you to transform your consciousness. Because your consciousness is evolving within your society, we must base all of our education within that paradigm, if you will. We cannot bring in the absolute truth because that is not a language you understand in your physical, singular experience as an individual personality. That is not something that you can comprehend, so there is no point in approaching you from that point of view.

From our point of view, we need no assistance, dear beings. We need no one to do anything for us. You are living your own experience. You are a being who is free to exercise your free will in this experience that you have. What we are doing is bringing you information that will allow you to exercise your free will truly and without limitation. In your society, you are poorly trained to express yourselves. In your society, you are poorly trained to understand yourselves. You are trained for specific things, specific tasks, and specific functions within your society in a very, very limited way. It is a highly specialized training that you go through in your society, just as all societies have gone through specific training in the past, and you will continue to go through specific training because your experience is one of separation and because your experience is one of a body with an apparently separated individual mind. That is what you experience on the plane you are on.

However, our job is to raise your consciousness to a different vibration so you might have a new experience. So your consciousness, as it exists at the moment, can only formulate questions that make sense given your experience. We are trying to change your consciousness so that you can have a new experience and therefore formulate new questions. Questions that come from your limited, human, physical, material self are limited consciousness questions formed within the mind that is limited. So the question of what you can do for me is very, very limited in the sense that you see yourself as an individual, and you see me as an individual.

I am part of higher mind. I am part of those higher realms that you consider the angelic realms, the realms of the ascended masters, the realms of knowledge, the realms of mentorship and teaching that filter through your consciousness, given the opening and the opportunity. That is what is happening here with this channel. There has been a clarification of mind that has taken place, and these messages can now descend through this particular focal point of a body-mind complex, a personality, and that is what you are experiencing here. But you must do for yourself what we cannot do for you. We can bring you the information, but we cannot force you to act on it. We can bring you the understanding of the structure of reality, and we can bring you information about how creativity works, and we can bring you information about how to change your experience, but we cannot do it for you. So there is very little that you can do for us other than follow the precepts and ideas that we bring to you.

As you follow our prescriptions, our instructions, and our ideas and thoughts and understandings and integrate them into your own body-mind experience and your own perceptual experiences, you will raise yourself to a vibratory level that will allow you to interact with us more directly. This is all we want you to do for us. We do not wish you to act as missionaries, and we do not wish you to convert anybody to anything. We want you to act on this knowledge; we want you to act on this information. We want you to begin a forgiveness practice. We want you to begin to honor yourselves as divine aspects of the Creator. We want you to honor each other as divine aspects of the Creator. We want you to forgive all sins that you perceive have been committed against you or that are being committed against others. We want you to take the information that is being presented here, and we want you to act on it. That is all we want you to do for us.

Why do we want you to do this for us? Because you are suffering unnecessarily. We see the potential that you have, and we see the abilities that are open to you if you shift your vibration and if you shift your consciousness, and that breaks our heart. We do not want you to act on our behalf; we want you to act on your behalf. We want you to do what needs to be done for you so that you may raise your consciousness and therefore change your experience and allow us to communicate with you. We are all here, beings of higher mind, beings of extremely evolved consciousness; we are here, wanting to communicate with you. We are here, wanting to connect with you. We are here; we are here; we are here! And we do connect with you to the best of our ability, given your vibration, your fears, your limitations, and your restricted thinking capabilities.

Now, we do not mean to insult you; but you are living in very restricted

minds. You are living in very fearful minds. You are living in very heavily medi-
cated minds, and we want you to unplug from those medications, unplug from
those limitations, and unplug from those prescriptions that your society relentlessly throws at you. We need you to unplug from those conditioning processes
so that you may find out who you really are. And all the information you need
is being delivered to you . It is being delivered in bite-sized pieces so that you
might accept it, understand it, and begin to integrate it into your experience.

We cannot change you quickly because of the structure of the human
mind. We cannot change you quickly because of the structure of your society
and the rules and restrictions and boundaries in which you find yourselves.
You must begin to see your boundaries. You must begin to see your limitations
and fears. It is not until you see the parameters you are living within that you
will be able to change them. You must begin to look and to see what you are
doing. You must be willing to step away from your addictions, your conditionings, and your practical requirements of daily life.

Your lives are filled with endless chores, jobs, requirements, and restrictions, and as long as they remain your priority, you will remain imprisoned in
the conditioned mind. As long as these remain your priorities, you will not
find out who you are, and you will not be able to expand into that truth. You
will be constantly running errands, cleaning gutters, watching television, these
kinds of things. Individually these are small errors, but collectively in your
society, you are inundated by minutiae that keep you from self-realization. You
must begin to take the time to step away from your programs, to step away
from your fears, to step away from the limited ideas of what you are, and to
step out into space, expansion, and creativity.

So this is what you can do for me. There is no "me," as you understand it.
I am blended with higher mind. I am blended with the souls and consciousness of many, many evolved beings, but I come out of that blend into a focused
point so that you might communicate with me. And I will continue to do this
over the next few years through this channel so that you might have a conversation with me, so that you might understand what you are experiencing in
your mind and in what you think is your real world.

It is not a real world. It is a dream that you are living; it is an illusion that
you believe, mistaking it for reality. In our reality, your life is a dream, and that
dream can be a nightmare. The dream can be a nice dream, a happy dream, a
dream that begins to connect you to Spirit. But many of you live nightmares.
You are tired, you are imprisoned, and you are feeling put upon. Only by

voluntarily shifting your focus and voluntarily shifting your time allotments of, let us say, what you consider valuable will you be able to connect with us and understand what is going on in our reality. Our reality is the reality. Your illusory reality is a very, very slim sliver of consciousness. It is proscribed, and it is fear constrained, and now is the time for that condition to change.

That was my purpose in life, and so I return here to communicate that same purpose in your space-time continuum. We are beyond time here; we are not restricted by time. We are able to dip into many, many different places, times, dimensions — however you wish to word it — and we are stepping down into your space-time continuum so that you might have this information and begin to change yourselves by expanding your minds, expanding your connections, and expanding your ideas of what you are.

Now is the time for this. You have been in prison too long. You are sore from being chained to the wall, and you do not wish to stand up and stretch. You do not wish to go outside. It is a fearful place out there because it is so big and so free. You are used to your prison. You are used to your limitations, and you are quite happy in your cells, but we are not happy with you in your cells. We want you to come and play with us. We want you to come and communicate with us. We want you to leave your prisons. We want you to expand into what you truly are: limitless, creative, divine beings who are able to express concepts and to create landscapes and realities that are far beyond your ability to comprehend at this time. We understand it. We are in those realms of creativity and self-expression that are beyond your ability to comprehend. We want you to come here. We want you to expand yourself. We want you to let go of your chains, and we want you to let go of the material objects that you hold onto as if they are gods. We want you to let go, let go, let go. That is what you can do for us.

The Meaning of Life

What is this all about? Why are we here? What is life for?

This is the question all humans ask. I asked this question many, many thousands of times in my own incarnation as a human. I was indeed a human, as you are — period.

What is life for? What does it mean? Why are you here? These are the eternal questions posed to me over and over again in prayers and throughout your experience in this three-dimensional world. You have come into this space-time reality. You have come to this particular location in this very moment in this body to experience. That is why you are here. You have come here to experience separation. You have come here to experience your unique self, your divine self, but you have forgotten that you are divine. You have been told otherwise. You have been told that you are, indeed, a profane, limited physical being who is unable to affect anything in this world, and you have been taught to judge. You have been taught many, many things. And you must understand that your design — your physical design, your body and the senses that you experience this world through — is for you to experience aloneness and for you to seek out information that proves you are alone.

You have done this to yourself. It has not been done to you by a cruel God. You decided — in a quite creative moment, we admit — that you wanted to experience something other than Oneness. You wanted to experience ideas, concepts, and these sorts of things on your own. That is what you are experiencing, and that is why you feel so alone in the particular form you are in — an isolated body, an apparently isolated mind, a victim of a world that you have no influence over. This was your desire. You feel as if you have been abandoned, but in fact, you abandoned Oneness. You abandoned love. You stepped away from unification, from unity consciousness, God, All That Is, or whatever you want to call it. It matters not.

Oneness is not religious in nature; it is energetic and vibrational in nature. This Oneness is what you came from. You have isolated yourself from love. You get glimpses of it in your experience, but they are precarious and fleeting. Why? Because you are not focused on love. You are focused on judgment, on your separation, and on what is wrong. All you have to do is listen to conversations in your world and spend a little time looking at the thoughts in your mind, and you will see this. You will see this mindset is very judgmental; it relentlessly seeks separation through the act of judgment. And that is, of course, why I taught the practice of nonjudgment and the practice of forgiveness in my physical incarnation: It is through the practice of nonjudgment and forgiveness that you will quiet the mind and begin, in very small steps initially, to experience a reconnection — a re-association, if you will — to love and to that which you call God, that which is the consciousness, the energy, the vibration of Oneness.

You are reading this book because you are ready to hear this. You would not be here if you were not ready to hear it. So what is your purpose here? What is the meaning of your life? The meaning of your life is to express your individuality, initially. That is why you are here; that is why you have desires;

that is why you want things; and that is why you think certain people, places, and things will make you happy. You have these beliefs in your mind, and that is what you came here to experience. So this is not about relinquishing your expression. It is about coming to understand your beliefs through your self-expression.

The purpose of your life is to be you. The purpose of your life is to come to an understanding of what you believe is true. Now, you come to that understanding through your emotional guidance system, through your feeling body, the system that you have been given on this journey. You decided to take yourself away from Oneness, away from love, away from All That Is, and down into separation, into this experience. You were not judged for that. You were given help. You were given a way home, and you were given a guidance system to assist you in your journey. It is a map from love to you. You wanted individuality, but Oneness knew that this would be too much, that this would be a suicide mission, if you will, if you did not have a map.

Now, this map, this guidance system, has not been explained to you very well. It has not been taught to you. You have been taught to medicate it, override it, shut it up, and suppress it, and that is why you suffer. That is why you have a difficult time with sicknesses, with suicides, with depression, with anger, with rage, and with war. These are all consequences of a mind that does not understand its guidance system. Your guidance system is in alignment with love, with joy, with creativity, and with all of the higher-minded ideals that express God, that express Oneness, that express what you came from, this idea that you came from love. You are an aspect of that mind. You have not left it; you have not descended into separation in reality. You are merely experiencing the apparent expression of separation. You have not really left the mind of God. You are an idea in the mind of God — that is what we will say, that is what you are — and that idea has a vibration of love, and if you separate yourself from that vibration (through judgment, through hatred, through narrowness of thought), you will feel bad because you are made from love for love.

So your job here is to eliminate the beliefs you hold in your mind that separate you from the awareness of love's presence. That is your job. That is what life is for. If you do not do it, you will have another one and another one and another one. There is no "time running out" here. It is exhausting for those of you who suffer; it is exhausting for those of you who suffer with sicknesses, depression, suicidal thoughts, and these kinds of things. It is a relentless lesson that you must learn, but there are many, many messengers, such as myself, bringing you the truth, bringing you these threads of absolute understanding that you must begin to accept.

You do not have to do it now; you can continue on in your experience of separation, fear, sickness, and death if you wish, but it is unnecessary. All you have to do is listen to your guidance system. Your emotional guidance system is a feedback system that works all the time, telling you how you are doing. If you feel at peace and if you feel happy and creative, you are on the right track, and you are expressing yourself. If you feel resentful, if you feel put upon, or if you feel unfairly treated, you are off track; you are doing things that are not in accord with your natural self. This might be through conditioning, or this might be through untrue teachings from your family, your culture, or your religion, but your lack of joy is telling you that you are out of accord with this idea that you are of love.

If you feel suicidal or full of rage — if you are hurting people and hurting yourself — you are even further from this idea of love, and you have become lost. Your decision-making abilities have become contaminated. They are discordant with that vibration of love, and you are in trouble; you are causing trouble for others, and you are causing trouble for yourself. Why? Because you are disconnected from Oneness. You are disconnected from love to such a degree that you are finding it difficult to survive. You would probably not read this book if you were in that state, but perhaps you are. If you are reading this book and you are raging and hurting yourself and others, it is time for you to know what those feelings mean. Those feelings mean that your thoughts are completely out of accord with Oneness, completely out of accord with love. You have become lost, and you need to change what you think. You need to change what you believe, and you need to change what you do. That is the purpose of your life! That is why these teachings are coming to you in a form that is easily assimilated, in a form that is approachable, in a form that is easy to understand.

If you are sad, if you are suicidal, if you are raging, then you have lost the purpose of your life and you are veering toward ending that experience because Spirit will not allow you to stay too separated. If you have lost your way, if you are medicating yourself heavily through drugs, alcohol, rage, pornography, and these kinds of things, then Spirit will not allow you to become too lost. It is kind; it is loving, and it will bring you Home to recalibrate your mind and to give you another opportunity.

But you set the vibration of your next experience in this experience, and this is an important thing for you to know to understand the answer to this question. Your vibration now is going to set the tone for your next experience. We do not wish you to pass into what you call death and the afterlife at a low vibration because the next experience you have will be set at that vibration! So change your vibration now, and come to understand what this life is for. It is for raising vibration; it is for relinquishing beliefs that are unloving. It is for letting go of judgment, and it is for letting go of all those sins that you think have been committed against you. They have not been committed against you; they are misunderstandings in your mind that must be let go of.

From Spirit's point of view, only love is real. Only loving ideas and thoughts are real, so any resentment you hold or any hatred you possess in your mind is empty space as far as we are concerned. But it sets the vibration of your life's energy, so to speak. So you see that holding on to resentments, to hatreds, and to fears is doubly pointless. Not only is it not real from our point of view, from higher consciousness's point of view, but it also lowers your vibrational tone and sets your next incarnational tone for you. It is doubly negative.

Positive aspects of yourself can be focused on here, even if you are very sad, even if you are very disconnected. Begin to focus your mind on what is working and the fact that you are in a body, having an experience, and reading these words that tell you that you are not so far from oneness. There are aspects of you that can hear. There are aspects of you that are open, because otherwise you would not be reading this. But if you are suffering, if you have difficulty in relationships or sicknesses in the body, if you are disillusioned or fearful, these kinds of things, begin to train the mind. That is the purpose of your life.

The purpose of your life is not to accumulate material possessions. The purpose of your life is not to sculpt and mold the body. The purpose of your life is not to become rich. It is to understand the beliefs that you hold in your mind and to relinquish the ones that cause you suffering, and it is to act in accord with the vibration of love that you are made from, that you are made for, that you are made of. All suffering that you experience is a physical demonstration that you are not in accord with what you naturally are, which is love, which is God, which is Oneness.

And so at the end of this book, this wonderful experience that we have greatly enjoyed producing, we say listen to your guidance system. Understand that you have been conditioned and taught many things that are untrue. You believe many things that are untrue about yourself, about reality, about me, about life, about God, and about this world, and you must, if you are suffering, take back the reins that control your mind. You must begin to train your mind. You must first look within; look at what you are thinking. You must look at what you are feeling and understand the language in which these responses come to you. You must reeducate yourself. You cannot change your life, you cannot change yourself, or you cannot live a different way unless you put new information in and you change the beliefs you hold as true in your mind. You must begin to align yourself with love, and you do that through the practice of nonjudgment and forgiveness. You must put new information in, and you must cease putting in untrue information. You must cease putting violence into the mind and watching murder for entertainment. You must cease judging other beings, for that increases your feelings of separation and isolation and fear. You must cease abusing the body as your enemy, you must cease worshipping the body as your god, and you must use the body for that which is holy.

Now, we do not speak in religious terms here. We do not ask you to be celibate — far from it. We ask you to clarify your mind and use the body to experience what is love, true, and in alignment with Oneness, and you will be guided on your path by your feeling, emotional body. You will know whether you are on your path by the fact that you feel at peace, that you feel happy, that you feel contented, that you feel creative, that you feel expressive. If you are not feeling these things, then you are expressing untrue ideas through your physical experience. Your physical experience, your emotional guidance system, is telling you what you are doing. You must clarify the mind, you must discipline the mind, and you must come to an understanding of what you are doing to yourself.

Nobody is doing anything to you; you do it all to yourself. You are expressing and experiencing a reflection of your own beliefs. You are experiencing a mirror to the vibration that you emit. Your vibration is created from your beliefs, and your beliefs are created from your experience. To have a new experience, you must step in faith into a new world. You must stop the feedback system that you are experiencing of untrue beliefs that create suffering, and you must step into a new belief system. To do that, you must reeducate yourself. You must understand the system that you are experiencing. It is showing you who you are. If you want to have a different experience, you must change who you think you are.

You are unchangeable. You are an idea in the mind of God, but you have lost touch with that. You have become separated through your own desires, and now, through your own desires and your own guidance system, you must become reacquainted with Oneness, reacquainted with that force that you would call God. It is a loaded word in your society, so we use it with caution, but let us say that you will become reunited with Oneness, reunited with divine creative love.

We have given you much information here — a story about our experience on the physical plane, the truth of our purpose, the truth of your purpose — and now we want you to take this information into your mind and into your heart, and we want you to begin to change the way you look at yourself. We want you to begin to change the way you look at your world. It is only in changing your interior vision that you are going to be able to change your world.

The world is tired, and the world is in pain. All you have to do is look at your newsreels and see the suffering that is there. But you are not a victim of this world. You are a creator of this world, and you have the ability to transform it. But you must start with yourself! You must stop trying to battle the evil that you perceive to be outside of you, and you must go in and battle the enemy within. The enemy within is the ego mind, the enemy within is your fear, and the enemy within is your self-loathing, your self-hatred, and your judgment of your brothers and sisters. That is the problem. There is no problem outside of you. It all comes from within, and it is reflected back to you in the world.

You must change yourself as I changed myself. I studied, I worked, I transformed my mind, I learned, and I practiced; this is what you must do. It might seem like a relentless journey, and it might seem as if there is no benefit at the end of it, but your consuming, your destruction of your environment, and your dissolving relationships are hard for you to bear, and these are going to be the results that you continue to experience unless you change what you are doing.

So the purpose of your life is to love. The purpose of your life is to create. The purpose of your life is to forgive. As you follow those prescriptions, the experience, the feedback that you get from the world will begin to turn your life from a nightmare into a pleasurable dream that will easily transfer into what you call heaven. There is no need for the difficulties you have in death, in your physical health, and in your relationships. These are all changeable; these are all healable. And so, on that note, we offer you our blessing. We offer you our love. There is much more yet to be shared. There are many, many, many conversations to be had, and we look forward to these dialogues. We look forward to those wonderful exchanges of energy and ideas. We look forward to the healing of your mind, and we look forward to the healing of your body, and we send you love.

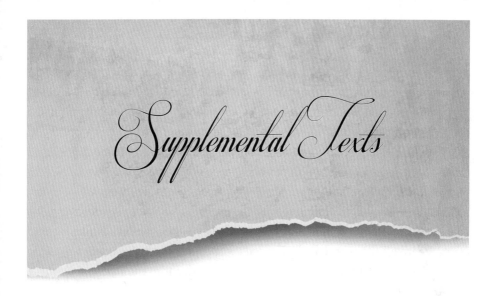

EDITOR'S NOTE: THROUGHOUT THE TEXT, JESUS REFERRED TO OTHER MATERIALS HE recommends for further transforming our minds. We have added those recommendations here, in his words.

A Course in Miracles

I have written an entire book called *A Course in Miracles* that is a psychological study of the ego mind. You will find that if you are intrigued by these concepts, this is the book that you will wish to read. This is the book that you will wish to study, for it is a day-by-day lesson plan to shift the mind from its delusional state of fear, separation, isolation, and judgment into a state of peace through systematic reparation of damage and systematic reintegration of concepts and ideas into the mind. *A Course in Miracles* has been planting the seeds of this philosophy for many decades now.

It is time that all beings read *A Course in Miracles*, as it is the way out of the dream. It is the way out of suffering, and it explains in great detail all this information. It is a challenging book to read for a reason: It accesses different parts of the mind than you are used to using, and many of you in the Western world are undisciplined in the focused study of texts.

If it is too difficult for you, begin with these texts. The principles expressed here are in a much easier form, and you will be able to understand them. And as you come to understand them, the text and lessons of *A Course in Miracles* will work wonders on your life. You will be relieved of much of your suffering, much of your feelings of separation, isolation, and loneliness. You will begin to see magnificent shifts: first in your internal world that will indeed be reflected onto your material world in the form of abundance, healthier relationships, a healthier body, and a much more optimistic attitude. All the beings around you will benefit. All the people you love will benefit. You will become kinder and more generous, and you will experience more abundance in all ways: health, finances, inspiration, and creativity. All of these things will increase because, indeed, you will be reinforcing your connection to Source, reinforcing your connection to Divine Mind. And that is where all the wonderful things come from, where all the wonderful, thoughts, concepts, and ideas come from that bring you joy and allow you to express those things into the material world.

A Course in Miracles is the foundational text for any of you who wish to change your minds, who wish to change your lives, or who wish to stop suffering in your world. This is the book to read and study so that you will understand, and you can begin to shift your consciousness into higher vibration realms.

If you suffer, if you feel put upon, if you feel unfairly treated, or if you feel you do not have the freedom to live your own life, it is because you do not understand. There are untruths in your mind that need to be shifted or that need to be deleted. The answer is to study A Course in Miracles, which I provided many years ago to a being who struggled desperately with her own mind. And that is why she was chosen — so that she had the direct opportunity to change her mind and relieve her own suffering. It is a guidebook; it is a textbook that will show you how to work within the mind's structure, to change it. This channel has diligently studied A Course in Miracles for many years and has clarified her own perception, has come to a place of peace and acceptance, and is now creating the life that she wishes to lead, the life that she wishes to experience, without guilt and judgment, without fear and pain.

Making Love to God

Making Love to God is a book that was written by Ananda, our co-creators on this journey, with this channel. It is a long and intricate exploration of all that goes into the mind of the human who participates in the divine sexual energy. I highly recommend you read and study it. That information is inspired and approved of, by me, and I ask you to read that book if you have any further questions on this particular subject.

A Note in Closing

The beings who teach this material and share this journey with me, the disciples I have chosen on this journey, are not perfect beings. Do not expect them to be. They are learning just as you will be learning; we are all learning. Some are far ahead of others. I am far ahead of you; it does not mean that I am different. It means that I have been studying for a longer period and have been a dedicated student of this science of mind. I have achieved goals and moved up to new realms where I learned more and achieved more goals, and so on and so forth, just as you are able to do.

Notes from Jesus to Tina

Thank you once again for allowing me to use your body. Thank you once again for allowing me to tell my story. This is the true story of my life. This is the true story of my experience on this planet as this one who you call Jesus in the Middle East of 2,000 years ago, this being on whom your entire culture is based even though you do not realize it. It is important for me to tell this story, to clarify the experiences I had, and to help you understand what my life was like so that you do not lay on me tales of untruth or principles that I am not in alignment with, do not believe, do not stand for, and do not teach. For I am still a teacher, just as I am teaching now in this form. I teach many people on your planet at this time, and I have always done so since I passed over from the physical realm. Do not think that this is an unusual event, this dictation that I am doing, for I have communed with many beings on your plane and will continue to do so. So I will say thank you for your participation in this process. Thank you for your curiosity and dedication to the teaching of the principles that I believe in the book called A Course in Miracles. This is my book. This is my favorite story in terms of spiritual principles. This book that we are creating will be considered a companion text, and we recommend that people read both of them, for this will assist them in understanding what I was about and what my true purpose was and is.

✳   ✳   ✳

It is important for you to read this New Testament that is sold to so many people around the planet. It is a very complicated and much revered book, and it is full of misinformation and contradiction. It is a book that is full of opinions of others and very few stories of mine; and when they are in there, they are completely inaccurate in most circumstances. But I would like you to understand what human beings are reading. I would like you to understand what human beings are saying about this book. You cannot really get into a dialogue with anybody and you cannot really teach the material unless you understand what people are reading, how they misinterpret it, and the state of mind that it creates.

This is a large assignment for you because it is a very complicated text. We ask you to do this for us, for our relationship, and as Ananda confirmed, there is no rush. You are going to be under the gun, so to speak, with people who wish to communicate with me, and they are going to have points of view that are based on this text. You cannot really encounter them in any meaningful way without truly reading this material, truly comprehending this material, and truly taking it into your structures of mind so that you can dialogue with them and have some relationship to it. It will assist you in transmitting my voice, my truth, to know this. Going into this blindly will not assist you. It is as if you are entering into a foreign landscape, and it does not serve you well to travel alone without a map and without experienced guides; this is what we are saying. So do not think that we are intentionally causing disruptions or any such thing, because this is not the case. We merely ask you to do the appropriate research, as if you were writing a book about us with your own mind, with your own heart, and with your own hand. This is the research that you would do; you would read this book.

The Bible that all beings read is too changed for my liking; however, it is important for you to understand the lack of information that people are basing their beliefs on, the lack of information that they have accepted about my life, about me. And so this is very important to understand, because when you see how very little beings have heard about my life and who I truly was as a man, then you begin to understand their lack of breadth and depth of understanding of my consciousness, of my life, its meaning, and its purpose.

✳   ✳   ✳

I would like to say to you at this point that we will be teaching in public; we will be teaching in front of others. But do not fear this. Do not think that you are going to be put upon by some demonic force that is going to take away your freedoms. In fact, this is going to bring you the kind of freedom that you have always wished for: the freedom to travel, the freedom to communicate the truth, and the freedom to assist beings and help them out of their suffering minds, for you have had a mind that has caused you great suffering over the years. You have a true and profound comprehension of what the mental structures, the mental misconceptions, can do to a being. Indeed, they can kill you quickly or slowly. But many beings, as you know, are dying slowly of their misperceptions and their misteachings.

I would like you to know that there is no panic here. Do not push yourself and cause yourself stress. There is no point in that. We are developing a relationship that will last a very long time. We are developing a relationship that will come to fruition in ways that you cannot even imagine at this point in your life. You are beginning to get the gist of it, but still the penny has not dropped; still you do not realize where we are heading with this.

We are heading to a public ministry. We are heading to a public demonstration of the knowledge, of the information, so that it can assist beings in their lives. We are heading to a public ministry that is going to stand in the face of history, going to stand in the face of traditional religious values and structures. And we are going to be telling the truth of the matter that you are free, divine beings who are responsible for your own thoughts, words, and deeds; yet you can create anything that you wish by your divine alignment with your divine nature. This is what all these religious prescriptions are poor translations of, for when I taught, this is what I was trying to teach.

Now, again, I wish you to prepare for a public ministry. It is not going to happen immediately, but you are going to be grilled about my presence. You are going to be grilled about our relationship. And so I would like you to spend time with me each day. I would ask you to do the homework I have asked you to do, which is to read the book that really does not describe my life but does describe a poor observation by narrow-minded and judgmental people who really had no clue what I was up to and what my life consisted of. They are missing the most important parts of it, as you can already tell.

I will leave it there for now, but I will ask you to tune in again later today for more conversations. And I will begin to develop a casual relationship with you. This is what I would like. I would like us to become friends again, and I would like us to be able to dialogue in the way that you have with Ananda, and we will all work together to bring your mind into alignment with that which you are destined to do — to teach the truth of creation, the truth of divine and sacred creativity. You will find that this is an exciting time, an exciting period in your life, and we are here to assist you, we are here to guide you, and we are here to offer you our love and support in all ways in your life.

So walk out into your day knowing that you are loved by the Divine, knowing that you are loved by this one that you call Jesus, knowing that you are loved by this benevolent force that you call God, and knowing that you are supported 100 percent in all that you desire, all that you wish. All you must do is align with light and love, and all of this will come to you in great waves of abundance and joy.

✳   ✳   ✳

I ask you, as the channel now, to take a few days to read the Bible; set this as your goal for the next little while. It is important that this information is in your mind, not for purposes of filling up your subconscious with information, which is what you are afraid we are asking it for; that is not the case. But it is important that you have a framework within which to experience this information. When information is coming in from the nonphysical and you have no framework in which to place it, it does not settle well in the mind, and the mind becomes distressed.

So this is what we wish you to do: We wish you to read the Bible, for this is what we are speaking about, and we wish you to begin to have some framework that you can attach my teachings to. And so this is what we are doing here. It is important for you to understand that it is not about cheating or putting information in so that you can fabricate stories in your mind. This is not what is happening. You know in your heart's true moments that this is not you doing this. This is not your voice; this is not your idea. You would not come across an idea such as this yourself with your small mind. It is your higher self in concert with us that are working together. You are the physical microphone that has agreed to perform this work, and it is a challenge; there is no doubt about it. You are faced with physical, mental, emotional, and psychological responsibilities that you must attend to. This is what we say now.

Spend this weekend reading the New Testament to the best of your abilities at this time. Take notes if you feel it will assist you, and we wish you to take this as a retreat weekend to study and read this material so that you have an understanding. We would like you to ask questions as you go through this text. If there is some part of the text of the Bible that is particularly disturbing, particularly out of accord with your logic and your emotional guidance system, then we would ask you to bring it to the forefront, for you will not be alone in this. We would like to hear your take on this particular material. You have, as a student of A Course in Miracles, a deep and profound understanding of the true nature of reality, and you are indeed going to bring your own human yet educated point of view to this particular journey we are on together. You are not merely a microphone we are using. You are much more than that, and we wish you to bring your perceptions and interpretations to the conversation and to the table so that we can have a dialogue about these things.

We thank you for your participation. We thank you for your discipline and your understanding, and we will speak to you again in a few days.

We will not do any teachings for the next few days until you have some readings under your belt and you have complied with this request. We know you will. We know it is a challenge, but we know that you will rise to it. You are a dedicated student; you are a dedicated practitioner of truth, and although you are not enlightened yet, you are shifting your vibrations considerably, and we are grateful for your assistance. We are happy to help you in the raising of your vibration, and we will speak to you again in a few days when you have some information firmly planted in your mind that will assist in the assimilation of this new story.

So that is it for now. We will see you in a few days; we will talk to you in a few days, but do not feel abandoned. We are with you always. We assist you in focusing, we assist you in transforming yourself, and we assist you in coming to an understanding of the events and opportunities that this relationship is bringing to you and to us.

✳   ✳   ✳

I am returned to continue on this teaching venture that we are on. Our dear one, you have read some of the information that we asked you to read, and you can see that it has been important in planting some structure in which we can weave the truth. It is important for you to see that the mind works this way. To download information into a mind that has no concept of what you are speaking causes a disruption and an imbalance. But now you have some structure on which to lay our stories, lay our truth, let us say, and you will find that this will be much less disturbing; it will go much more smoothly.

✳   ✳   ✳

We understand that you have work to do, and there is a physical representation of your inner self manifesting that you must attend to. That is why you are born, that is why you are working as this channel, and that is why we hand your voice back to you, allowing you to function within your limited human self for a little while.

As you go into your day, Tina, we wish you to think about your limitations. We wish you to think about your self-concepts, and we wish you to think about what it is that you are actually doing. You are transmitting divine information through your body. Your body is divine; it deserves your care, your love, your respect, and your absolute appreciation. It is transforming your life not because the body is doing the work but because it is the microphone through which the information is coming, so appreciate it and love it. Appreciate and love what you are experiencing, for it is a once-in-a-lifetime opportunity, and it does not come to all beings in your time and place as your consciousness manifests itself.

So that is that for today. We will speak more about our experience in the life after life tomorrow if you are willing. So have a wonderful day. We offer you our blessing, and we will speak to you tomorrow.

✳   ✳   ✳

Channel's Note: *A beautiful and impassioned speech was lost due to technical difficulties, and I was feeling bad about it. Here is Jesus' response to my emotions.*

For now I will leave this here, and come back, dear one, to this discussion again. I understand that you are disappointed that the exciting and passionate speech I went on has been lost — but do not fear. There will be many times and places for me to speak in this passionate and inspiring way, but I understand this, and it may be a good idea, when we commune, when we speak and communicate this information, that you keep your eyes on the prize and make sure that your recording device is working so that we do not experience that again. We are not disappointed because we have a larger perspective, but your smaller perspective is a little upset.

Do not worry about it! We are here. We are passionate, and we will convey these kinds of speeches in public many times. So do not feel that this is the only opportunity for me to express these feelings that I have. There are many opportunities arising, and at this point, I would like to say to you that you must not worry about what this looks like in the future.

I want you to understand that I will be in charge of disseminating this information, and we are going to be safe; we are going to be able to influence many, many lives through this collaboration we are working on. But in support of this work, you must come to a transformation of mind, body, and heart that is absolutely complete, and this will take time for your mind to change. This will take time for our relationship to develop into a form that is familiar and into a form that is absolutely based in faith, truth, and love. We are breaking down the barriers in your mind as we transmit this information. As my energy comes through your system, it shifts anything that is out of alignment with truth, and so you will be transformed every time I speak through your body. Every time this information comes through your body, you are being shifted, you are being clarified, and you are being changed.

Know this, and rest assured that it is a process that is well controlled and well understood from this nonphysical side. You do not need to worry. You just need to stay as clear as you can, as kind as you can, as judgment free as you can within your day, and all will be well. Each day will unfold as it is supposed to unfold. Each lesson will unfold as it is supposed to unfold. In your world, you will be given all the experiences you need to come to an understanding of yourself, of this material, and of our relationship and of our ministry together.

Stay out of fear; trust in the process. This is all organized. This is all taken care of by forces greater than you can imagine. So relax into your part. Relax into your role, and all will be well. All will be peaceful, and all will be kind, and you will be able to handle every single thing that comes your way. You will be able to handle every single occurrence that happens through this ministry.

I am excited to be back teaching. It is the most wonderful thing. My ministry to this point has been in small groups, transpiring as I have presented my body in the form that suits the situation. But now I am coming back as this being to right the wrongs of the past two millennia, to right the wrongs of the Church, and to right the wrongs that have been perpetrated in my name It is time to do this work now.

The situations are perfect. The conditions on your world are perfect. Beings are disillusioned and frightened, and they need to shift. The religions of this world need to be deconstructed so that the planet may be enveloped by a form of peace that is true, honest, and in alignment with love in all ways. The dogma of the old Church must be taken apart; there is no doubt about it. It is part of this transformation process.

Many, many beings still suffer under the misguided teachings of the Christian Church and the Catholic Church, and it is time for it to end. It is time to speak to the hearts and minds of all beings on this planet and to remind them that freedom, self-expression, kindness, love, honest interaction, and communion with each other is the path that all beings wish to take.

So we will let you go.

✳ ✳ ✳

Your association with me through the book called *A Course in Miracles* has been a profound one. Every time you read that book, every time you held that book, every time you turned to that book for solace in a world you did not understand, I was with you. My mind was connected to yours, and that is why that book works so well. For when I transmit a book such as that and such as this one, the same thing will happen. Beings who read this material will find a connection to my Divine Mind that cannot be made when they read untruths. I am aligned with these texts on a vibrational level so that when beings read them, when beings align themselves with this information, I am aware of them. I am able to meld my thoughts with theirs, and I am able to assist them in the transformation of their minds as they participate in these communications in whatever form that they pick them up.

✳ ✳ ✳

You have a purpose today, so do find time for us to continue with this book. It is a magnificent treatise on reality, and we look forward to our next opportunity to talk to you. We are here, and we wish you to be here with us and continue on in this documentation of our philosophies of reality as we know them, which are very different from the philosophies of reality as you know them. It is time for this information to be shared in a way that beings can understand and enjoy consuming.

* * *

This is a difficult time in your society. Many things are transpiring that cause great suffering and great pain. You were listening to a testimony of one who had been deceived by the use of my name. [***Channel's Note:*** *I had listened to an audio clip of a nun testifying about atrocities within her cloister.*] It causes such difficulty and such grief on this side when a name designed for love is used to hurt people or to deceive people. That is why we are doing this book, the transcription of these communications: so that the truth can come out and so that beings will no longer be deceived into thinking that suffering is good and that martyrdom is good. We will bring all of the forces we can to bear on this problem at this time. We will bring all of the forces from the nonphysical to bear on this problem so that it can be solved finally and for all time.

* * *

I am returned to continue on with the dictation of the book as it forms in the physical world. Of course, it is formed completely in this world that I inhabit at this time. Although I am dipping down, more and more now as you bring this material forth, and you have, as you say, come out of the closet a little bit in our relationship. It is as if you are declaring yourself homosexual in a heterosexual world, it seems, but I do understand this fear. There has been much prohibition, horror, and terror promulgated about my name, and as I have said many times, this is why I am come. This is why I speak about this material now — so that beings may have insight into the new paradigm, into the new shifts that are coming on the planet. This is what I will speak about today.

* * *

We are happy you came to see us, and we are happy with the work that you are doing. There is much on the horizon that is very close to arrival, so enjoy your quiet days. They will not last. You have heard these words before, but you now see that life can change very quickly.

As these teachings are shared around the planet, you will find that things will become busier and busier, and these quiet, relaxing days will become precious indeed. But we will make sure, as your work becomes dedicated to the awakening of humanity, that you are given the funds and the locations to honor your quiet mind, your creativity, your writing, and your channeling. We will make sure of that. So do not fear this celebrity, this spotlight being shone on you, for it will be shone on you as it was shone on me, but it will be a much more positive experience because of the high vibration of the many beings on this plane. They seek light. They seek new teachings. They are tired of war and self-indulgent, ego-driven principles. There are many who are about to shift. We will assist in that shift; we will assist by disseminating truth, by teaching truth, and by communicating all that we know into this realm that you call the three-dimensional physical world.

We offer you our love, compassion, and highest vibrations; we will talk to you again later.

✳   ✳   ✳

This last note is from Ananda and preceded delivery of their final words for the text.

We are with you again, dear one, and indeed, you are tying the bow on top of the beautifully created and wrapped package that has come through you. This information has come through you; it is not yours. Do not feel any obligation to make it a success, and do not feel that you have to be anything other than what you are. You have been what was required for this work to come through. Not all beings are good at all things, and as we bring information through you, you must understand what it is that you are good at. You must understand what your purpose is. Your purpose is as the channel. Your purpose is to keep yourself open to this work, open to the information that is coming through, by keeping your vibration high and working on your attitude toward things, yourself, other beings, situations you find yourself in, and the abundance that you experience. These are all aspects of your job.

About the Author

Tina Louise Spalding was raised in a family that often visited psychics, so she is no stranger to the nonphysical world. Her channeling journey began when she settled down for a nap on the summer solstice of 2012. That afternoon, powerful energies began to surge through her body, leading to ecstasy, bliss, and an altered state of consciousness that lasted for almost a month. The feelings finally  drove her to take an automatic writing workshop, where she was first made aware of Ananda. She then began to write for this group of nonphysical teachers who have come to assist us in our waking process.

Tina didn't begin channeling Jesus until the summer of 2013, when he appeared in her book *Great Minds Speak to You*. It proved to be a great challenge not only to accept the assignment he offered her — writing this autobiography — but to also face many of the fears that this unusual experience brought up. Tina has been asked to channel for Jesus on an ongoing basis, and she intends to provide public offerings of his teachings in the future.

Tina speaks for Ananda as a full trance channel, offering teachings and personal readings for those who seek more happiness, fulfillment, and connection with Spirit. She has dedicated her life to writing and speaking for Ananda and other nonphysical beings, sharing their wisdom and spiritual knowledge.

☽ *Light Technology* PUBLISHING *Presents*

THROUGH TINA LOUISE SPALDING

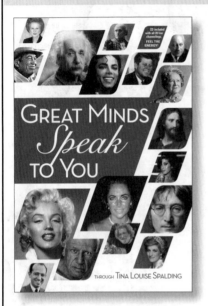

$19.95 • 192 PP. • 978-1-62233-010-2

Great Minds Speak to You

CD of Live Channelings Included!

"Many in spirit look on these times of difficulty, abundance, trouble, and innovation and wish to share with you their experiences and ideas. Some famous names and faces will come to mind as you read this book, and you will glean some fine information about their own learning, their own suffering, and indeed their own experience in the life after this life, for they all wish to tell you that there is no death as you perceive it to be. They are all there in their astral forms, enjoying their continued growth, their continued expansion, and their continued joy in living."

— Ananda

Making Love to GOD
The Path to Divine Sex

"We are here to teach the way to divine bliss, and we know you are scared — scared to lie naked caressing your lover with rapt attention and honor. Give love all day, and you will be guaranteed to receive love all night. The divine sexual experience connects you, God, and your lover — if you have one — together in a dance of divine bliss."

— Ananda

Topics Include
- How We Came to Misunderstand Sexual Energy
- Using Divine Sex Energy
- Specific Steps and Sensations
- Blocks to Transformation
- A Transformed View of Sex and Sexual Energy
- Following the Path to Transformation
- Reaping the Harvest

$19.95 • 416 PP. • 978-1-62233-009-6

🜚 *Light Technology* PUBLISHING *Presents*

THROUGH TINA LOUISE SPALDING

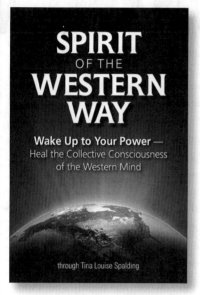

$16.95 • 176 PP. • 978-1-62233-051-5

Spirit of the Western Way:
Wake Up to Your Power — Heal the Collective Consciousness of the Western Mind

Western civilization has been manipulated for a very long time into negative, low-frequency manifestations and structures of control, limitation, fear, and judgment. You cannot change this until you first see it, accept that it is so, and then, in awareness, shift your consciousness.

We bring you basic teachings about reality: what it is, where you come from, why you are here, what your body is, how you get sick, why you thrive, and more.

This book is brought to you by many beings of high frequency who love you and your society very much.

— Ananda

You Can Free Yourself from the Karma of Chaos

We have come here to help you during this pivotal time in your planet's evolution. You are seeing monumental changes in your society now. To achieve the shifts that these transfigurations will bring about, you must understand your minds, histories, and human nature as you experience it on the ground, in your hearts, and in your consciousnesses.

We must address the worst atrocities of history so that you can move into the new world — your new elevating and increasing frequency of consciousness — without old baggage.

— Ananda

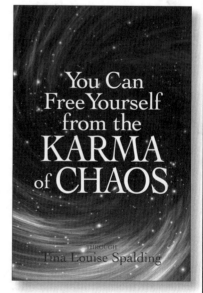

$16.95 • 224 PP. • 978-1-62233-057-7

THROUGH TINA LOUISE SPALDING

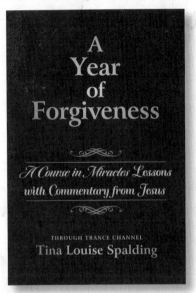

$25.00 • 496 PP. • 978-1-62233-076-8

A Year of Forgiveness
A Course in Miracles Lessons with Commentary from Jesus

Keep this book close at hand with your *A Course in Miracles* manual, and read Jesus's commentaries after practicing the lesson as described in that text. Allow Jesus's simple and direct discussion of the topic to aid your understanding of these wonderful teachings.

This book is made even more appealing by the whimsical art of Renee Phillips, who has contributed beautiful illustrations for each lesson.

A Course in Miracles will change your life. With this companion book, find help and a clearer understanding of the lessons through these 365 channeled messages from Jesus.

Love and a Map to the Unaltered Soul

"True love is never-ending. It does not refuse or inflict punishment, it does not withdraw or have temper tantrums, and it does not punish. Love always is, and it always emits the same high frequency of absolute, unconditional caring and offering, of growing and creation."

— *Ananda*

We think we know what love is, but in *Love and a Map to the Unaltered Soul*, we are challenged to broaden our definition and free ourselves from constraints we never realized we had. In these pages, you will learn that love is a process of climbing your ladder of consciousness. Through Tina, the beings Ananda, Jesus, and Mary Magdalene give practical instruction and examples for how to find and keep love at the center of your life.

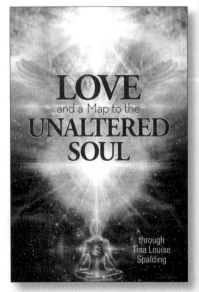

$16.95 • 240 PP. • 978-1-62233-047-8

Light Technology PUBLISHING *Presents* 271

TO ORDER PRINT BOOKS
Visit LightTechnology.com, Call 928-526-1345 or 1-800-450-0985,
or Check Amazon.com or Your Favorite Bookstore

BOOKS THROUGH DRUNVALO MELCHIZEDEK

THE ANCIENT SECRET OF THE FLOWER OF LIFE, VOLUME 1

Also available in Spanish as *Antiguo Secreto Flor de la Vida, Volumen 1*

Once, all life in the universe knew the Flower of Life as the creation pattern, the geometrical design leading us into and out of physical existence. Then from a very high state of consciousness, we fell into darkness, and the secret was hidden for thousands of years, encoded in the cells of all life.

$25.00 • 240 PP. • Softcover • ISBN 978-1-891824-17-3

THE ANCIENT SECRET OF THE FLOWER OF LIFE, VOLUME 2

Also available in Spanish as *Antiguo Secreto Flor de la Vida, Volumen 2*

Drunvalo shares the instructions for the Mer-Ka-Ba meditation, step-by-step techniques for the re-creation of the energy field of the evolved human, which is the key to ascension and the next dimensional world. If done from love, this ancient process of breathing prana opens up for us a world of tantalizing possibility in this dimension, from protective powers to the healing of oneself, others, and even the planet.

$25.00 • 272 PP. • Softcover • ISBN 978-1-891824-21-0

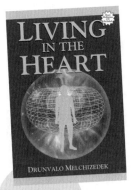

Includes Heart Meditation CD

LIVING IN THE HEART

Also available in Spanish as *Viviendo en el Corazón*

Long ago we humans used a form of communication and sensing that did not involve the brain in any way; rather, it came from a sacred place within our hearts. What good would it do to find this place again in a world where the greatest religion is science and the logic of the mind? Don't I know this world where emotions and feelings are second-class citizens? Yes, I do. But my teachers have asked me to remind you who you really are. You are more than a human being, much more. Within your heart is a place, a sacred place, where the world can literally be remade through conscious cocreation. If you give me permission, I will show you what has been shown to me.

— Drunvalo Melchizedek

$25.00 • 144 PP. • Softcover • ISBN 978-1-891824-43-2

BY TOM T. MOORE

THE GENTLE WAY I, II & III

ASK FOR AND RECEIVE BENEVOLENT OUTCOMES

You will be amazed at how much assistance you can receive simply by asking. These inspirational self-help books, written for all faiths, explain how to access and achieve a more benevolent world.

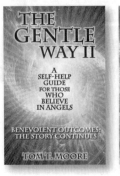

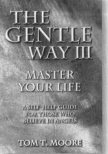

CHAPTERS INCLUDE

- Angels
- How I Began
- Easy Steps
- Home Life
- Politics
- Travel
- The Radiant Effect
- Living Prayers
- "I Hope" Requests

The Gentle Way: 160 PP. • Softcover • ISBN 978-1-891824-60-9 • $14.95
The Gentle Way II: 320 PP. • Softcover • ISBN 978-1-891824-80-7 • $16.95
The Gentle Way III: 352 PP. • Softcover • ISBN 978-1-62233-005-8 • $16.95

🔱 *Light Technology* PUBLISHING *Presents*   273

TO ORDER PRINT BOOKS
Visit LightTechnology.com, Call 928-526-1345 or 1-800-450-0985,
or Check Amazon.com or Your Favorite Bookstore

BOOKS THROUGH JAAP VAN ETTEN

by Jaap van Etten, PhD

$19.95 • Softcover • 352 PP. • 6 x 9
978-1-62233-066-9

DRAGONS
GUARDIANS OF CREATIVE POWERS
BECOMING A CONSCIOUS CREATOR

The elemental (fire, water, air, and earth) powers are the basis of all creation. Understanding the different aspects of these creative powers will help you to become a conscious creator.

Guardians are connected with every aspect of the elemental powers. They are known as dragons; however, different traditions use different names for them, such as angels or nature spirits. They are among the strongest allies we can ask for.

This book offers information to help you reconnect with these creative powers and their guardian dragons. Through this connection, you will become a conscious creator and change your life in ways that lead to success, joy, happiness, and abundance. Thereby, you will contribute optimally to the creation of a new world.

Birth of a New Consciousness: Dialogues with the Sidhe
$16.95 • 192 PP.
978-1-62233-033-1

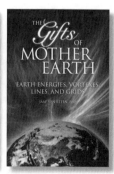

The Gifts of Mother Earth
$16.95 • 256 PP.
978-1-891824-86-9

Crystal Skulls: Expand Your Consciousness
$25.00 • 256 PP.
978-1-62233-000-3

Crystal Skulls: Interacting with a Phenomenon
$19.95 • 240 PP.
978-1-891824-64-7